Faculty Advising Examined

Faculty Advising Examined

Enhancing the Potential of College Faculty as Advisors

Gary L. Kramer
Editor

Brigham Young University

Anker Publishing Company, Inc.
BOLTON, MASSACHUSETTS

Faculty Advising Examined

Enhancing the Potential of College Faculty as Advisors

ISBN 1-882982-63-0

Composition by Nicolazzo Productions
Cover design by Frederick Schneider/Grafis

Anker Publishing Company, Inc.
176 Ballville Road
P.O. Box 249
Bolton, MA 01740-0249 USA

www.ankerpub.com

TABLE OF CONTENTS

About the Editor — *vi*
About the Contributors — *vii*
National Academic Advising Association Endorsement — *xiii*
American Association for Higher Education Endorsement — *xiv*
Preface — *xv*
Acknowledgments — *xxiv*

1 Advising as Teaching — 1
Gary L. Kramer

2 Faculty Advising: Practice and Promise — 23
Wesley R. Habley

3 The Importance of Faculty Advising: A CEO and CAO Perspective — 40
Robert E. Glennen

4 Expectations and Training of Faculty Advisors — 55
Faye Vowell and Phillip J. Farren

5 The Role of Evaluation and Reward in Faculty Advising — 88
Victoria A. McGillin

6 Organizational Models and Delivery Systems for Faculty Advising — 125
Margaret C. King

7 Managing and Leading Faculty Advising to Promote Success — 144
David H. Goldenberg and Steve B. Permuth

8 Resources to Improve Faculty Advising on Campus — 173
Betsy McCalla-Wriggins

9 Outstanding Faculty Advising Programs: Strategies That Work — 201
Franklin P. Wilbur

10 Evolution and Examination: Philosophical and Cultural Foundations for Faculty Advising — 223
Susan H. Frost and Karen E. Brown-Wheeler

11 Practical Legal Concepts for Faculty Advising — 245
Wesley R. Habley

12 Faculty Advising and Technology — 258
Eric R. White and Michael J. Leonard

Bibliography — *284*
Index — *302*

ABOUT THE EDITOR

GARY L. KRAMER is associate dean of student academic and advisement services and professor in the Department of Counseling Psychology and Special Education at Brigham Young University. A former dean of students at Trident Technical College in Charleston, South Carolina, he received his Ph.D. from Oregon State University. He has published 70 refereed journal articles, book chapters, book reviews, monographs, grant proposals, ERIC and institutional reports, as well as more than 50 scholarly papers in ten different refereed journals. He is also the editor of four monographs, the author of six monograph chapters, and chapters in books published by Jossey-Bass and the Society for College and University Planning (SCUP). He has delivered more than 100 professional papers, including keynote addresses for 11 different professional organizations, and edited a book on student academic services for Jossey-Bass. In addition to having served as the National Academic Advising Association's (NACADA) president, he has received the association's awards for researcher of the year, distinguished service, and excellence in the field.

ABOUT THE CONTRIBUTORS

KAREN E. BROWN-WHEELER received her undergraduate degree from Rutgers College and is pursuing a doctorate in English literature at Emory University. Her main research interests are British Victorian and Irish literature, and she is currently completing her dissertation on the role of ghosts in Victorian fictional autobiographies titled *The Afterlife of Romanticism: Haunted Victorians.* She advised students for nearly three years as an academic counselor with Emory University, and for more than five years taught introductory English courses to first-year students. She served on the President's Commission on the Status of Women at Emory University as the student-concerns committee chair, with a particular interest in addressing the need for mentors for female students and faculty. She has also served at Emory as the program coordinator for the University Advisory Council on Teaching and as the project manager for the Commission on Research.

PHILLIP J. FARREN is vice president for student affairs and dean of enrollment management at Western New Mexico University. He earned his Ph.D. (1969) in higher education from the University of Northern Colorado. He has presented papers and published numerous book chapters and journal articles in the areas of the fiscal impact of advising, the marketing of advising, the future of advising, and the centrality of academic advising to all aspects of the campus community.

SUSAN H. FROST is vice president for strategic development and an adjunct professor at Emory University. She received her undergraduate degree from Agnes Scott College and her doctoral degree from the University of Georgia. Since joining Emory University in 1991, she has organized and developed the university's first central institutional planning and research effort, designed and implemented major planning initiatives, and conducted comprehensive studies of faculty work and life at the university. She is the author or editor of three books on higher education: *Using Teams in Higher Education: Cultural Foundations for Productive Change; Inside College: Undergraduate Education for the Future* (with Ronald Simpson); and

Academic Advising for Student Success: A System of Shared Responsibility. Her articles have appeared in the *Journal of Higher Education and Research in Higher Education,* among others. Her current research interests include strategic development of universities and the nature of the intellectual community. She consults with colleges and universities on issues related to their strategic development and on the academic advising of undergraduate students.

ROBERT E. GLENNEN is president emeritus of Emporia State University. During the 1998–1999 academic year, he served as the Jones Distinguished University Professor in the Jones Institute for Educational Excellence at Emporia State University. He was interim president of the University of Southern Colorado, where he was also an interim provost for 18 months. He has been a college academic advising and student retention consultant for more than 35 colleges, universities, and community colleges across the United States, and he has received numerous awards for his work in and support of advising and teacher education. His presentations and publications have focused on the areas of academic advising, student retention, and enrollment management. He was instrumental in establishing the National Teachers Hall of Fame in Emporia, Kansas, and served as its president from 1989 to 1997.

DAVID H. GOLDENBERG serves as professor and dean of Hillyer College within the University of Hartford. He has been a faculty member, department chair, dean, chief academic officer, and chief executive officer at both private and public universities. He is the author of one text, four monographs, and a variety of articles on administration in higher education.

WESLEY R. HABLEY directs the Office for the Enhancement of Educational Practices at ACT, Inc. Prior to joining ACT in 1985, he served first as academic advisor and later as director of the Academic Advisement Center at Illinois State University and also as director of academic and career advising at the University of Wisconsin–Eau Claire. He holds a B.S. in music education, an M.Ed. in student personnel from the University of Illinois–Urbana Champaign, and an Ed.D. in educational administration from Illinois State University. He has served in NACADA in a variety of roles, including treasurer and president, and is the recipient of awards for outstanding contributions to the field of advising and for service to the association. He is the lead researcher and author of monographs on four ACT national surveys of campus practices in academic advising. Additional publications include more than 30 journal articles and book chapters. He has served as consultant to or workshop leader at more than 130 colleges in the United States, Canada, and the Middle East.

MARGARET C. KING is associate dean for student development at Schenectady County Community College, where she provides leadership for the Division of Student Affairs as one of three associate deans reporting directly to the president. In her position she directs the Student Development Center, which includes academic advising, counseling, and job placement services. She received a B.A. in history from Ursinus College and an M.S. and Ed.D. from the State University of New York at Albany. A founding member of NACADA, she was its president from 1991 to 1993. She has been a faculty member of the Summer Institute on Academic Advising since its inception in 1987, and serves as a consultant on academic advising for both two- and four-year colleges and universities. She was editor of the New Directions for Community Colleges' publication *Academic Advising: Organizing and Delivering Services for Student Success* (1993), and has also authored a number of chapters and articles about academic advising in two-year colleges and organizational models and delivery systems. She received the State University of New York Chancellor's Award for Excellence in Professional Service, the NACADA Award for Service to NACADA, and the association's Virginia N. Gordon Award for Excellence in the Field of Advising.

MICHAEL J. LEONARD is assistant director of the Division of Undergraduate Studies at Pennsylvania State University, from which he received a master's degree in educational psychology. He is the chair of NACADA's Technology in Advising, and has contributed to the *NACADA Journal,* Academic Advising News (the association's quarterly newsletter), and a monograph on technology in advising. He has presented numerous sessions and workshops at professional conferences and has provided consulting services to higher education institutions on the topic of technology in advising. He is general editor of *The Mentor: An Academic Advising Journal,* an award-winning electronic publication.

BETSY MCALLA-WRIGGINS is director of career and academic planning at Rowan University. She earned her B.S. (1969) in home economics education and her M.S. (1974) in educational psychology at the University of Tennessee, Knoxville. Before coming to Rowan University, she was an assistant director of promotion and education at Butterick Fashion Marketing Company. At Rowan, she has been responsible for the career development, counseling, student work, cooperative education, and academic advising units. In 1992, she created the CAP Center, which fully integrates the academic advising and career development functions. She is on the faculty at the ACT/NACADA Summer Institute on Academic Advising and currently serves as president of NACADA.

VICTORIAL A. MCGILLIN is dean of academic advising and an adjunct professor of psychology at Wheaton College (Massachusetts). She earned a B.S. (1971) and an M.S. (1973) in psychology from Pennsylvania State University and a Ph.D. in clinical psychology (1979) from Michigan State University. Prior to Wheaton College, she served as the associate dean of the college and director of academic advising at Clark University, where she was also on the graduate faculty of the Department of Psychology. She has held graduate faculty appointments at the University of Connecticut and Michigan State University. She has served on the board of directors of NACADA as private university representative, northeast regional representative, chair of the research committee, and since 1999, vice president for member services. She has served on the editorial board of the *NACADA Journal,* and has published numerous articles on advising and higher education, as well as in the field of psychology. Her current research includes the study of student risk and resilience in higher education, gender differences in patterns of support and self-efficacy, and developmental patterns in advisor evaluations.

STEVE B. PERMUTH is professor of educational leadership and policy studies at the University of South Florida. He has served in faculty and administrative roles at both private and public universities and is the author of four texts and 50 articles in the areas of policy and education law.

FAYE VOWELL is provost and vice president for academic affairs at Western New Mexico University, which is noted for its application of quality principles to higher education. She has been active in advising and has been with NACADA since 1984. She has authored a number of articles and edited a variety of monographs on advising, as well as led a team of advisors in the creation of a video training program for faculty advisors. She is currently leading a NACADA initiative to help college and university presidents and vice presidents understand the importance of advising.

ERIC R. WHITE earned his undergraduate degree in history from Rutgers University and his M.S and Ed.D. in counseling psychology from the University of Pennsylvania. He joined the Pennsylvania State University staff in 1970 as a psychological counselor and coordinator of counseling services at the Delaware County campus. After moving to the University Park campus in 1975 as coordinator of the Freshman Testing, Counseling, and Advising Program, he was named director of the Division of Undergraduate Studies in 1986 and then executive director in 1999. He has been active in NACADA, serving as the multiversity representative to the board of directors, chair of the placement committee and the Commission on Standards and Ethics in Advising, a member of the Consultants Bureau, and currently as treasurer. He was also president of the Association of Deans and Directors of University Colleges and Undergraduate Studies. He is an affiliate assistant professor of education at Penn State, author of monograph chapters and journal articles, and coeditor of the monographs *Teaching Through Academic Advising: A Faculty Perspective* (1995) and *Teaching Through Mentoring* (2001), both published in the Jossey-Bass New Directions for Teaching and Learning series. He has also written a chapter for the NACADA/Jossey-Bass publication *Academic Advising: A Comprehensive Handbook.*

FRANKLIN P. WILBUR, as associate vice president and executive director of the Center for Support of Teaching and Learning at Syracuse University, has campus-wide responsibilities for improving the quality of the academic experience, with particular focus on learning outcomes assessment. For many years, he has led an all-university effort to improve undergraduate academic advising, strengthen lower-division instruction, build international linkages and programs, and strengthen school-university-community relations. Since 1973, Wilbur has also administered Project Advance, a nationally known school-college partnership serving schools throughout the Northeast. As an associate professor in Syracuse University's Graduate School of Education and the College of Arts and Sciences, he has taught courses on instructional development, planning and managing change and innovation, project management, technology in education, and educational administration. He has also served as a freshman forum instructor for more than 12 years, helping students make an effective transition from high school to university life. A frequent speaker at national and regional meetings, Wilbur has consulted with and served as a program evaluator for schools, colleges, and industry throughout the country on such topics as improving academic advising, assessment, retention of students, and innovation in teaching and learning. He has written extensively on topics such as school-college partnerships, advising, and educational reform. He is active in many community and national organizations and currently serves on the boards of several foundations, including the Syracuse-based Samaritan Center. In 1993, Wilbur was named a Senior Research Fellow of the American Association for Higher Education.

One Dupont Circle, Suite 360
Washington, DC 20036
Ph 202/293-6440 Fax 202/293-0073
www.aahe.org

Dear Colleague,

"This book is a long-awaited resource for higher education. Too often faculty members are left to sink or swim when it comes to effective student advising—they are blamed for something they lack the professional training to do. This book provides a 360-degree look at what faculty members, department chairs, deans, advising directors, and vice presidents need to know and do to have significant impact on the student retention and successes that institutions of higher education across America are striving to achieve." These words by Yolanda Moses, president of the American Association for Higher Education, affirm the importance of the role of advising and of this book in advancing the effectiveness of that role.

As part of its own contribution to higher education, the American Association for Higher Education (AAHE) centers on fields that include excellent student advising as part of support for student learning. AAHE's fields of inquiry and action are learning about learning, assessing for learning, organizing for learning, and partners in learning. Excellent advisors base their work on what they know about how students learn, assess the outcome of their advising in order to improve it, situate their work within the other institutional support systems, and collaborate with other educators on their campus. Advisors and those who support them, therefore, are important constituents of AAHE.

AAHE's work is based on a set of operating principles. These values—learning, boldness, collegiality, collaboration, diversity, innovation, and service—govern the ways in which we interact with each other and with our members to enact our mission and fulfill our vision. They are values that also underlie the best in advising.

Sincerely,

Barbara L. Cambridge

Barbara L. Cambridge
Vice President

National ACADEMIC ADVISING Association

Fall 2002

Dear Colleague,

The National Academic Advising Association (NACADA) is pleased to endorse *Faculty Advising Examined,* edited by Gary L. Kramer. As student success and student retention draw increasing attention on college and university campuses, it is imperative that we recognize and understand the vital role that faculty contribute through effective academic advising. Additionally, it is important to recognize that faculty need support and recognition for their advising role. This timely book addresses those issues and provides important discussions on the administration of faculty advising and model programs.

Established in 1979, NACADA is an organization of professional advisors/counselors, faculty, administrators, and students working to ensure the educational development of students. NACADA strives to champion the educational role of academic advising to enhance student learning and development in a diverse world; to affirm the role of academic advising in supporting institutional mission and vitality; to address the academic advising needs of higher education; to advance the body of knowledge on academic advising; and to encourage the contributions of all members and promote the involvement of diverse populations. The association addresses this mission by directing its efforts and resources toward student development through professional development and education, participation by members, generation and dissemination of knowledge, and advocacy for advising programs and advisors.

NACADA welcomes individual advisors, faculty members, administrators, and graduate students to join us in enhancing the development of students through effective academic advising. Please visit our web site (www.nacada.ksu.edu) for complete information about NACADA and the many facets of our work—services, publications, professional development opportunities, professional networks, and the many other benefits of membership in NACADA.

Sincerely,

Roberta "Bobbie" Flaherty
Executive Director

Kansas State University, 2323 Anderson Avenue, Suite 225, Manhattan, KS 66502-2912
Phone 785-532-5717 FAX 785.532.7732 E-mail nacada@ksu.edu
Web site http://www.ksu.edu/nacada

PREFACE

Faculty advising is largely an unexamined activity, yet it has been an integral component of the higher education system since it began at Johns Hopkins University in 1877. This book not only examines faculty advising as a potential contributor to student college success, but more important, provides information on how to organize, deliver, and improve overall faculty advising on the modern campus. It is intended as a resource for academic leaders in addressing issues of accountability, training, delivery, evaluation, and recognition and reward in faculty advising.

Research indicates that at most institutions, faculty are either the only source of academic advising for students or such faculty function as part of a larger advising system administered by centralized or decentralized advising professionals. While national research shows an increasing involvement of faculty in advising students, advising is mostly uneven and unsatisfactory. The areas of accountability and clearly defined expectations, evaluation and assessment of individual and program performance, reward and recognition, and training—all of which are emphasized in this book—are the most significant methods for improving advising, but they are the components in which current campus advising programs are least effective (Habley & Morales, 1998).

However, as other research has pointed out, when faculty advising works well, it significantly impacts student retention, success, and satisfaction with the college experience (see, for example, Astin, 1997; Light, 2001a; Pascarella & Terenzini, 1991; Tinto, 1987, 1990, 1993, 1998). As Richard J. Light (2001b) states, "Of all the challenges that both faculty and students choose to mention, providing or obtaining good academic advising ranks number one. In fact, good advising may be the single most underestimated characteristic of a successful college experience" (p. B11). There is no question that faculty play an essential role in the institution's advising program, but how does effective faculty advising come about?

Given that most institutions care deeply about student growth and success, what key concepts of faculty advising must receive attention in order to achieve individual- and program-advising quality? Taking the institutional perspective, this book intends to provide academic leaders with a resource guide to strengthen and reaffirm faculty advising. The chapters focus on improving the practice of faculty advising by presenting advising as not only a form of teaching but also as a defined and examined activity that includes resources, best practices, national data, delivery methods, and faculty-advisor development through strategic and tactical efforts.

Since 1994, the American Association for Higher Education (AAHE) has invited some of our contributing authors to present workshops on faculty advising roles. Similar workshops are given at the American Association of Collegiate Registrars and Admissions Officers (AACRAO), the Association to Advance Collegiate Schools of Business (AACSB International), the National Orientation Directors Association (NODA), the Freshman Year Experience Conference, and the National Academic Advising Association (NACADA) Summer Institute. In 1995, NACADA published a monograph titled *Reaffirming the Role of Faculty in Academic Advising,* in response to the organization's interest in expanding the national discussion on faculty advising. Just a year before, NACADA had established an external relations committee charged with extending information about the association's services and programs to academic colleagues from a variety of institutional settings and backgrounds. The committee also used the monograph to reach out to other organizations that focused on faculty issues. Although *Reaffirming the Role of Faculty in Academic Advising* has served its original purpose well, the content needed to be updated. To handle that and to broaden the monograph's audience, the editor was approached by Anker Publishing in 2001 to join together the monograph and AAHE workshop materials and expand the topic of faculty advising into a new book.

AUDIENCE

This book is primarily aimed at individuals who are responsible for the support or direction and coordination of faculty advising programs at the campus, college, or department level. This includes

- directors or coordinators of advising offices that use faculty advisors
- vice presidents (or associate or assistant vice presidents) in academic or student affairs with responsibilities for the coordination of or support for campus faculty advising

- deans (or associate or assistant deans) who have college-level responsibilities for coordination of or support for faculty advisors
- department chairs
- individuals responsible for faculty development programs

The book will also assist individual faculty advisors in learning more about the important role they play in advising students. Considerable emphasis is given in this book to developing faculty's potential as advisors, clarifying role expectations, and using resources to improve advising performance.

CHAPTER SUMMARIES

The 12 chapters represent every important facet of faculty advising. They are authored by experts who are experienced faculty, researchers, and leaders in the field well equipped to share their expertise in these areas. The book begins with the presentation of a framework, or lens, of advising as teaching, then proceeds through detailed discussions on each of the framework's components: expectations and faculty advisor development, assessment evaluation and reward, campus collaboration, delivery and resources, and the use of technology in advising.

Chapter 1. Advising as Teaching, *by Gary L. Kramer*

In 1972, Burns Crookston introduced the concept of developmental advising. He pictured advising as prescriptive learning and developmental teaching. In this context, advising is effective when it is based on the premise of student growth and success. Chapter 1, based on this concept, sets the philosophical framework for the chapters that follow. In particular, it advocates that quality faculty advising and teaching are based on similar principles, ones that provide a lens through which faculty can view advising as a form of teaching. The chapter also takes into account that student diversity and needs place high demands upon faculty time, while higher education's multiple and vertical infrastructures add complexity, if not barriers and challenges, to the content and delivery of effective advising. Nevertheless, there are some things faculty advisors can do to make a difference in the lives of the students they advise. A model in this chapter will help faculty advisors become aware of the distinctive advising needs of each academic class.

Chapter 2. Faculty Advising: Practice and Promise, ***by Wesley R. Habley***
A review of the literature on faculty advising leads to three major conclusions: Faculty advising is 1) a constant in American higher education, 2) the predominant form of delivery of advising, and 3) a critical factor in student success and institutional effectiveness. However, Habley argues that faculty advising has yet to realize its full potential. Furthermore, he states, many contend that faculty advising receives far too little attention, and decision makers and resource allocators remain largely uninformed regarding effective advising practices. The chapter provides a review of data on the status of faculty advising taken from ACT's Fifth National Survey of Academic Advising. The author, a respected national leader of the advising movement, also shares data from other sources on students' perceptions of their faculty advisors.

Chapter 3. The Importance of Faculty Advising: A CEO and CAO Perspective, ***by Robert E. Glennen***
Drawing on his experience as academic vice president, provost, and president of three different institutions, Robert Glennen provides the chief academic officer (CAO) and the chief executive officer (CEO) a perspective on the importance of faculty advising. The chapter emphasizes a strong academic advising system as an effective approach to increasing enrollments and improving graduation rates, the primary concerns of academic officers. The author takes the reader beyond the verbal commitments of developing and maintaining an active advising system to practical means of managing and leading faculty advising efforts, such as providing resources, personnel, space, and rewards for advising. When the program faces obstacles, Glennen advocates the intervention of the CEO and CAO. It is their responsibility to guarantee that students receive significant faculty advising.

Chapter 4. Expectations and Training of Faculty Advisors, ***by Faye Vowell and Phillip J. Farren***
Divergent expectations of advising are often held by faculty advisors and their student advisees. Two great challenges faced by an institution are first to create a commonly held vision of advisor and

advisee rights and responsibilities, and second, to elevate advising from its status as a little-regarded add-on to a faculty load already heavy with the obligations of research and teaching. Two areas related to faculty expectations and training are addressed in this chapter: 1) expectations of the advisor's role and level of performance in relationship to the culture of the institution, and 2) clearly stated expectations of and a climate of support for advising. These expectations naturally shape the goals and objectives of an advisor training or education program. The authors, vice presidents of academic and student services and teaching faculty, not only present ideas for providing a comprehensive advisor-training or development program in an institution, but they also strongly suggest that it all begins with a thoughtful consideration of expectations and role definition.

Chapter 5. The Role of Evaluation and Reward in Faculty Advising, *by Victoria A. McGillin*

Evaluation and reward of faculty advisors go hand in hand with defining their role and training. An institution's approach to evaluation or assessment grows out of its culture and may be affected by such things as tradition, outcomes assessment, and continuous improvement. Appropriately stated expectations, training of faculty to enable them to meet their expectations, sensitive and sensible evaluation procedures, and appropriate rewards for their performance as advisors are all factors in improving faculty advising. From a discussion of best practices on assessing and rewarding faculty advising on the campus, the chapter moves directly to the question of how to improve faculty advising, and specifically, the role of assessment and reward in faculty-advisor development. Written from the perspective of a dean and faculty member, McGillin uses practical applications and scholarly research to present what deans, department chairs, and provosts need to know about promoting change in their faculty advisors' approaches.

Chapter 6. Organizational Models and Delivery Systems for Faculty Advising, *by Margaret C. King*

How advising services are organized and delivered on college campuses varies from institution to institution, yet closer inspection reveals many similarities, particularly in regard to the involvement of faculty. Four key factors greatly influence the way in which advising services are organized and delivered: 1) institutional mission, 2) student population, 3) the scope of the faculty contract, and 4) the complexity of institutional programs, policies, and procedures. Insights on the coordination, effectiveness, and strengths and weaknesses of several advising models are discussed in this chapter. The chapter also focuses on seven organizational models of academic advising, and note is made of other groups on campus that can provide effective advising in partnership with faculty. The author, a former president of NACADA, lends her advising expertise to a discussion on how delivery methods used by faculty advisors, regardless of the organizational model, are critical links in helping students reach their goals. And when students achieve their goals, she asserts, the institution achieves its goals as well.

Chapter 7. Managing and Leading Faculty Advising to Promote Success, *by David H. Goldenberg and Steve B. Permuth*

Chapter 7 addresses three questions: 1) How can faculty who serve as academic advisors be more effective in this role? 2) What attitudes and practices contribute to advising effectiveness? and 3) How can advising programs be structured to introduce these attitudes and practices? Overall, the chapter's emphasis is on strategies that contribute to advising effectiveness. The chapter takes into account planning for success by addressing the following strategic questions: Who are the students we serve? What resources do faculty advisors need to accomplish their advising role? How can collaboration be used effectively? What are concepts of shared responsibility? David Goldenberg, a current faculty member (Hillyer College of the University of Hartford) and a past provost in two university systems, and his colleague Steve Permuth, a professor of educational leadership at the University of Southern Florida, demonstrate that leadership requires one or more members of the organization to envision a different, and better, manner of achieving student success through academic advising.

Chapter 8. Resources to Improve Faculty Advising on the Campus, *by Betsy McCalla-Wriggins*

As colleges and universities continue to be challenged to improve the quality of their faculty advising programs, identifying resources helpful in this process is of paramount concern. A number of significant resources are presented in this chapter, in particular, the CAS Academic Advising Program Standards and Guidelines, developed by the Council for the Advancement of Standards in Higher Education (CAS). The author, the current president of NACADA, describes some significant national resources that focus on the elements of academic advising, career-life planning, and leadership. All three elements, the author states, are critical in creating a vision for a comprehensive, integrated, campus-wide academic advising system. NACADA's information resources and programs, including publications, training materials, the National Clearinghouse on Academic Advising, Consultants Bureau, and its awards programs, are identified and summarized in the chapter.

Chapter 9. Outstanding Faculty Advising Programs: Strategies That Work, *by Franklin P. Wilbur*

Associate vice president and executive director of the Center for Support of Teaching and Learning and a faculty member at Syracuse University, Franklin Wilbur distills in this chapter the best faculty advising models, the ones that offer students and faculty additional opportunities to connect in meaningful ways. Academic advising on college and university campuses has changed significantly over the past 20 years. For more than a decade, NACADA has recognized advising programs throughout the country. Using NACADA's Outstanding Advising Program Award as a base of information, Chapter 9 reviews the overall effectiveness of several faculty advising models. Syracuse University's all-university program to strengthen academic advising, in particular, is presented in depth. The intent of this chapter is to encourage readers to envision a plan for strengthening, maintaining, and assessing various aspects of advising on their own campuses and to begin to prioritize the areas most in need of attention.

Chapter 10. Evolution and Examination: Philosophical and Cultural Foundations for Faculty Advising, *by Susan H. Frost and Karen E. Brown-Wheeler*

Perhaps no one is more qualified to write this chapter than Susan Frost, vice provost and associate professor at Emory University, and her colleague and advising leader Karen Brown-Wheeler. They examine faculty advising in both its historical and current settings, and place emphasis on the philosophical foundations and culture of faculty advising in higher education. The chapter explores advising as a vital, organic part of the culture of teaching and considers the opportunities teaching intrinsically provides for advisement. The authors examine whether current systematic support for academic advising may actually hinder faculty advising by casting advising as an obligation rather than as a form of teaching. Through a discussion of internal and external motivations to teach, they explore more organic ways to support and enhance faculty advising.

Chapter 11. Practical Legal Concepts for Faculty Advising, ***by Wesley R. Habley***

In an increasingly litigious society, faculty advisors need to be concerned about the possibility that the advice they give might lead to legal action by students. Although the courts are generally reluctant to intercede in academic matters, advisors must be aware of several important legal issues. The chapter reviews the principle of judicial nonintervention, potential sources of litigation, the basic principles of contract law as they relate to academic advising, and records management and student privacy.

Chapter 12. Faculty Advising and Technology, ***by Eric White and Michael J. Leonard***

Internet technology, through the electronic medium of computers and communication lines, now connects the world in ways never thought possible just a few years ago. The electronic connection of computers and databases has created an "e" factor that has transformed and significantly enhanced the advising process. In essence, the "e" factor has moved faculty advising beyond the routine and changed the concept of advisors as just information disseminators. While personal contact is essential to the advising process, information technology can add value and economy for both the advisor and advisee. The authors bring to and incorporate into this chapter not only nationally recognized advising technology, including that of Penn State, but also their expertise as leaders of the advising system at university, regional, and national levels.

REFERENCES

Astin, A. W. (1997). *What matters in college? Four critical years revisited.* San Francisco, CA: Jossey-Bass.

Crookston, B. B. (1972). A developmental view of academic advising as teaching. *Journal of College Student Personnel, 13,* 12–17.

Habley, W. R., & Morales, R. H. (1998). *Current practices in academic advising: Final report on ACT's fifth national survey of academic advising* (Monograph Series No. 6). Manhattan, KS: National Academic Advising Association.

Kramer, G. L. (1995). Redefining faculty roles for academic advising. In G. L. Kramer (Ed.), *Reaffirming the role of faculty in academic advising* (pp. 3–9) (Monograph Series No. 1). Manhattan, KS: National Academic Advising Association.

Light, R. J. (2001a). *Making the most of college: Students speak their minds.* Cambridge, MA: Harvard University Press.

Light, R. J. (2001b, March 2). The power of good advice for students. *The Chronicle of Higher Education,* p. B11.

Pascarella, E. T., & Terenzini, P. T. (1991). *How college affects students: Findings and insights from twenty years of research.* San Francisco, CA: Jossey-Bass.

Tinto, V. S. (1987). *Leaving college: Rethinking the causes and cures of student attrition.* Chicago, IL: University of Chicago Press.

Tinto, V. S. (1990). Principles of effective retention. *Journal of the Freshman Experience, 2,* 35–48.

Tinto, V. S. (1993). *Leaving college: Rethinking the causes and cures of student attrition* (2nd ed.). Chicago, IL: University of Chicago Press.

Tinto, V. S. (1998). Colleges as communities: Taking research on student persistence seriously. *Review of Higher Education, 21* (2), 167–177.

ACKNOWLEDGMENTS

I would like to thank my author-colleagues, who have shared their experience and scholarship on faculty advising. Without them there would be no book! We hope that this collection of insights will help others as they seek to rethink, renew, and revitalize faculty advising on their campuses. My colleagues have challenged us with ideas and strategies to improve advising services for students.

Specific thanks go to NACADA and AAHE for sponsoring this volume as a contribution to the profession. I owe much to Peter Gardner and Shannon Openshaw of Brigham Young University (BYU) for their assistance in editing the manuscript and in organizing all the detail associated with this book project. Many, many thanks for providing editorial feedback and for the long hours spent in final manuscript preparation.

And finally my colleagues at BYU and my family, especially my wife, Lauri, deserve special recognition for their support, patience, and love. I am grateful for their adjustments of need and expectation, at moments inconvenient, that allowed me the time and energy to complete this work. Thank you for understanding.

Gary L. Kramer
September 2003

1 ADVISING AS TEACHING

Gary L. Kramer

Advising as teaching is not a new concept. Since the beginning of higher education in America, faculty advising has been an integral component. However, it was Burns Crookston, in a landmark article published in 1972, who first described academic advising as a teaching function. The teacher-advisor role advanced by Crookston focused on stimulating students toward a positive, shared, active approach to both intellectual and interpersonal learning. Later, Richard Light (2001), after a ten-year study of more than 90 institutions of higher education, validated Crookston's work when he concluded, "Students who get the most out of college, grow the most academically, and who are happiest organize their time to include activities with faculty members" (p. 10). This chapter—indeed, this book—will give meaning to how students and faculty organize their time and effort to get the most out of academic advising. Our focus is on how faculty advisors make a difference in the lives of the students they advise, especially since, other than teaching, no other college activity seems to enjoy more legitimacy than academic advising.

This chapter explores the notion of faculty-student interaction through a framework, or lens, of advising as teaching. The first section lays the foundation for faculty advising as an integral component of higher education, while the second presents and discusses the framework's components. The concluding section examines the changing role of students, the services they come in contact with, and the impact of faculty advising on their lives.

Detailed discussions on each of the following components of the advising-as-teaching framework are provided in subsequent chapters. For example, for information on expectations and faculty-advisor development, see Chapter 4; for assessment, evaluation, and reward, see Chapter 5; for best practices and strategies see Chapter 9; for faculty advising and the use of technology see Chapter 12; and for campus collaboration, delivery, and resources, see Chapters 6 and 8.

This chapter takes into account that student diversity and needs, high demands upon faculty time, and higher education's multiple and vertical infrastructures add complexity, if not barriers and challenges, to the content and delivery of effective academic advising. Unfortunately, perhaps unknowingly, institutions with such conditions oftentimes disconnect students from the very services and people the students need to be successful academically. At the same time, higher education, in both the long and short run, is driven to deliver cohesive, coherent, and connected services. This tension will not be resolved in this chapter or book, but it is hoped that the readers will find among the following pages a noteworthy idea or two to improve their performance as advisors to students or advising directors.

FACULTY ADVISING AS AN INTEGRAL COMPONENT OF HIGHER EDUCATION

In general, higher education has been critically viewed as a service to be purchased, one which is composed of organizations like any other commodity. Its customers are students, governments, and businesses. Higher education is expected to be timely, efficient, and effective in its delivery of services. A less critical and perhaps more proactive view is that higher education is a leader in and servant to society. In some aspects, it can even be visionary. What expectations does this view place on colleges and universities, in particular, in relation to advising as teaching? One response is that colleges should be proactive in engaging faculty to seek out relevant issues and then help define and address them. Extending beyond university walls, this can mean joining with other social agencies to improve society. Within its walls, it can mean that faculties and departments join together in collaborative and collegial ways to improve the institution, especially in the delivery and improvement of advising on the campus.

Regardless of institutional mission or size, faculty are an integral part of the advising process. They may be the only source for assisting students, or they may function as part of a larger centralized or decentralized advising system. Wes Habley points out in Chapter 2 that faculty advising continues to be the predominant advising delivery mode at all types of institutions, although it has taken on many forms and various levels of importance through the years. The first formal and recognized system of faculty advising dates back to 1877 at Johns Hopkins University. Informal incidences date back even further, as evidenced by Rutherford Hayes's description of a rule adopted by Kenyon College in 1841. The rule stipulated that each student would choose a faculty member who would be an advisor and friend, as well as a medium of communication with the faculty as a whole (Hardee, 1970). The following are some significant dates and events that had an impact on the system of faculty advising up to the mid-20th century:

- 1862: The Morrill Act established land-grant colleges, making a college education more accessible.
- 1877: Johns Hopkins University created the first formal, recognized system of faculty advising.
- 1888: Harvard University initiated a program of faculty advising for freshmen.
- 1899: Johns Hopkins University president appointed the first "chief of faculty advisors."
- 1901: University of Illinois appointed the first dean of men to handle disciplinary duties and extracurricular activities and to resolve academic problems.
- 1920: Harvard and Johns Hopkins Universities reported the use of counselors to supplement the work of faculty advisors.
- Post–World War II: The dramatic influx of students created a need for more comprehensive consideration of the academic-advising needs of a more academically diverse student body.
- Beginning in the 1950s: A dramatic shift gave emphasis to the student point of view.

For further information on the evolution of faculty advising, see Chapters 2 and 10.

The student-counseling and student-centered frameworks of the 1950s and 1960s, and especially the developmental theorists of the 1960s, most likely paved the way for Crookston's model of developmental advising and the role of faculty as advisor-teacher. These topics are presented in the next section.

A DEVELOPMENTAL VIEW OF ACADEMIC ADVISING AS TEACHING

Burns Crookston, a University of Utah faculty member, introduced the terms and expanded the model for developmental advising. He distinguished between prescriptive learning, a much-used and trite form of teaching that still plagues higher education today, and developmental teaching or advising, a more holistic and learner-centered approach. His description separated the tenets of prescriptive learning from developmental teaching, as shown in Figure 1.1.

FIGURE 1.1

DIFFERENCES BETWEEN PRESCRIPTIVE LEARNING AND DEVELOPMENTAL ADVISING-TEACHING

Prescriptive Learning	Developmental Advising-Teaching
• Advisor has primary responsibility • Focus is on limitations • Effort is problem oriented • Relationship is based on status • Relationship is based on authority and the giving of advice • Evaluation is done by advisor	• Advisor and student share responsibility • Focus is on potentialities • Effort is growth oriented • Relationship is based on trust and respect • Relationship is based on equal and shared problem solving • Evaluation is a shared process

In validation of several tenets of Crookston's "developmental teaching," Frost (1995) wrote that as developmentally advised students move through an academic institution, they increase their own responsibility for educational planning and decrease their reliance on the advisor. Thus, the promotion of concepts of "shared responsibility" (phrase coined by Frost) for the student, the advisor, and the institution can lead to student learning, rather than merely to advisors' supplying answers to specific questions; students' involvement in their own academic and career futures; and a collaborative planning that engages and motivates students to plan for success through strategic and quality efforts. Similarly, Stark (1989) commented on the importance of helping students take responsibility for their own education, claiming that effectiveness in advising depends partly on advisors' and institutions' adjusting their goals to the goals that students set for themselves. Or, according to Chickering (1994), effectiveness is helping students increase their capacity to take charge. He suggested that advisors do this by raising questions, sharing perceptions, and suggesting resources. Advisors help students think through short-term decisions and long-range plans, which enables students to eventually "take charge" of their educational careers.

Furthermore, Light (2001) suggested that quality faculty advising is distinguished from poor advising by the asking of hard and personally meaningful questions. Graduating seniors in an assessment study reported that the kind of advising critical for their success was the result of advisors asking unexpected questions that helped them connect their personal, academic, and career interests. These three concepts of shared responsibility—aligning institutional and student goals, helping students increase their capacity to take charge of their educational career, and showing concern for students by asking questions that help them make connections—sum up the basis of developmental advising.

Other findings from Light's (2001) assessment study that both support and expand upon Crookston's model of developmental advising, suggest that effective advising

- Is interested in what matters to students
- Asks questions that unite
- Assists students in connecting academic work to their interests and passions
- Tailors advising to students' unique situation
- Develops a mutually rewarding human relationship
- Helps students think about the relationship between academic work and their personal lives
- Personalizes advising by asking about students' goals in college

- Discusses how students spend their precious time
- Encourages students to join a campus organization
- Advocates ethical and professional conduct in academic endeavors

Some faculty who perceive developmental advising as a counseling/psychology-based approach have dismissed this framework of advising as being foreign or requiring too much involvement with students' personal lives. Others complain that they are not prepared (trained) to offer advising of this sort. Ironically, as Crookston pointed out, good teaching and advising share the same principles. For faculty advising to be effective, faculty must 1) engage the student; 2) provide personal meaning to students' academic goals; 3) collaborate with others or use the full range of institutional resources; 4) share, give, and take responsibility; 5) connect academic interests with personal interests; 6) stimulate and support student academic and career planning; 7) promote intellectual and personal growth or success; 8) assess, evaluate, or track student progress; and 9) establish rapport with students. These principles are also at the heart of the successful classroom experience. Their application to advising is why Crookston coined the term "advising as teaching." Thus, faculty who perceive advising-as-teaching as an amorphous and unrelated concept to their teaching and research duties may need to revise their advising perspective to include the above attributes—regardless of whether such concepts are used in the classroom or in some other individual or group student advising setting. The next section more specifically translates developmental advising concepts into the teaching-learning infrastructure.

A FRAMEWORK FOR FACULTY ADVISING AS TEACHING

Most course syllabi describe objectives and outcomes of the course, teacher-learner responsibilities and the learning environment or strategies, and methods of assessment or grade distribution. Most faculty adopt, adapt, or create a teaching style or framework for presenting course material. What parallels exist between course preparation, classroom delivery, and faculty advising? Advisors should ask themselves, "How well do I teach and advise now, and what changes will make my teaching and advising better?" "Does my preparation for teaching, or, in the context of advising as teaching, does my advising help students to become more effective and successful?" For example, if student success in the classroom depends on a framework or organization for teaching, can similar preparations and teaching strategies be applied to the advising situation? In this context, just as our teaching should be first class, shouldn't our advising of students be at that same level? While we explore ways to draw connections between good teaching and good advising, we should be able to learn what students can do as a result of advising as teaching.

This background and these questions set the stage for the balance of this section, in which I propose a model for faculty advising preparation and practice that is similar to teaching. Germane to this discussion and in the context of advising as teaching, faculty advisors might consider the process of developing a new course. Some general questions usually considered are 1) What is the course purpose? What are the learning-teaching methods? What is the student-learning assessment strategy? What are the course expectations? 2) What knowledge and skills must students attain? 3) Are there effective processes for listening to and connecting the personal and career interests with student academic pursuits? 4) What processes are in place to assess faculty performance? and 5) What is the administrative commitment and support provided to the teaching of the course?

Figure 1.2 outlines both the aspects of a course syllabus and advising as teaching. It is followed by a discussion of each principal component identified in the figure.

FIGURE 1.2

A FRAMEWORK FOR COURSE SYLLABUS DEVELOPMENT AND ADVISING AS TEACHING

I. Vision (Purpose)
II. Role (Definition)
III. Assessment and Evaluation
IV. Skill Development (Preparation) and Campus Collaboration
V. Technology Interface

Vision (Purpose)

As the syllabus is the roadmap to what a course is all about and the outcomes to be achieved, an "advising syllabus" is just as important to identify purpose and the framework for advising students. For example, the advising syllabus might have a vision statement that includes such goals for students as 1) persistence to timely graduation, 2) an expectation for quality effort, 3) advising as a shared responsibility, 4) involvement in the academic community, 5) an accounting on how time is spent, 6) an interest in their own growth and success, and 7) getting to know at least one faculty member per semester or term. Such goals statements expand the traditional advising notion of mere course scheduling. Without a clearly defined purpose or vision statement to identify, evaluate, and respond to student advising needs, advising winds up being nothing more than information dissemination. (Other insights on developing a mission for faculty advising on the campus are found in Chapters 3 and 7.)

About the same time Crookston introduced advising as a form of teaching and concepts of developmental advising, O'Bannion (1972) proposed a vision for academic advising in general. Like Crookston, O'Bannion set the expectations and tone for advising by elevating advising beyond just information dissemination and class scheduling. And similar to Richard Light's (2001) findings three decades later, O'Bannion advanced the notion that advising begin with exploring the needs of the student and helping them to connect personal, academic, and career goals. Only then, according to O'Bannion, is the student positioned to select a program of study, select courses, and schedule classes.

Figure 1.3 adds another dimension to this component: knowing, in general, student needs and the tasks students are required to complete. This model distinguishes by academic class both the emphasis of advising and the unique needs of freshmen, sophomores, and so on. It also provides some general guidance to advisors on gauging student development and progress and preparing students for successful transition from one academic year to the next. There is some evidence that students move successfully through the stages of college life when they are guided to formulate plans of action and make commitments to educational goals (Upcraft & Kramer, 1995).

FIGURE 1.3

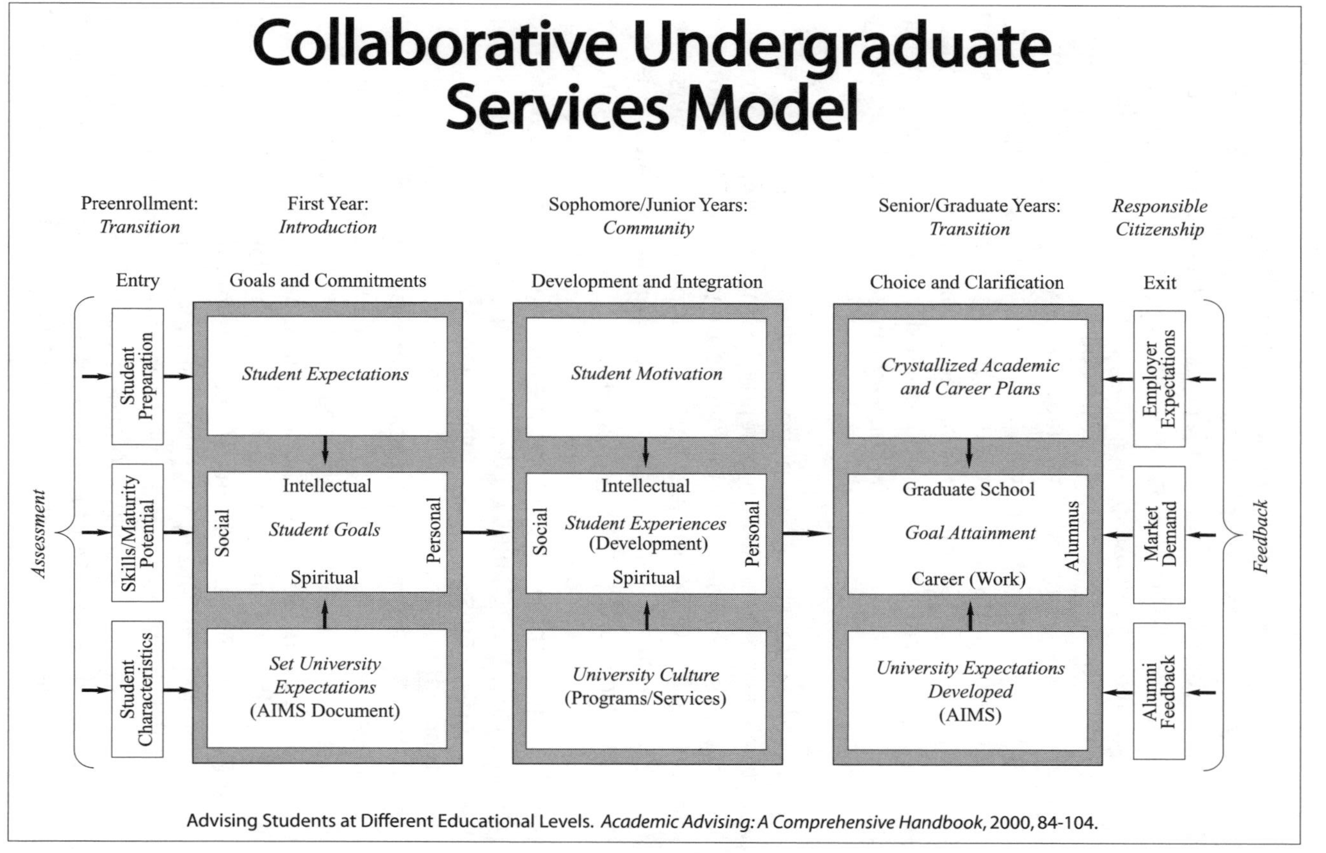

Advising Students at Different Educational Levels. *Academic Advising: A Comprehensive Handbook*, 2000, 84-104.

Role (Definition of Roles in Advising)

In good course management, there is an understanding of stewardship and the teaching-learning process. Likewise, in faculty advising a definition of roles and responsibilities is clearly needed. In the advising-as-teaching process and in advising on the campus in general is a lack of definition about what is meant by advising, who delivers advising services, and what the institutional, advisor, and advisee responsibilities are. In Chapter 9, Frank Wilbur describes the interrelationship of a campus statement on advising and the improvement of the advising system. The agreement, he states, on what advising is and how it should occur on the campus is vital not only to meet the needs of students but also to clarify responsibilities and ensure their academic success. It's easy to understand why faculty advising or any kind of advising on the campus is so uneven across institutions, as Wes Habley points out in Chapter 2. Simply stated, academic advising is not clearly defined. Furthermore, most college catalogs, the institutional authority on policies and procedures, give the reader only minimal clues concerning advising roles and responsibilities.

Wilbur's example of the Hamilton College statements on advising roles is helpful for institutions that are reviewing their own statements on advising. This step of defining the campus advising system is an important one, especially as it includes expectations for advising to be stated upfront in the college catalog as in the Hamilton example on three levels of responsibility (Figure 1.4).

Assessment, Evaluation, and Reward

Integral to course development and student learning and development is assessment. For a more detailed presentation of this essential component of the advising-as-teaching framework see Chapters 5 and 8. The reader will want to pay particular attention to the Council for the Advancement on Standards and the National Academic Advising Association Core Values on Academic Advising among the host of faculty-advising-assessment resources described by these authors. Both of these resources provide qualitative and comprehensive expectations and assessment procedures related specifically to improving academic advising. Also, the National Student Engagement Survey (NSSE), headed by George

FIGURE 1.4
SAMPLE RESPONSIBILITIES ON ADVISING

Institutional Responsibility
- Identify academic advisement policies, procedures, and resources.
- Publish timely and accurate information on program requirements.
- Connect academic, career, and personal planning services.
- Monitor and track timely student graduation.
- Support advisor professional development.
- Evaluate campus academic advising services.
- Recognize and reward outstanding advisors.

Advisor Responsibility
- Look for potential in students; ask questions.
- Collaborate across the academic community to support student academic planning.
- Monitor student progress.
- Assist students to identify and connect personal and academic goals.
- Motivate students to take responsibility for their own academic career; promote shared responsibility.
- Establish a relationship with students by personalizing the advising process.
- Take the student development or success point of view.

Student Responsibility
- Prepare for and keep appointments.
- Establish and follow academic plan.
- Use institutional resources.
- Review academic progress.
- Attend and participate in class.
- Get involved in campus and community events.
- Take responsibility for decisions.
- Get to know at least one faculty per year.

Kuh (2001), assesses such aspects of the student experience as a supportive campus environment, enriching educational experiences, and student interactions with faculty. The NSSE's "College

Student Report" asks students about their educational activities and backgrounds. It focuses squarely on the teaching and learning activities that personally and intensely involve all types of students at all types of colleges and universities. This instrument is an excellent tool to be used in assessing the campus student-learning environment. Another noteworthy tool is Loyola University's (New Orleans) Senior Exit Survey (Voigt, 2002), which is linked to the university's student-records system. Their assessment approach is "it takes a campus to graduate a student." By involving both students and the university community in collaborative ways, this survey has led to a dramatic rise in Loyola's key measures of success along with a transformation in the way the campus thinks about assessment and institutional effectiveness.

These tools provide a way of reviewing the advising program and focus on what Trudy Banta (2002) advocates: 1) say what you do, 2) do what you say, and 3) provide institution-specific and comparative evidence. Good assessment, like good advising and teaching, is good research and should be used to ask students, the institution, and providers, 1) Is advising more effective? 2) Are students learning more? 3) Are students more satisfied? 4) Are faculty more satisfied? and 5) Do outcomes justify costs?

Above all, assessment is effective when it asks students directly how the institution can improve the academic experience and tailors its findings to improving the institution's academic-advising program. Critical to the credibility of any assessment program is that action steps for improvement and organizational changes be derived from student concern. Just as important is reporting back to them, closing the communication loop and reassuring students that their views are taken seriously by management. To bring about an active role of students and others in the improvement process, feedback and resulting actions must be made publicly available. One way of doing this is to form an institutional advising-steering council that involves student leaders, faculty, administrators, and perhaps even alumni and staff in the assessment process as well as in promoting advising as teaching.

Finally, Banta (2002) offers several principles in building an effective outcomes-assessment plan. She divides these characteristics into three phases and several principles. Effective outcomes assessment begins with a planning phase. Then comes careful attention to implementation. Finally, there is the improving and sustaining phase of assessment. Improvement, not just accountability, is the bottom line in assessment. Banta and her colleagues succinctly outline the processes of involvement, leadership, and actual improvement in the system (please note that in Figure 1.5 only a sampling of the principles are given).

FIGURE 1.5

AN ASSESSMENT MODEL

Planning

- Involves stakeholders (faculty, administrators, students) from the outset to incorporate their needs and interests and solicit their later support.
- Begins when the need is recognized; timing is crucial.
- Has a written plan that is related to goals people value and to conditions that promote change.

Implementation

- Has knowledgeable, effective leadership.
- Recognizes that assessment is essential to learning and improvement.
- Assesses processes as well as outcomes.
- Is undertaken in an enabling and supportive environment.
- Incorporates communication with constituents concerning activities and findings.
- Effective outcomes assessment produces data that guide improvement on a continuing basis.

Improving and Sustaining

- Produces credible evidence of learning and organizational effectiveness.
- Ensures that assessment data are used continuously to improve programs and services.
- Provides a vehicle for demonstrating accountability to stakeholders.
- Encompasses ongoing evaluation and improvement. (Adapted from Banta, 2002)

Skill Development and Campus Collaboration

Setting expectations for learning is part of the academic curriculum. As with any course of instruction, aligning course purposes with delivery of content is of obvious importance. To be equally effective in advising as teaching, purposes or expectations for advising must be also be aligned with content and delivery. How and when advisor skill development should take place is discussed in Chapters 4 and 8. Areas of expectations discussed in these chapters include support for faculty advising, funding, facilities, collaboration, communication, and the use of technology, time, qualifications, and training or development of faculty for advising as teaching. Both chapters point out key resources and sample training material.

Part of skill development is helping faculty become aware of and know how to enlist the aid of the available campus services to meet students' diverse needs. Advising as teaching necessarily involves collaboration with all segments of the campus community. Figures 1.3 and 1.6 illustrate key academic needs of students by academic class (for example, freshmen, sophomore) and show campus services organized around the student point of view.

Technology Interface

Chapter 12 is an excellent resource for the technology component of the advising-as-teaching framework, presenting a variety of technology uses that faculty can incorporate into the advising process.

Today's information technology, particularly web technology, is a viable tool or enabler not only for enhancing the classroom experience but also for improving faculty advising. Using the web, students can access academic-planning data themselves and seek advice from professional staff and faculty members as needed. Self-service is a preferred mode of service delivery for many students, because they often need information at times when college or university offices are closed. Students also prefer convenient access, available at any place and at any time. Likewise, for faculty advisors, using information technology to provide students with timely and convenient access to academic information relieves them of the mundane task of providing routine data for students (Kramer, 2002).

FIGURE 1.6

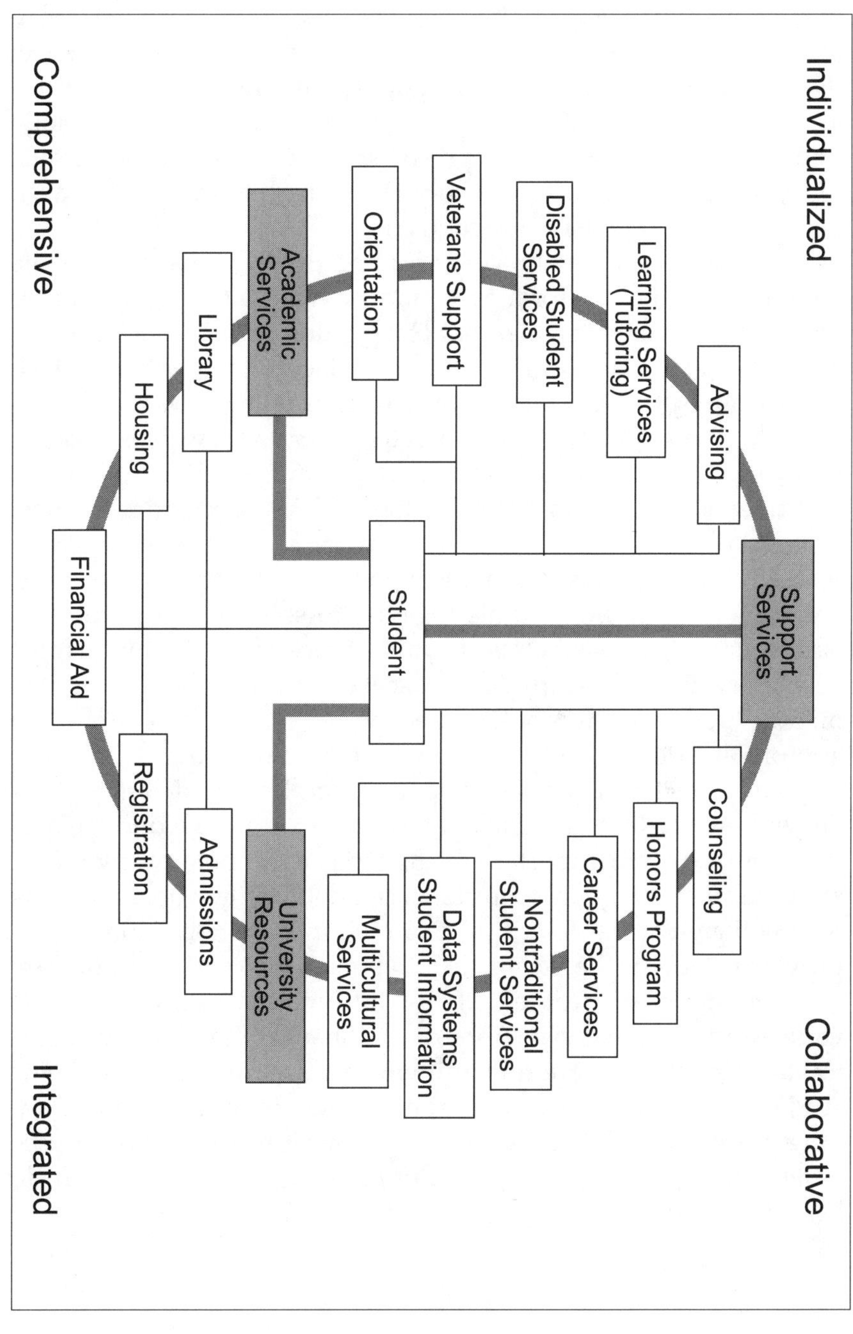
Individualized
Collaborative
Comprehensive
Integrated
Advising
Learning Services (Tutoring)
Disabled Student Services
Veterans Support
Orientation
Academic Services
Library
Housing
Support Services
Student
Financial Aid
Counseling
Honors Program
Career Services
Nontraditional Student Services
Data Systems Student Information
Multicultural Services
University Resources
Admissions
Registration

Furthermore, information technology can complement the institution's goal of encouraging students to be self-reliant while positioning faculty advisors to help students make informed, responsible decisions and set realistic goals. Thus, technology becomes effective only as it is integrated into, supports, and humanizes the service environment for advisors and students; however, as technology transforms the way we do things, so too must faculty advisors transform themselves. Their focus should be on high touch as much as, if not more than, high tech and high effect.

One note of caution, however, is appropriate at this point: While the above may be true for most faculty advising situations, there are times when technology may not bring value to the advising situation and may in fact present barriers to faculty to student contact. Faculty advisors must play a role in determining how technology can help support student needs. On the other hand, web technology is having an impact on how campus departments define themselves and how students gain access to them. That is, historically, most campus departments have defined themselves in a hierarchical model. Web technology has made it possible to flatten organizations and thus bring multiple units together to solve student problems (see Figure 1.7). Nevertheless, the human face of the institution must be preserved. Each institution must work to find the appropriate mix of information technology and personalized services that are appropriate for the institution's goals and culture (Kramer, 2002).

When appropriately defined and implemented, technology allows both students and faculty advisors to move beyond the routine. Perhaps more important, using today's technology anywhere, anytime, and at any pace, students can determine where and how they will gain access to critical planning information. Moreover, it provides students the means to both personalize and monitor their academic (degree) progress. Thus, information technology adds value to advising when it supports or enhances the delivery of critical academic information in a timely and accurate way and helps students and advisors to engage one another in the academic-planning process. The challenge for institutions is to effectively balance what computers can do best with what faculty advisors can do best.

FIGURE 1.7

Student Academic Services

Vertical vs. Horizontal Collaboration

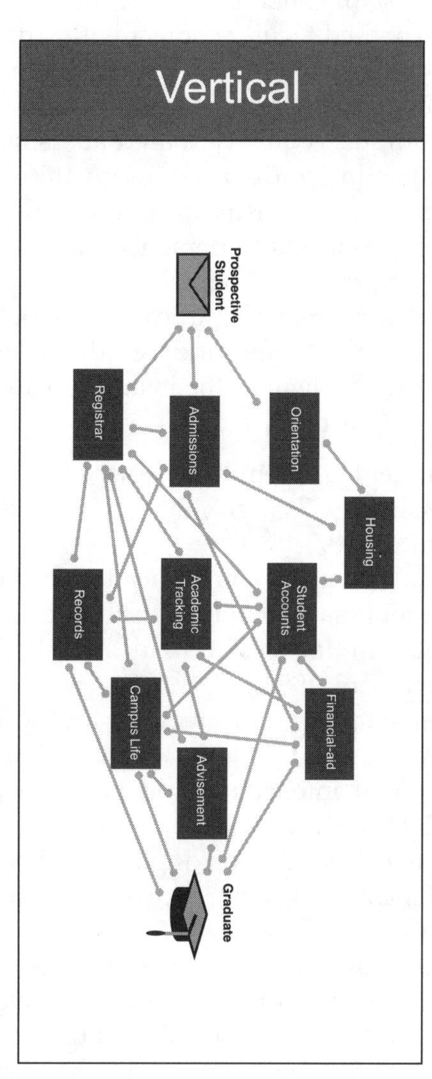

VS.

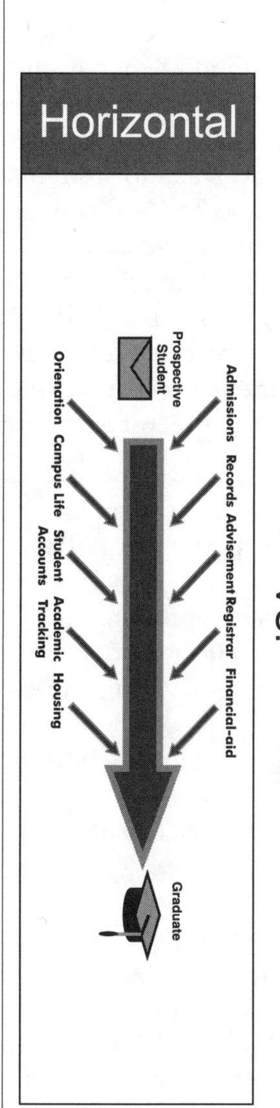

CONCLUSION

Richard Brown noted that "the most important factor in retention rates is a relationship with an adult on campus. Usually, that means a faculty member" (Altschuler, 2001, p. 17). Others who have researched faculty contact with students tend to concur with Brown's retention notion. They conclude that the best success case for students is when they are involved with faculty and involved on the campus. A quality shared-advising effort leads to students' persistence to graduation; motivation to succeed in college; involvement in the institution; satisfaction with college, academic, and career connection; personal and academic success; academic achievement; and cognitive development (Kramer, 1995). Specifically, there is significant and positive research on these aspects of the student-undergraduate experience. For example, student involvement in the institution and regular faculty-student interaction positively affects

- Student academic success, satisfaction, and retention (Astin, 1997; Light, 2001; Pascarella & Terenzini, 1991; Tinto, 1987).
- Student achievement, academic skill development, and general satisfaction with the undergraduate experience (Pascarella & Terenzini, 1991; Volkwein, King, & Terenzini, 1986).
- Satisfaction with faculty and quality of instruction (Astin, 1997).
- Student intellectual and personal growth (Astin, 1997; Light, 2001).
- Career decision making (Astin, 1997).
- Nonclassroom or cocurricular activities (Light 2001; Pascarella & Terenzini, 1991).

Indeed, as Chickering and Reisser (1993) commented, "students who reported the greatest cognitive development were also most likely to perceive faculty as being concerned with teaching and student development and to report having a close, influential relationship with at least one faculty member" (p. 322).

Clearly, the frequency and quality of faculty and student interaction significantly affect student satisfaction within the college experience. As the barriers that prevent faculty-student contact are removed, studies confirm positive correlations with other areas—student success, achievement, retention, and satisfaction with faculty, the quality of instruction, and in attending college altogether.

As the authors point out in the respective chapters that follow, the areas of faculty advisor development, role definition, evaluation, recognition and reward, and the use of technology are the most significant methods through which advising services can be improved, but, unfortunately, these are still the least effective components of the campus advising program (Habley & Morales, 1998).

Amid this discussion on what faculty can and should do, students can certainly help the advising process by adjusting their expectations. That is, rather than looking for Mr. Chips, a surrogate parent or friend, as Altschuler (2001) noted, they can view advising as teaching as an extension of the classroom. Furthermore, when they share the responsibility of advising they come prepared as they would for a course of study, they take initiative, keep appointments, and participate in the evaluation of advising.

A challenge, however, that all academic institutions and faculty advisors face is the diverse makeup of the student body. To be effective, it is important that advisors focus on inclusion of student diversity in the teaching-advising process. Recognizing, including, or even celebrating the diverse backgrounds of students in advising as teaching has great potential to enhance the student-faculty relationship and broaden the institutional and student perspectives and growth (El-Khawas, 1996; Light, 2001; Moore & Upcraft, 1990). Faculty find the same diversity among students in the classes they teach, so this is nothing new; but the reality is that a single faculty—even one who rigorously practices student-development principles—cannot meet diverse students needs alone. Fortunately, it takes a campus to graduate a student. Campus-wide collaboration in advising students is the key.

Furthermore, these challenges can be met, according to Chickering and Gamson (1987), through establishing and emphasizing campus-wide the following principles of good practice in undergraduate education: 1) regular student-faculty contact, 2) student cooperation and responsibility for their education, 3) active learning, 4) prompt feedback, 5) reward and recognition of time on task, 6) high expectations, and 7) respect of diverse talents and ways of learning.

In conclusion, along with implementing the advising-as-teaching framework, faculty advising can be strengthened and positioned for improvement as advising as teaching by the following conditions:

- There is campus leadership and vision that build a campus culture based on student caring.
- Students are involved not only in assessing programs put in place for them but also in having an active role and voice in improving advising performance.
- Campus leaders encourage innovation and evaluation of faculty advising and reward, recognize, and disseminate successful innovations.
- Faculty are supported as integral partners in the advising enterprise.
- There are thoughtful, purposeful efforts to get in students' way—to be intrusive. Rather than get out of the way of students, Light (2001) suggests that faculty advisors should get in students' way. Students should do many things on their own, he contends, but faculty should not hesitate to help. Faculty can play an important role in helping students evaluate and reevaluate their choices.
- The advising program is well defined and based on the premises of student growth and success and the student-development point of view. From the classroom to one-on-one advising, advising as teaching can use the same learning goals. Such goals usually include helping students clarify, connect, and crystallize life (personal), career, and academic goals; establishing and developing a thoughtful educational plan; maximally using available resources; becoming involved in the academic community; and regularly evaluating individual progress.
- Faculty advising is motivated by high expectations and standards.
- Diversity is embraced and founded upon the principle of inclusion.

How can each faculty advisor make a difference in the lives of students? Referring to the digital society in which we live,

Rosabeth Kanter (2001) observed: "It will require a deeper emphasis on human skills that build meaningful community out of mere connections" (p. 12). Indeed, in behalf of the students who depend on us, the theme of all of our efforts to improve faculty advising on the campus might be to make meaningful community out of mere connections with students. The framework for advising as teaching is one practical and faculty-relevant way to add value and purpose to student-faculty contact.

REFERENCES

Altschuler, G. C. (2001, November 11). Take this advice, or don't. *New York Times,* [Educational Life Section] p. 4A.

Astin, A. W. (1997). *What matters in college? Four critical years revisited.* San Francisco, CA: Jossey-Bass.

Banta, T. W., & Associates. (2002). *Building a scholarship of assessment.* San Francisco, CA: Jossey-Bass.

Chickering, A. W. (1994). Empowering lifelong self-development. *AAHE Bulletin, 47* (4), 3–5.

Chickering, A. W., & Gamson, Z. F. (1987). Seven principles for good practice in undergraduate education. *AAHE Bulletin, 39* (7), 3–7.

Chickering, A. W., & Reisser, L. (1993). *Education and identity* (2nd ed.). San Francisco, CA: Jossey-Bass.

Crookston, B. B. (1972). A developmental view of academic advising as teaching. *Journal of College Student Personnel, 13,* 12–17.

El-Khawas, E. (1996). Student diversity on today's campuses. In S. R. Komives & D. B. Woodward, Jr. (Eds.), *Student services: A handbook for the profession* (pp. 64–80). San Francisco, CA: Jossey-Bass.

Frost, S. H. (1995). Designing and implementing a faculty-based advising program. *NACADA Journal, 1,* 27–32.

Habley, W. R., & Morales, R. H. (1998). *Current practices in academic advising: Final report on ACT's fifth national survey of academic advising* (Monograph Series No. 6). Manhattan, KS: National Academic Advising Association.

Hardee, M. D. (1970). *Faculty advising in colleges and universities.* Washington, DC: American Personnel and Guidance Association.

Kanter, R. M. (2001). *Evolve!: Succeeding in the digital culture of tomorrow.* Watertown, MA: Harvard Business School Publishing.

Kramer, G. L. (Ed.). (1995). *Reaffirming the role of faculty in academic advising* (Monograph Series No. 1). Manhattan, KS: National Academic Advising Association.

Kramer, G. L. (2002). Online advising. *ECAR Research Bulletin, 15,* 2–10.

Kuh, G. D. (2000). *National survey of student engagement: Conceptual framework and overview of psychometric properties.* Bloomington, IN: Indiana University, Center for Postsecondary Research and Planning.

Light, R. J. (2001). *Making the most of college: Students speak their minds.* Cambridge, MA: Harvard University Press.

Moore, L. V., & Upcraft, M. L. (1990). Theory in student affairs: Evolving perspective." In L. V. Moore (Ed.), *Evolving theoretical perspectives on students* (pp. 3–23). New Directions for Student Services, No. 51. San Francisco, CA: Jossey-Bass.

O'Banion, T. (1972). An academic advising model. *Junior College Journal, 42* (6), 62–69.

Pascarella, E. T., & Terenzini, P. T. (1991). *How college affects students: Findings and insights from twenty years of research.* San Francisco, CA: Jossey-Bass.

Stark, J. S. (1989). *Student goals for colleges and courses: A missing link in assessing and improving academic achievement* (ASHE-ERIC Report No. 6). Washington, DC: George Washington University.

Tinto, V. (1993). *Leaving college: Rethinking the causes and cures of student attrition* (2nd ed.). Chicago, IL: University of Chicago Press.

Upcraft, M. L., & Kramer, G. L. (Eds.). (1995). *First-year academic advising: Patterns in the present, pathways to the future.* Columbia, SC: University of South Carolina, National Resource Center for the Freshman Year Experience and Students in Transition.

Voigt, L. (2002). *Using assessment to foster a campus learning cycle and institutional effectiveness.* Paper presented at the Assessing Quality in Higher Education Conference, University of Vienna.

Volkwein, J., King, M., & Terenzini, P. (1986). Student-faculty relationships and intellectual growth among transfer students. *Journal of Higher Education, 57,* 413–430.

2 FACULTY ADVISING: PRACTICE AND PROMISE

Wesley R. Habley

Although the roles and functions of academic advising services providers reflect the development of American colleges and universities, one historical constant in academic advising is that faculty have always played a prominent role. Informal advising of students was a role of faculty members in the earliest American colleges, both private and church-related (Rudolph, 1962). Until the last half of the 19th century, the informal, and largely unorganized, role of the faculty advisor/mentor was predominant. In 1876, however, Johns Hopkins University initiated what is believed to be the first system of faculty advising based primarily on an influx of new students. And in 1888 Harvard College initiated a program of faculty advisors for freshmen. Indicating a need to coordinate the effort of faculty advisors, the president of Johns Hopkins appointed the first "chief of faculty advisors" in 1899 (Cowley, 1949). For nearly a half century, the role of faculty advisor as informal mentor remained relatively consistent. Yet, during that time period, it also became obvious that faculty members could not respond to all the complex student concerns that confronted them. As a result, the first deans of men and deans of women positions began appearing on college campuses in the early 20th century. The deans' role included handling disciplinary duties, providing extracurricular activities, and resolving academic problems.

As American higher education approached the middle of the 20th century, a number of factors were reshaping its organization and the role of faculty. The first factor that influenced the role of faculty was the increasing diversity of post-secondary institutions and of the students those institutions served. A uniquely American system of higher education included public and private universities, small liberal arts colleges, city colleges, church-related colleges, two-year colleges, and technical colleges. Each institutional type and even some institutions within types differed perceptibly in mission, goals and objectives, curricula, organization, and means of financial support. In addition, fueled by the concept of American democracy, higher education became increasingly seen as an opportunity for all members of society, not just a privilege extended to the children of the elite. And, particularly following World War II, students from more diverse socioeconomic and cultural backgrounds not only contributed to a college enrollment boom, but also provided significant challenges for those who were to provide advice and counsel to them. These factors of diversity clearly shaped the faculty's perception of their role in advising and mentoring students, since timeworn assumptions about student background and academic preparation were no longer unilaterally applicable to their students.

In addition to the increasing diversity of institutions and students has been an evolution of the curriculum in American colleges. In colonial times, preparation programs were few, the curriculum was clearly defined and sequenced, and there were no electives. The proliferation of institutional types led to dramatic increases in fields of study and in the breadth of course offerings. As a result of the new breadth, flexibility, and complexity of the curriculum, faculty advisors were no longer in a position in which they could intimately know and interpret the curriculum for all programs within the institution.

A final factor that was to reshape the role of the faculty advisor was the continued broadening of expectations for faculty performance. To the faculty member's role as teacher and mentor were added ever-increasing expectations for him or her to be researcher, writer, grant procurer, and participant in faculty governance and other activities. Although these roles were defined and rewarded differently in the various institutional types, it became clear that college faculty were expected to be proficient in multiple roles, with advising only one of many.

With these many changes, many people wondered whether faculty members had the information, the time, and in some cases, the interest in serving as academic advisors. Some of these people concluded that individuals other than faculty members should serve as such advisors. There is evidence of counselors supplementing the work of faculty advisors as early as 1920 at Harvard and Johns Hopkins Universities (Rudolph, 1977), but it is only since World War II that there has been a decided trend toward individuals other than instructional faculty delivering academic-advising services. Currently, many campuses report using counselors, full-time advisors, peer advisors, and paraprofessional advisors to provide academic advising (Habley, 1992).

Trends notwithstanding, however, faculty advising services remain a constant in American higher education. In American College Testing's (ACT) most recent survey of advising practices, Habley and Morales (1998) discovered that on 48% of the campuses surveyed, faculty members were the only individuals who delivered academic advising, while in 42% of the institutions surveyed, faculty advisors and staff in an advising office shared advising responsibilities. And even on those campuses with advising offices, 39% reported that faculty members were utilized to provide services within those advising offices as either primary service providers (18%) or as a supplement to primary service providers (21%). These data suggest that faculty members are responsible for somewhere between 75% and 90% of all the academic advising that takes place on American campuses.

There is also widespread support for faculty members being involved in academic advising. Chickering and Gamson (1987) assert that "frequent faculty-student contact in and out of the classroom is the most important factor in student motivation and involvement" (p. 4). And because academic advising is the only structured activity on campus that encourages ongoing, individual interaction between the student and a concerned representative of the institution, it naturally follows that advising can become a potent strategy for promoting informal out-of-class contact between students and faculty. Frost (1991) underscores this concept. She suggests that advising, unlike most out-of-class activities, is a service provided to most students; advising provides a natural setting for out-of-class contacts to occur; and advising involves intellectual matters, the most important area of concern for students.

This history makes it clear that faculty advising is a constant in the history of American higher education, that it is the predominant method for delivering advising services, and that it is a critical factor in both student success and in institutional effectiveness.

Despite this, many people contend that faculty advising receives far too little attention and that decision-makers and resource allocators remain largely uninformed about effective advising practices. The remainder of this chapter focuses on the status of faculty advising practices and the opinions students have of faculty advisors.

FACULTY ADVISING PRACTICES

Data on the status of advising practices are taken from ACT's *Fifth National Survey of Academic Advising* (Habley & Morales, 1998) and, where possible for comparative purposes, ACT's *Fourth National Survey of Academic Advising* (Habley, 1992). Since the data contained in the 1998 report are voluminous (more than 50 tables), this chapter includes only observations on the data. Although the report provides data cross-tabbed by institutional types, the primary focus here will be on institutions nationally. Readers who wish either to understand the methodologies or to delve more deeply into the data should consult the references listed above.

The 1987, 1992, and 1998 ACT advising surveys each included a section on academic advising in the academic unit or department. The survey questions were intended to provide a description of existing advising practices in the following areas: delivery of advising services, advisor load and student contact, training of faculty advisors, evaluation of faculty advisors, recognition and reward for faculty advisors, and faculty advisor information sources. Respondents were asked to indicate whether a characteristic or activity existed in all departments on campus, in some of the departments on campus, or in none of the departments on campus. National survey observations for each of these areas are provided below.

Delivery of Advising Services

Items in this part of the survey dealt with the identification of individuals who serve as academic advisors, the prevalent roles of those advisors, and the utilization of group advising formats to deliver advising services to students.

Observations on advisor types and the extent of their involvement within academic units:

- Instructional faculty continue to be the primary deliverers of advising services in academic departments.

Fifty-five percent of campuses use full- or part-time non-teaching advisors in at least some of their departments. Fourteen percent use clerical staff to advise in at least some of their departments.

- Although there is a slight decrease in use of paraprofessionals, 23% of campuses use paraprofessionals to deliver advising in at least some of their departments.
- After a significant decrease in peer advising, only 15% of campuses use peer advisors in at least some of their departments.

Observations on the methods by which faculty members become involved in academic advising:

- Across all institution types, faculty members are generally required to advise.
- There are some indications that advising by faculty is becoming a voluntary activity in at least some departments on campuses.

Observations on the extent to which group advising formats were utilized to deliver advising services:

- There have been dramatic declines in the use of group advising formats in academic departments.
- The dominant form of group advising, used in about a third of the institutions, is the small group meeting during orientation or registration.
- Only one in eight institutions provides coursework to augment advising in the academic department.

Advisor Load and Student Contact

For a faculty advising program to be effective, several factors related to advisor-advisee contact need to be taken into account. First, the faculty advisor must have a reasonable number of students to advise. Second, the faculty member must devote time to the function of academic advising, allowing for more than perfunctory schedule approval once each academic term. Finally, institutional policies and procedures should maximize the potential for interaction between the advisee and the faculty advisor.

Observations on the typical advisor load in academic departments:

- Faculty advisor loads are as variable within institutions as they are across institutions.
- The modal advising load for faculty with full-time instructional loads is between 20 and 40 advisees.
- The mean advising load for full-time instructional faculty across all institutional types is 26.4 advisees.

Observations on the amount of time faculty spend in the advising function:

- Data from the 1998 survey seem to refute the commonly held opinion that for a typical faculty advisor about 5% of his or her workload is spent in advising responsibilities.
- The mean percentage of faculty time reportedly spent in advising is consistent across all institutional types, with a range of 10.5% (two-year public institutions) to 11.8% (four-year private institutions).

Observations on the frequency and degree of intrusiveness of advising in the academic departments:

- The mean number of student contacts with a faculty advisor is 4.0 per term.
- In general, the occasions when students are required to contact their faculty advisors have remained stable over the past decade.
- At half or more of the campuses in the fifth survey, contact with faculty advisors is required for registration (80%), dropping/withdrawing from a class (66%), adding a class (64%), changing a major (59%), approving graduation plans (59%), and declaring a major (53%).

Training of Faculty Advisors

Because training of faculty advisors is a significant factor in the effectiveness of their advising, a set of items on the survey dealt with the existence of training programs, the formats they utilized, and the topics included in such training.

Observations on the existence of training activities for faculty advisors:

- About one-fourth of college campuses require training for faculty advisors.
- About one-third of college campuses provide training

for faculty advisors.

Observations on formats for training faculty advisors:

- The most common format for faculty-advisor training is a single workshop of one day or less per year.
- A significant proportion of faculty-advisor training is delivered through individualized training based on faculty member needs.

The final aspect of training for faculty advisors that was explored in the national survey dealt with the topics included in the training programs. The topics were organized to include three training content areas: conceptual skills, informational skills, and relational skills. "Conceptual skills" are defined as the ideas that advisors must understand. For the purpose of this survey, these included the importance of advising and the definition of advising. "Information skills" are defined as the things an advisor must know. For survey purposes, these included academic regulations, policies and registration procedures, campus referral sources, career and employment information, and the use of information sources. "Relational skills" are defined as those behaviors an advisor must exhibit in the advising interaction, and include counseling skills, interview skills, and decision-making skills.

Observations on training topics for faculty advisors:

- The most common topics included in faculty-advisor training focus on information and facts, while some time is also given to such concepts as the definition of advising. Topics that focus on building strong relationships with advisees receive very little attention.
- The data on faculty-advisor training support the traditional definition of academic advising as giving information that leads to the selection and scheduling of courses.

Evaluation of Faculty Advisors

Observations of the evaluation and frequency of individual faculty advisor performance:

- Fewer than three in ten (29%) campuses evaluate the performance of faculty advisors.
- Only 23% of colleges systematically evaluate faculty advisors (every term, every year, or every other year).

Observations on the types of evaluation:

- Student evaluation is the primary evaluation strategy. Even so, only 24% of campuses report that this strategy is in place for some or all of their departments.
- Only 15% of institutions rely on supervisor evaluation of faculty advisors in some or in all academic departments.

Recognition and Reward for Faculty Advisors

Observations on recognition, reward, or compensation provided for faculty advisors:

- Fewer than one in three (31%) campuses recognize, reward, or compensate faculty for academic advising.
- The most commonly cited reward strategy is to make advising a minor consideration in promotion and tenure. Yet, only 8% of all campuses employ this method in all departments.
- There was a consistent decline in all types of recognition strategies for faculty advisors from the 1987 and 1992 data.
- Campus-wide recognition, reward, or compensation for faculty advisors declined between the 1992 and the 1998 surveys.

Faculty-Advisor Information Sources

Because access to reference tools and information about advisees is critical to the advising process, respondents were asked to assess the extent to which faculty advisors were provided with those information resources.

Observations on reference materials routinely provided to faculty advisors:

- Support or reference materials made available to faculty advisors is on the decline.
- The only support tools that more than half of the institutions provide for faculty advisors in all academic departments are planning worksheets (65%), advising handbooks (56%), and campus-referral directories (53%).
- Fewer than four of ten campuses provide access to student retention data, student-population descriptive data, employment-outlook projections, record-keeping forms, or articulation worksheets to advisors in all departments.

Observations on the availability of information about individual advisees:

- Providing student information resources to faculty advisors appears to be in slight decline as indicated by an increase in information sources reported under "no departments provide."
- Faculty advisors are more likely to be provided with admission-test scores, college transcripts, and placement test scores.
- Faculty advisors are less likely to be provided with the admission application, high school transcript, and noncognitive information collected through the admission testing process.

Commentary on Faculty Advising Practices

Commentary on faculty advising included in the final reports of previous surveys optimistically focused on slight incremental gains in practices that support faculty advising. Yet, a review of data from the fifth survey provides less support for optimism on continued incremental gains. Only a few elements of quality faculty advising improved between the 1992 and 1998 surveys. Among observable improvements were increased involvement of faculty, increased tendency to require contact with faculty advisors, and expansion of the information resources provided to faculty advisors. Some very important facets of quality faculty advising have not changed since the 1992 survey. Those are the number of contacts per term, advisor-advisee ratios, evaluation of advisors, reward for advisors, and faculty time spent in advising.

Finally, there have been declines in the most critical areas of faculty advising: training, evaluation, and recognition and reward. While many individuals believe that faculty advisors provide effective advising, others believe that advising by faculty is perfunctory and ineffective. And, indeed, one can probably find both good and bad examples of faculty advising on any college campus. In reality, it is not individual faculty performance that is at issue here. The problem is that practices that support faculty advising are inconsistent and unsystematic. Data from the fifth survey support the contention that existing problems in faculty advising are systemic to each campus. Indeed, the lack of a systematic, campus-wide approach to critical advising practices may very well be the root cause underlying the inconsistency in faculty advising. This situation is particularly acute in training, evaluation, and recognition and reward. Only 23% of campuses nationwide require training for faculty advisors. And only 29% of campuses nationwide regularly evaluate the faculty member's performance in academic advising. Finally, only 31% provide any form of recognition or reward for those doing faculty advising. Unless key administrators place a high priority on the implementation of consistent campus-wide practices for training, evaluating, and rewarding faculty advisors, improvements in advising by faculty will rely on happenstance and be piecemeal at best. Other chapters in this book provide focus on training, evaluation, and reward.

STUDENT OPINIONS OF FACULTY ADVISORS

The data reported here are based on a sample of 41,293 student records from 93 colleges in 38 states that administered ACT's Survey of Academic Advising between January 1, 1995, and September 30, 1999. Normative data of this type are often referred to as "user norms," since they simply represent a composite of the data obtained by a number of institutions that administered an instrument over a particular period of time. Not all instruments processed by ACT during the period have been included in the sample. Approximately 2,920 student records were eliminated to guarantee that no single institution would be overrepresented in the data. The colleges in the sample include large and small, public and private, and two- and four-year institutions.

Several important qualifications are necessary with respect to the data presented in the sample. First, the data are not based on a random or preselected sample of students or colleges. While a variety of institutions are represented in the sample, ACT did not attempt to alter the sample to provide a nationally representative data set. Second, the survey instruments were administered in different ways to different groups of students from the various institutions represented. Consequently, the response rates obtained by the institutions using the survey vary widely. The effects of the varying administration modes and response rates on the normative data are not known. Finally, the number of cases and institutions represented in the report was limited; therefore, comparisons based on the data must be interpreted with caution. Of this sample, 29,836 students reported on academic advising they had received from a faculty advisor. The results reported below are from two of the four sections of the survey: "Academic Advising Needs" and "Impressions of Your Advisor." The observations that follow on these two survey sections are based on data reported in Appendix 2.1 and Appendix 2.2, respectively.

Academic Advising Needs

The academic advising needs section of the survey (see Appendix 2.1) included 18 items and was divided into two parts. In Part A, students were asked to identify the extent to which the listed topics were discussed with their current faculty advisors. Part A included three possible responses: 1) have not discussed and do not need to; 2) have not discussed, but should have; and 3) have discussed. Students who had discussed a particular topic with their advisors were then asked in Part B to rate their satisfaction with the advisor's assistance by checking one of five possible responses: 1) Very Dissatisfied, 2) Dissatisfied, 3) Neutral, 4) Satisfied, 5) Very Satisfied. In Appendix 2.1 we see the percentage of students selecting each of the three possible responses allowed in Part A. The last column, based on answers given in Part B, indicates the mean satisfaction level—on a scale of 1 to 5—of the students with the responses they received.

Have not discussed and do not need to. The percentages of students selecting this response ranged from a low of 10.8% to a high of 75.5% on the 18 items.

Items with the lowest percentage of students selecting this response were

- Scheduling/registration procedures (10.8%)
- My academic progress (17.1%)
- Meeting requirements for graduation, student teaching, certification, etc. (19.5%)

Items with the highest percentage of students selecting this response were

- Withdrawing/transferring from this institution (75.5%)
- Dealing with personal problems (71.1%)
- Obtaining remedial/tutorial assistance (67.6%)

- Obtaining employment on campus (66.2%)

Have not discussed, but should have. The percentage of students selecting this response ranged from a low of 7.4% to a high of 32.3% on the 18 items.

Items with the lowest percentage of students selecting this response were

- Scheduling/registration procedures (7.4%)
- Dealing with personal problems (7.7%)
- Dropping/adding courses (8.7%)
- Withdrawing/transferring from this institution (9.9%)

Items with the highest percentage of students selecting this response were

- Finding a job after college/job placement (32.3%)
- Identifying career areas which fit my skills, abilities and interests (26.5%)
- Continuing my education after graduation (26.3%)
- Matching my learning style to courses and instructors (25.3%)

Have discussed. The percentage of students selecting this response ranged from a low of 10.1% to a high of 75.9% on the 18 items.

Items with the lowest percentage of students selecting this response were

- Withdrawing/transferring from this institution (10.1%)
- Obtaining employment on campus (13.6%)
- Obtaining remedial/tutorial assistance (13.9%)

Items with the highest percentage of students selecting this response were

- Scheduling/registration procedures (75.9%)
- My academic progress (60.7%)
- Meeting requirements for graduation, student teaching, certification, etc. (56.3%)

Mean ratings for satisfaction of academic advising needs. Of those students who had discussed particular topics with their faculty advisors, the mean ratings (from 5=very satisfied to 1=very dissatisfied) ranged from a low of 3.98 (obtaining financial aid) to a high of 4.31 (dealing with personal problems). Mean ratings on 16 of the 18 items were at or above 4.00 (satisfied).

Items with the lowest satisfaction levels were

- Obtaining financial aid (3.98)
- Withdrawing/transferring from this institution (3.99)
- Obtaining remedial/tutorial assistance (4.04)
- Obtaining course credit through non-traditional means (4.06)

Items with the highest satisfaction levels were

- Dealing with personal problems (4.31)
- Identifying career areas that fit my skills, abilities, and interests (4.20)
- Matching my learning style to particular courses and instructors (4.18)
- Clarifying my life/career goals (4.15)

Student Impressions of Advisors

In the "Impressions of Your Advisor" section of the survey (see Appendix 2.2), students were asked to rate their current faculty advisors on 36 advisor traits and/or characteristics. The 5-point scale included the following descriptors: 1) Strongly Disagree, 2) Disagree, 3) Neutral, 4) Agree, and 5) Strongly Agree. Students were also given a "Does Not Apply" response option. The mean ratings for impressions of faculty advisors ranged from a low of 3.25 (Takes the initiative in arranging meetings with me) to a high of 4.08 (Respects my right to make my own decisions). The mean of means for all impressions of faculty advisors is 3.83, which falls between "neutral" and "agree" on the rating scale.

Items with the lowest satisfaction levels were

- Takes the initiative in arranging meetings with me (3.25)
- Encourages my involvement with extracurricular activities (3.41)
- Encourages me to talk about myself and my college experiences (3.45)
- Helps me explore careers in my field of interest (3.49)
- Anticipates my needs (3.52)

Items with the highest satisfaction levels were

- Respects my right to make my own decisions (4.17)
- Is a good listener (4.10)

- Knows who I am (4.09)
- Is approachable and easy to talk to (4.09)
- Keeps personal information confidential (4.08)
- Has a sense of humor (4.08)

Commentary on Student Responses to Advising Needs and Impressions of Faculty Advisors

A review of the data on student opinions of their advisors leads to four important observations. First, the data point to the conclusion that faculty advisors are satisfactorily meeting student needs, while also identifying areas where advising could be strengthened. Faculty advisors would do well to focus on the advising needs with the highest percentage of student responses of "have not discussed, but should have." Those items are finding a job after college/job placement; identifying career areas that fit my skills, abilities, and interests; continuing my education after graduation; and matching my learning style to particular courses and instructors. The second observation is that students generally have positive impressions of their faculty advisors. The data also suggests, however, that the following areas need improvement: taking the initiative in arranging meetings, encouraging involvement in extracurricular activities, taking the time to talk about personal experiences, assisting the advisee to explore careers, and anticipating advisee needs. The third observation is that the data should cause critics of faculty advising to reject anecdotal evidence as being representative of all faculty advising. Finally, these data underscore the conclusion of an earlier study by Habley (1994) that compared student evaluations of faculty advisors to ratings of other advisor types. That study suggested that on all dimensions, faculty advisors perform as well as, if not better than, other advisor types.

CONCLUSION

The information presented in this chapter might lead to a variety of conclusions about the state of academic advising. Yet, in the mind of this author, there is only one viable conclusion and that conclusion is best captured by an "if-then" question: If practices that support faculty advising are far from exemplary and if students believe that faculty advisors are satisfactorily meeting their needs and the students have generally favorable impressions of their faculty advisors, then what impact would faculty advising have on students if practices supporting faculty advisors were strengthened? The answer to the question is almost overpowering and should serve as strong leverage for enhancing the quality of faculty advising on every college campus.

REFERENCES

American College Testing. (1994). *Normative report of the survey of academic advising.* Iowa City, IA: Author.

Chickering, A. W., & Gamson, Z. F. (1987). Seven principles for good practice in undergraduate education. *AAHE Bulletin, 39* (7), 3–7.

Cowley, W. H. (1949). Some history and a venture in prophecy. In E. G. Williamson (Ed.), *Trends in student personnel work* (pp. 12–27). Minneapolis, MN: University of Minnesota Press.

Frost, S. H. (1991). *Academic advising for student success: A system of shared responsibility* (ASHE-ERIC Higher Education Report No. 3). Washington, DC: ERIC Clearinghouse on Higher Education, George Washington University.

Habley, W. R. (1992). *Fulfilling the promise? Final report of the fourth national survey on academic advising.* Iowa City, IA: The American College Testing Program.

Habley, W. R. (1994). FIRE! (Ready–Aim): Is criticism of faculty advising warranted? *NACADA Journal, 14* (2), 25–31.

Habley, W. R., & Morales, R. H. (1998). *Current practices in academic advising: Final report on ACT's fifth national survey of academic advising* (Monograph Series No. 6). Manhattan, KS: National Academic Advising Association.

Rudolph, F. (1962). *The American college and university.* New York, NY: Knopf.

Rudolph, F. (1977). *Curriculum.* San Francisco, CA: Jossey-Bass.

APPENDIX 2.1
ACADEMIC ADVISING NEEDS

Situations	Not Discussed No Need %	Not Discussed Should Have %	Have Discussed %	Mean Rating Satisfaction
1. My academic progress	17.1	16.5	60.7	4.08
2. Scheduling/registration procedures	10.8	7.4	75.9	4.10
3. Dropping/adding courses	34.8	8.7	51	4.14
4. Obtaining course credit through nontraditional means (CLEP, PEP, job experience, etc.)	56.7	20.4	17.2	4.06
5. Selecting/changing my major area of study	55.6	10.2	29.2	4.11
6. Meeting requirements for graduation, student teaching, certification, etc.	19.5	18.5	56.3	4.13
7. Improving my study skills and habits	55.6	20.2	19.1	4.11
8. Matching my learning style to particular courses, course sections, or instructors	47.6	25.3	21.6	4.18
9. Obtaining remedial/tutorial assistance	67.6	13.6	13.9	4.04
10. Clarifying my life/career goals	38.3	21.6	35	4.15
11. Identifying career areas that fit my current skills, abilities, and interests	37.5	26.5	30.4	4.20
12. Coping with academic difficulties	49	19.4	26.3	4.16
13. Obtaining financial aid	57.2	20.1	17.3	3.98
14. Obtaining employment on campus (work study, assistantships, etc.)	66.2	14.9	13.6	4.12
15. Finding a job after college/job placement	44.5	32.3	17.9	4.10
16. Continuing my education after graduation	42.6	26.3	26.3	4.15
17. Withdrawing/transferring from this institution	75.5	9.9	10.1	3.99
18. Dealing with personal problems	71.1	7.7	16.2	4.31

APPENDIX 2.2

STUDENT IMPRESSIONS OF FACULTY ADVISOR

1. Knows who I am	4.09
2. Is a good listener	4.10
3. Expresses interest in me as a unique individual	3.88
4. Respects my opinions and feelings	4.05
5. Is available when I need assistance	3.85
6. Provides a caring, open atmosphere	3.99
7. Checks to make sure we understand each other	3.89
8. Respects my right to make my own decisions	4.17
9. Provides me with accurate information	4.01
10. Keeps me up to date on changes in academic requirements	3.67
11. Refers me to other sources from which I can obtain assistance	3.76
12. Encourages me to assume an active role in planning my academic program	3.98
13. Accepts constructive feedback concerning his or her effectiveness as an advisor	3.62
14. Encourages me to achieve my educational goals	3.99
15. Helps me identify the obstacles I need to overcome to reach my educational goals	3.74
16. Takes the initiative in arranging meetings with me	3.25
17. Is on time for appointments with me	3.99
18. Clearly defines advisor/advisee responsibilities	3.67
19. Allows sufficient time to discuss issues or problems	3.96
20. Is willing to discuss my personal problems	3.64
21. Anticipates my needs	3.52
22. Helps me select courses that match my interests and abilities	3.85
23. Helps me to examine my needs, interests, and values	3.68
24. Is familiar with my academic background	3.74
25. Encourages me to talk about myself and my college experiences	3.45
26. Encourages my interest in an academic discipline	3.70
27. Encourages my involvement in extracurricular activities	3.41
28. Helps me explore careers in my field of interest	3.49
29. Is knowledgeable about courses outside my major	3.70
30. Seems to enjoy advising	3.91
31. Is approachable and easy to talk to	4.09
32. Shows concern for my personal growth and development	3.83
33. Keeps personal information confidential	4.08
34. Is flexible in helping me plan my academic program	3.95
35. Has a sense of humor	4.08
36. Is a helpful, effective advisor whom I would recommend to other students	3.92
Overall mean	3.83

3 THE IMPORTANCE OF FACULTY ADVISING: A CEO AND CAO PERSPECTIVE

Robert E. Glennen

Having served as an academic vice president, a provost, and president of three different institutions, the author can offer perspectives on faculty advising from the view of a chief academic officer (CAO) and a chief executive officer (CEO) of a university. A CAO usually has supervision of all academic areas, including the deans of colleges and schools, all academic departments, and the directors of academic-support units. The library, technology services, and international programs usually report to the CAO. If a CAO is titled provost, then student services, and sometimes financial services, will also report to him or her. He or she is generally second in command on a college campus. The CEO, called the president or the chancellor, is the person designated by the governing board to head the institution and provide leadership. This board delegates operational authority to the campus CEO, and it is that individual's responsibility to ensure that academic advising is high on the institutional list of commitments and priorities.

Both the CAO and the CEO need to understand the importance of academic advising to the campus. Annually, institutions across the nation are experiencing budget reductions and declining enrollment. One successful approach to combating declines in enrollment is to increase student retention. The highest attrition takes place during the freshmen year, when approximately 40% of students drop out (Carnegie Commission, 1980). A strong academic advising system has proven to be an effective retention approach to increasing enrollments. For advising to be most effective, CAOs and CEOs should not only verbally commit to developing and maintaining an active advising system, but also provide resources, personnel, space, and rewards for advising.

MANAGING AND LEADING FACULTY ADVISING EFFORTS

In order to be effective and responsive, the CAO and CEO must be visibly supported by the faculty advising program. That support can be manifested in a number of ways. Glennen (1975) points out that administrative support for advising does indeed affect student satisfaction, especially when administrators communicate to the campus community that advising is a high priority and that time spent advising students is a positive investment in the future of the students and the institution. The administration must articulate the importance of advising to the faculty and assure them that retention efforts are not synonymous with the reduction of academic standards, but rather, generally, an increase in them. The most effective way to show the importance of advising is to make it part of the faculty recognition, tenure, and promotion process. Often it is the CAO or CEO who provides the leadership role and the funds for this to happen. Other rewards may include reassigned time for advising, release from committee work, or salary supplements.

The CAO or CEO could also embed advising into the institution's mission statement and strategic plan, and include an advising mission statement in the catalog and on the school web site. In more than 40 consultancies the author has conducted on academic advising, most institutions state that they do have a policy on advising. But while these policies exist in the school catalog, many are not put into practice.

Other ways to show institutional support include providing advisors with computers with access to an integrated student information system, good secretarial support, and adequate training. Having the CAO or CEO attend or present an advisor-training session can have a powerful impact on faculty advisors. Mentioning faculty—in faculty addresses and in comments and presentations to governing boards—who have received advising awards, given presentations on advising, or published articles on advising is a good way to show support for advising. Finally the CAO or CEO must evaluate the success of the advising program and share those results broadly with faculty, staff, students, parents, and other stakeholders. In academia, that which is measured is respected and deemed important.

The CAO or CEO of an institution needs to ensure that there is an advising mission statement and a definition of advising that is appropriate to the institution and that these are communicated to all stakeholders of the institution. In addition, to effectively manage and lead a faculty advising effort, the CAO or CEO should be knowledgeable about the role of faculty advisors, ethical considerations in advising (especially those discussed in the NACADA Core Values), the types of advising services offered, the impact of advising on fiscal considerations, strategic planning, considerations in selecting an academic advising director and faculty advisors, and faculty development or training issues. These essentials will be discussed in the sections that follow.

The Role of the Faculty Advisor

Faculty have been advising students since higher education began. However, not all faculty are good advisors. Some faculty may be excellent teachers or good researchers or contribute abundantly in service—but not be effective advisors. Therefore, the CAO or CEO would be wise to create a system that selects faculty who want to be involved in advising, who can easily establish rapport with students, and who are willing to put forth time and effort to assist students.

The role of faculty advisors is to provide academic advice, help establish student goals, provide career guidance, assist students in selecting a major course of study, clarify graduation requirements, disseminate information, and generally assist students in achieving academic success. Good advising is critical to the life of the campus and the success of its students. Because academic advisors are the principal interface between students and the institution, they must know the institution and be able to relate to students on a one-on-one basis. Academic advisors have a responsibility to humanize the school for their advisees, to be available, and to be willing to spend time helping individual students solve their academic problems. Advisors should be "models" for advisees to emulate—successful faculty members who are able to draw upon their own past experience as students in helping advisees to be successful. A faculty advisor's own academic experience influences the advice and direction he or she gives to their advisees.

Academic advisors provide the following types of information and services in individual advising sessions: academic information, academic counseling, career information, career counseling, assistance with personal and social concerns, information regarding institutional regulations and procedures, and referrals to other professionals such as counselors, faculty, and health-care workers. Academic advisors are not psychological counselors. When they become aware of problems requiring the expertise of a psychologist or a psychiatrist, the proper course of action is to refer the student for appropriate professional help.

Ethical Considerations in Advising

The author's philosophy on advising is that higher education must be sensitive to the needs, the desires, and the aspirations of our students. Students come to college for many reasons, and their potential for growth and development varies greatly in both kind and quantity. The institution has a great obligation to help students identify and fulfill their potential, whatever it may be, but it also has an obligation to society that goes beyond helping individuals fulfill their human potential. Society looks to higher education to provide graduates with the high-level skills and breadth of understanding required in today's society. Institutions exist to serve not only the needs and aspirations of individual students, but also the needs of society—to serve the common good.

Much of the time, fortunately, the aspirations of individual students and the needs of society coincide, and the institution is able to serve both at the same time. At other times, however, individual student aspirations conflict with the needs of society. In such situations the institution, if it is to be true to its mission, must weigh the legitimate claims of both as it attempts to resolve the conflict in an equitable way.

An institution that attends only to the aspirations of individual students, ignoring the needs of society, is socially irresponsible. One that is insensitive to the aspirations of its students, seeking only to satisfy the needs of society, is repressive and authoritarian. Inherent in higher education is a certain amount of tension as students and society try to push it toward one extreme or the other.

As members of the faculty, who share the responsibility for fulfilling the institution's mission, advisors must live and work in the midst of this tension. Sometimes, when the considerations supporting the aspirations of students appear more weighty than those supporting the claim of the community, it is necessary for advisors to stand with students against the community, whose rules, requirements, or procedures may be inhibiting students. On other occasions, when the weightier considerations are on the side of the common good, advisors may find it necessary to stand with the community against students whose desired behavior may be unduly wasteful of public resources or may be unfair to other students whose interests are also at stake.

Faculty academic advisors can escape this tension only by becoming something other than educators. They could escape it, for example, by defining their role simply as regulators, or interpreters and enforcers of rules. Such a position, however, would err on the side of authoritarianism and would rightly be resisted in the name of individual rights. The tension could also be avoided if advisors defined their role purely and simply as that of student advocate, whose task it is to support students' requests, no matter what they might be. Such a position, however, would err on the side of social irresponsibility and would rightly be opposed in the name of society's legitimate expectation that those who conduct the affairs of the institution give due consideration to the effective use of limited resources. It could also be opposed on the ground that educators have a responsibility to consider not only what students desire to do, but also what they as faculty judge to be in the best interest of students.

Academic advisors, as educators, represent both the interests of students and the wider interests of society. Ideally, academic advisors are people who find life in the midst of such tension not a frustration but a perpetual challenge in response to which they can do their finest work. The CAO and CEO must support advisors in these efforts. Indeed, they must initiate discussion of such ethical considerations on their campuses.

NACADA core values. All advisors should be aware of the NACADA Statement of Core Values of Academic Advising (1994). Upholding the ethical standards described in this document will ensure that advisors practice the highest level of conduct in their relationship with students, faculty colleagues, and the campus community. In order to serve students well, academic advisors need to understand that they are responsible to many constituents who make up the academic community.

CAOs and CEOs establish the tone for the advising program on campus. If they know and practice the core values, the use of appropriate ethical standards among advisors is likely to follow. These administrators must make certain everyone on the campus is committed to making students feel wanted and "at home"; this includes the faculty, administration, academic divisions, financial services office, library, student union, residence halls, campus police and safety, clerical, and maintenance staff.

Types of Advising Services

The CAO's or CEO's concern with various types of advising is that the types used be appropriate to the needs of the institution and the student and that they be effective. The administrator must evaluate different advising methods to document their effectiveness.

Group advising. Group advising sessions provide opportunities for students to interact with other students and to share ideas, feelings, and concerns. Advisors share basic common information with a number of students in one setting, such as at orientation, preregistration, or registration, and students share academic information and develop group camaraderie. Academic-advising orientation or first-year-experience courses provide academic information in more depth, support for vulnerable students, opportunities for students to develop rapport with and confidence in the advisor, and credibility for the importance of advising tasks.

Computer-assisted advising. Computer-assisted advising provides better record keeping, information regarding special needs, a student database to match student records with degree requirements, greater accuracy of advising information, simplified access to records, and reduced personnel costs. It also releases advisors from monotonous, routine processes and provides interactive programs directed toward special populations. Computer-generated information allows students to demonstrate responsibility for their own academic planning and decisions. For example, computer-assisted advising at Brigham Young University includes 1) a listing of all university classes completed with an accompanying transcript, 2) a summary of general-education requirements completed and a listing of deficiencies, 3) a summary of college requirements with courses completed and courses deficient, 4) a summary of major requirements with courses completed and courses deficient, 5) and a summary of specialization courses with courses completed and courses deficient.

Advising as teaching. Faculty advising is another form of teaching. It is best provided on a one-on-one basis whereby advisors have special access to students' data (test scores, grades, previous course schedules, and planned major requirements) and can integrate this information into the students' academic goals and career aspirations. While it is best to match students to academic advisors in their proposed major, there are often faculty advisors on a campus who are generalists and can advise undecided freshmen and sophomores. This kind of advising might take place in a centralized advising center for freshmen and undecided students that is staffed by a faculty member from each department that has an undergraduate major. Such faculty advisors receive appropriate reassigned time and are cross-trained to be advising generalists. When faculty serve as advisors, they bring a wealth of skills from teaching that relate directly to advising.

Fiscal Implications of Advising

A CEO is interested in the fiscal health of the whole institution—which areas stay within the budget, which overspend, which generate income. Appropriate use of fiscal resources is even more essential today, with current budget reductions, declining enrollments, increasing operational costs, and decreasing state revenues. Institutions have to do more with less. Studying the impact of advising on the institution's bottom line can contribute to this fiscal picture. For example, Glennen, Farren, and Vowell (1996) found that increasing student retention through advising had definite positive fiscal implications for Emporia State University. Table 3.1 illustrates the financial benefits of the retention efforts at that institution. The study found that 7.54 million dollars in increased revenues returned to the institution over a ten-year period (after the cost of the centralized advising center was taken out). In addition, monies were generated from increased residency in dormitories, meal plans, bookstore purchases, snack bar expenditures, and ticket sales for various lectures, games, and concerts.

TABLE 3.1

FINANCIAL BENEFITS OF STUDENT RETENTION AT EMPORIA STATE UNIVERSITY

Year students matriculated	Additional State Funds, 2nd year	Additional State Funds, 3rd year	Additional State Funds, 4th year	Additional State Funds, 5th year	Total Additional State Funds	Cost of Student Advising Center (SAC)	Additional State Funds Minus Cost of SAC
1984	$64,336	$96,668	$153,782	$231,387	$546,173	$174,000	$372,173
1985	$162,578	$180,920	$272,220	$120,750	$736,488	$177,747	$558,741
1986	$280,426	$209,025	$209,025	$87,750	$853,958	$168,261	$684,697
1987	$90,740	$276,757	$268,125	$260,364	$856,124	$178,834	$677,290
1988	$371,600	$236,895	$515,721	$317,192	$1,609,138	$179,942	$1,429,793
1989	$219,375	$404,625	$491,136	$294,448	$1,470,610	$243,817	$1,226,793
1990	$165,321	$465,651	$425,898	$398,090	$1,255,251	$255,574	$999,677
1991	$117,668	$266,770	$352,594	$339,663	$1,151,695	$265,726	$551,591
1992	$131,450	$341,098	$352,934	*	$795,482	$243,891	$156,349
1993	$96,679	$310,878	*	*	$407,557	$251,208	$156,349
Total	$1,700,173	$2,789,287	$3,041,435	$2,049,644	$9,682,476	$2,140,00	$7,542,476

*Data in these columns is not available since they refer to time periods after the study was completed.

The Importance of Planning for Academic Advising

Strategic planning can foster a positive change regardless of the financial circumstances. Any college or university needs to develop and implement an effective strategic plan, and it should be developed by a campus-wide committee representing all the major constituents on campus—faculty, students, administrators, and classified staff.

An institution's strategic plan and mission statements should include academic advising. For example, at Emporia State University in Kansas, where the author served as president for 13 years, the mission statement included the following:

> A student-centered institution . . . assists students to achieve their potential through excellent instruction, through its nationally recognized advising and assessment programs, through a focused concern for individual and personal needs, and through special attention to the needs of persons with disabilities. (Emporia State University, 1993a)

Likewise, the institution's strategic plan contains several statements relative to the integration of academic advising in the institution:

> Strengthen recruitment and retention of programs for targeted populations such as the academically talented, minorities, transfer students, and non-traditional students through such activities as the honors program, diagnostic assessment, credit by examination, articulation enhancement scholarships, graduate assistantships and fellowships, and intrusive advising. (Emporia State University, 1993b)

Greenwood (1984) states that administrators and their boards must take responsibility for ensuring that the institution's mission statement presents a comprehensive rationale for the educational enterprise. The statement should emphasize academic and personal development of students and encourage facilitation of educational growth through advising and programming activities designed to be responsive to those needs. One of the best ways to ensure that students receive this kind of support from their advisors is to establish intrusive advising as a part of the campus culture.

Intrusive Advising

Once a school makes a commitment to developing an academic advising program, it must adopt a philosophy of advising. The author's personal philosophy has always been that an institution should practice intrusive, or outreach, advising. Such advising is based on the principle that students should receive academic advising throughout the year as necessary, not just once a year. A deliberate effort is made to watch over a student's academic career (Glennen, 1975). Simply stated, intrusive advising is actively concerned about the affairs of the students (Glennen & Baxley, 1985). Active concern means that the institution does not wait for students to get into academic difficulty, but takes the initiative to frequently call students in for advising. To be intrusive connotes a tendency to be deeply concerned about the affairs of others.

The first advising contact with a new student is often a frenetic experience. It typically occurs during new student orientation, at a time when the goal is to enroll students in a course load appropriate to their desires or that is dictated by the curriculum for full-time students. Circumstances are hardly ideal. Frequently, a single advisor is working with several students; classes are often closed; and for many students this might be a traumatic experience.

Thus, the initial interview, as opposed to the initial contact, is the first opportunity that advisors have to speak to students in a one-on-one setting. An integral part of intrusive advising, this interview differs greatly from advising that primarily schedules classes. It should be one of the most significant opportunities for student contact and for establishing a mentoring relationship. The research of Alexander Astin (1985) and others at the Higher Education Research Institute at UCLA suggests that frequent, meaningful, and individual faculty-student interaction is the single most significant determinant of student satisfaction during the baccalaureate experience. Hence, the initial interview can provide positive, latent outcomes that manifest themselves several years after the actual advising experience.

Some suggestions for conducting the initial interview include the following ideas. First, prior to the visit advisors should spend some time reviewing the contents of the student's advising folder, if possible. The folder might include a log, ACT or SAT scores, a placement form for the beginning English and mathematics courses, the student's semester class schedule, and a sheet completed at the time of orientation indicating past extracurricular and organizational involvements, intent for future participation, or other desires the student hopes to have satisfied during the undergraduate experience. Placement scores should correspond to class enrollments on the class schedule. Advisors should stay alert to the student's indicated major, degree, and career aspirations that appear on the ACT profile, the application form, and the information sheet completed at orientation, and should discuss with the student any differences that appear on the three relative to the major.

In the initial interview, advisors should let students know who they are and what their role is. They should give their name, note the department in which they teach, and the major(s) for which they advise (or that they do general advising for freshmen and undeclared students). To reinforce their name and department at that time, they might also give students their business card. They could also indicate that they will be the student's advisor until the student completes graduation requirements and leaves the institution.

Advisors should talk with students about the following topics: If a student has strong test scores, the advisor should point this out and stress the honors program. The advisor should review with the student the interest profile and comment on its congruence (or incongruence) with the indicated major. Discrepancies between the placement form and the class schedule for the current semester should be pointed out.

The advisor then should discuss the student's class schedule, ask about the names of instructors and grades on assignments completed, and have the student speculate about midterm or final grades. Advisors will also want to talk to the student about the student's total time commitments relative to employment, family responsibilities, commuting, or extracurricular activities or campus organizations.

When appropriate, an advisor can refer the student to other campus services. For example, if the student has concerns about a roommate, the advisor may explain to how to resolve such difficulties; if the student is struggling in a particular academic area, the advisor may wish to refer the student to a writing, mathematics, or reading lab. Other referrals might be made to the counseling center, the library, the student health center, or other available support services.

If the student is undeclared, the advisor should refer the student to services available to such students. Undeclared or undecided students have not selected a major or field of study. Undeclared students generally have a greater potential for withdrawal from the university and a greater dissatisfaction with their educational life than do students who know what major they want to pursue. These undecided students need more intensive intrusive advising, especially in exploring educational opportunities and career options. Such support can help students identify academic and personal goals and help them learn to accept and live with the decisions they make.

For declared students, advisors can assess the strength of the student's interest in the declared major and the level of achievement in related courses in which the student is currently enrolled. Advisors might give the student a copy of that major's curriculum guide.

Advisors should encourage students to contact them at the scheduled advising time if problems arise. Advisors should also explain that they will contact the student to schedule an advising session if the advisor has reason for concern, such as a student concern/action form from an instructor or an early-alert form. If no problems are perceived, the advisor and student could plan the next contact for preenrollment for the subsequent term.

Most important in this interaction is that advisors practice real advising, which transcends the signing of an advisement form. Advisors must develop an advising style and strategies that are consistent with their personality, but for maximal impact, these strategies should include intrusive, developmental advising.

Selection of Faculty Advisors and the Director of Academic Advising

There is no major in academic advising or courses in a doctoral program that would prepare faculty to be advisors, thus most advisors become so without any particular preparation or advising background, and they often lack knowledge of how to be a good advisor. It is therefore essential for the CAO, CEO, or appropriate advising administrator to select a competent, qualified individual to be the director of academic advising. The director must be capable of determining the right priorities, working well with people, selecting the faculty-advising team, delegating authority, paying attention to small details, using data and technology, supporting and motivating others, planning and involving others in planning, and making difficult decisions. Appointing him or her to selected university committees enhances information-exchange opportunities and strengthens communication links. The various committee appointments facilitate dialogue and help ensure that students are treated consistently throughout the university.

The director of academic advising may also have the responsibility for selecting faculty advisors. It is important to select faculty who are interested in working with students, and who demonstrate a personal commitment to advising, demonstrate organizational ability, are highly regarded among their peers, possess good written and verbal communication skills, exhibit good judgment, and display the ability to make decisions when advising undeclared students.

Faculty Development or Training

One of the prime responsibilities of the director of academic advising is to set up a professional development program for faculty advisors in the areas of conceptual, relational, and informational skills. Such a program would stress the development of interpersonal skills that would let them more readily establish rapport with advisees, and also teach them about the curriculum, rules, and regulations of the institution and about how to improve their advising techniques. Guest speakers from the ACT Corporation, psychologists and psychometrists, student-personnel workers, and financial-aid officers may be used. Faculty advisors should be made aware of sources for referral on campus and of how to refer students for support services. Such services might include the counseling and testing center, residence halls, admissions and records, the career center, financial aid, and the job placement office.

Advisors should be provided with a variety of professional periodicals and have the opportunity to view training films and videos. Additionally, there are conferences, workshops, and conventions that will help them improve their advising skills. And they should be encouraged to join NACADA, the professional organization for advisors. The role of the CAO or CEO is to show interest in the faculty development program and provide support as needed. This interest is often crucial in encouraging faculty to participate in development programs. A certificate of completion or letter from the CAO or CEO acknowledging participation in advisor development also helps.

STRATEGIC AND PRACTICAL ISSUES IN MANAGING AND LEADING FACULTY ADVISORS

As a CEO the author would expect advising administrators to provide a good rationale for their academic advising program; be well prepared for presentations to central administration (having done their homework); clearly define the budget requests and personnel, equipment, and space needs; demonstrate a personal commitment to advising; demonstrate the ability to organize events; be highly regarded among peers; and possess good written and verbal skills.

However, CAOs are mindful of other important consequences tied to the advising programs at their colleges and universities. First, the quality of advising is often a factor in receiving a good "institutional report card." Whether the evaluator is *U.S. News & World Report,* a regional accrediting association, or the state's commission on higher education, the consequences in terms of enrollments, reputation, and budgets can be enormous. Institutional evaluation processes at national, regional, state, and system levels typically include criteria such as retention and graduation rates, time to degree, credits earned over requirements, and student satisfaction. Good advising programs and processes have been linked to outstanding marks on these kinds of criteria.

Second, advising patterns can determine an academic program's viability. The advice, direction, and mentoring provided by advisors shape enrollment patterns in an institution. For instance, hundreds of content areas for study exist in higher education that do not exist at secondary levels. Entering students who have the general goal of "studying biology" need to be encouraged to explore related options as well (for example, biotechnology, biochemistry, forensics, molecular biology, neurosciences, and occupational therapy) before they make their final decisions. Indeed, the continued existence of these study options depends upon advisors educating students about them. Student demand is a key factor in an institution's decision to maintain a program and enrollments for it.

Third, advising affects the institution's revenues. In one way or another, variations in an institution's resources are tied to variations in the institution's enrollments. Increases in the conversion rate of accepted students to enrolled students, transfer-student enrollments, the first-year-to-second-year retention rate, and the proportion of full-time students to part-time students generally mean more revenue for the institution. A good advising program is key to all these factors (B. M. Montgomery, personal communication, October 13, 2001).

CONCLUSION

Advising, like all human endeavors, will always be an imperfect science and art. No advisor can "get it right" every time, and all can improve. Improving advising services and programs benefits both our students and our institutions in substantial and valuable ways. The CEO and CAO must provide the leadership, planning, and support to implement and promote academic advising on the campus. When obstacles arise that hinder the program, they must intervene. Their role is to guarantee that students receive this significant service.

REFERENCES

Astin, A. W. (1985). *Achieving educational excellence.* San Francisco, CA: Jossey-Bass.

Carnegie Commission. (1980). Carnegie council's final report. *The Chronicle of Higher Education,* pp. 9–12.

Emporia State University. (1993a). *Mission statement.* Internal communication.

Emporia State University. (1993b). *Strategic plan.* Internal communication.

Glennen, R. E. (1975). Intrusive college counseling. *College Student Journal, 9,* 2–4.

Glennen, R. E., & Baxley, D. M. (1985). Reduction of attrition through intrusive advising. *NASPA Journal, 22,* 10–15.

Glennen, R. E., Farren, P. J., & Vowell, F. N. (1996). How advising and retention of students improve fiscal stability. *NACADA Journal, 16,* 38–41.

Greenwood, J. D. (1984). Academic advising and institutional goals: A president's perspective. In R. B. Winston, Jr., T. K. Miller, S. C. Ender, T. J. Grites, & Associates, *Developmental academic advising* (pp. 70–71). San Francisco, CA: Jossey-Bass.

National Academic Advising Association. (1994). *NACADA statement of core values of academic advising.* Retrieved 2002 from http://www.nacada.ksu.edu/Profres/corevalu.htm

4 EXPECTATIONS AND TRAINING OF FACULTY ADVISORS

Faye Vowell and Phillip J. Farren

This chapter deals with expectations for and training of faculty advisors more broadly than might be expected. To ensure the success of the advising program, advising administrators especially need to be aware of the different expectations that a variety of stakeholders bring and to develop ways to address them. Expectations about advising may be based on prior personal experience or on the experiences of others. Expectations can also be further separated into two general categories: those that people bring with them and those that result from advisor training or development. Whatever their source, expectations must be understood by the advising administrator.

The quality of the relationships among those who have an interest in the advising process is crucial to good advising. Relationships are built on trust and clearly articulated and understood expectations. Expectations may vary widely or be commonly held. As relationships grow and mature over time, expectations may be modified, validated, or negated. A comprehensive advisor training or development program thus needs to begin with a thoughtful consideration of expectations.

EXPECTATIONS

Expectations about advising vary according to the differing cultures and histories of institutions. The most common differences are those occasioned by size, scope (two-year or four-year), geography (rural or urban), or classification (public, private, or proprietary). Other differences that shape advising expectations include the specific mission of the institution: Is there a liberal arts focus? Is it church-related? Is it a regional comprehensive? Or is it a research institution? Even within these categories, expectations are further influenced by the specific demographics of the institution. A school with a student body composed primarily of first-generation college students may have different expectations of advisors than one that is not so composed. External challenges the institution faces or has faced in the past will also impact expectations. For example, is there declining enrollment in a school that is funded on the basis of student credit-hour production, or is there an overabundance of students, causing an emphasis on reduction of time to graduation? The school's unique history has further impact on expectations in many ways: Was the school founded as a land-grant institution? Was it originally a normal school? Are the faculty and staff unionized? How long has the school been in existence? Has its role and population changed over time? Has the leadership of the institution been stable, or have there been frequent turnovers?

The expectations of different stakeholders in the advising process will be based on their individual personalities and their positions in the institution. Although advisors and their advisees are often considered the primary stakeholders, the web of relationships that supports a strong advising program includes many other people: parents and family; central administration; advising administrators; teaching faculty; staff in student, fiscal, administrative, and academic affairs; and such external constituencies as governing boards, legislatures, donors, and accrediting agencies. These groups have a number of different areas of expectation.

Areas of Expectation

Different areas of expectation include training, evaluation of advisors and advising programs, advising outcomes, and reward for faculty advising. There are also expectations about support for the advising process in the areas of personnel, budget, facilities, and technology. Other expectations deal with the organization of advising, planning, collaboration, time, sanctions for poor advising, communication, qualifications for advisors, and the advising of special populations. Some expectations are shared generally by all stakeholders, some by subgroups of stakeholders, and some are unique to particular stakeholder groups.

Expectations about support: Staffing, budget, and facilities. Expectations for support of advising are widely shared. Support can be defined as institution-wide acceptance of the importance of advising, which is demonstrated in incorporating the role of advising into such publications as the catalog and the schedule of classes as well as into the mission statement and strategic plan. The supportive institution will invest time and energy in selecting the appropriate advising model for its institutional mission and culture; provide funding, technology, personnel, and facilities to accomplish the mission; and establish a system for evaluating and recognizing outstanding performance in advising. A final element of support is that key administrators are willing to provide personal support for advisors, encouraging their growth and development. Admittedly, this level of support is an ideal, but it is nonetheless a worthy goal.

The advising model chosen by the institution will determine the number and kind of personnel associated with advising, faculty advisors as well as support staff. The support staff may consist of only the departmental secretary in a decentralized, totally faculty-based model, or a secretary and graduate assistants or work study students in a centralized model. Commonly shared expectations about support personnel are that there will be an appropriate number to accomplish the task efficiently and effectively, that they will be competent in their jobs, and that continuing assessment of the advising program or process will help determine the adequacy of staffing. Often there is an ongoing conversation about the ratio of advisors to advisees. According to the national data collected in the ACT national survey and discussed more fully in Chapter 2, this ratio varies widely both within an institution and across institutions.

Budget expectations include the areas of advisor and staff salaries, travel money, supplies and equipment money, money to fund training and professional development, and perhaps money for consultants. Advisors, students, and students' parents and families expect that the budget will be adequate to accomplish the task. The advising administration; the staff in academic, student, fiscal, and administrative affairs; and the faculty in academic departments are often compete for scarce resources. At times the advising administrator is expected to generate funds for the advising operation in creative ways, such as charging fees for orientation or for testing. External constituencies (the governing board, legislature, accrediting agencies) and the central administration expect proof that the allocated money is well spent and supports the institution's needs and mission.

Expectations about facilities involve office space, waiting areas, areas for training and storage, furniture, equipment, computers, and library materials. The size of the institution affects the kind of facilities stakeholders expect as does the advising model chosen. Advisors and students generally expect that facilities will be adequate in size and equipment, centrally located in a prominent place, and easily accessible. Centralized advising centers are usually expected to be located near other student services. Whatever the expectations, the central administration and advising administrators often deal with less than ideal circumstances. Advising facilities tend to improve as the entire institution realizes the impact of advising.

Expectations about collaboration and communication. Collaboration can be defined as a joint effort among peers or partners to achieve a desired end. All parties expect that collaboration will take place and that advisors and advisees will know about and use the expertise available from all parts of campus. This may be an ideal expectation that will need to be realized in advisor training.

Expectations about communication are often similarly ideal. Communication includes both interpersonal communication and the systemic communication that is part of the transfer of information in the advising process. Systemic communication includes the way advisors are informed about changes in university policies, procedures, and deadlines as well as curriculum changes. It also includes the system whereby advisors are informed about advisee grades, admission status, receipt of financial aid, use of support services, and other areas supporting the advisor's ability to help students make good academic decisions. The further removed a stakeholder is from the advising interaction, the less concerned he or she may be about the details of the communication process. But all expect that communication will work well, both interpersonally and systemically.

There also exists a shared, although often idealized, expectation that bad advising is known about; that sanctions are applied; and that remedies to address bad advising are in place. It is further expected that this sanction process is well known, clearly understood, and fairly administered. Effective sanctions include explaining the problem to the advisor, suggesting steps to correct it, and monitoring to observe the results. If good results are not forthcoming, the advisor may be required to take additional training, lose a pay increase, not receive tenure or promotion, or simply be removed from advising and assigned other commensurate duties. Such corrections of bad advising are more difficult to enforce on an advisor who is a tenured full professor. Also, if a faculty member is removed from advising, his or her advisees are often shifted to a good advisor, who then is overworked, the result being that the second faculty member is punished for being a good advisor. Advising administrators need to be aware of this dynamic and seek solutions appropriate within their own institution.

Expectations for the advising organization. Shared expectations also exist for the organization of advising or the advising model. Ideally, the advising organization should fit the institutional mission and resources, be efficient and effective, be evaluated regularly by all interested stakeholders and be modified if necessary. Advising needs should be considered in the institutional planning cycle, in the strategic plan, and in the enrollment management plan, and all planning should include needs assessment for the special populations the institution serves. The advising unit or advising administrator also must establish a planning process for delivering advising services.

Expectations about technology. The use of technology in advising has become important. Technology includes access to the student records on a student information system, degree audits, web searches for online resources, and even access to web-based classes. Central administration in concert with external constituencies (governing boards, legislatures, and accrediting agencies), staff in administrative, student, and fiscal affairs, faculty who do not advise, as well as families and parents expect that advisor use of technology resources will be adequate to meet students' needs.

Advisors expect that they will receive the equipment they need, that they will be trained to use it, and that they will have adequate technical support and timely repairs of technology problems. They further expect that key data will be available online and that the same information can be accessed from different offices as needed. Advisors want technology to support advising, but many are afraid it may replace the personal contact in advising, especially if they view advising as scheduling only.

Advising administrators generally expect that advisors will use available technology and will use it appropriately. Information retrieval should be timely and the data accurate. They believe that appropriate use of technology will help advising to become more than mere scheduling, since it will free advisors to devote more time to more complex issues of advising. Students expect that their data will be correct and secure and that advisors will have access to it and know how to use it. They are coming to expect such one-stop services as portals, web-based registration, online degree audits, and easy access to their records for decision-making.

Expectations about time. Expectations relating to time spent on advising have two dimensions: time for individual advising appointments and follow-up, and time in relationship to other activities. Even if they have no specific times in mind, parents and families, external constituencies, teaching faculty, and staff in administrative, student, and fiscal affairs expect adequate time to be allotted to advising. Central administration expects that the allotted time is adequate, will be provided for in the faculty contract, and faculty will be on campus to advise at the appropriate time, including the week before classes start or in the summer. Advising administrators expect that the faculty contract reserves adequate time for good advising and advisor training.

Advisors, on the other hand, expect that their schedules will be adjusted to allow sufficient time to do a good job of advising as well as to receive necessary training. This expectation can cause some frustration when advising is treated as another add-on to an already full load. Further compounding this frustration, students expect faculty advisors to be readily available for advising purposes during posted office hours. If advisors are using email to advise, students often expect that their email questions will be answered immediately, rather than the next day or later.

Expectations about advisor qualifications. Those not directly involved in the advising interaction do not usually have specific expectations about qualifications, defined as the interests, skills, and abilities that faculty may possess. Among those qualifications would be an interest in students, a desire to be proactive in helping the institution address student concerns, a willingness to be trained and evaluated in advising and to use technology to support advising, and possession of good interpersonal skills. They would also expect advisors to believe in the importance of advising and to commit themselves to improve its quality. Other expectations would vary with the specific institution and its chosen advising model.

Expectations about accountability. Advising outcomes, or the products of an advising system, are shaped by an institution's stance on the subject of accountability. Expectations for accountability have increased on the part of the general population, donors, legislatures, governing boards, and parents. Parents and families expect students to be satisfied with the advising they receive, to have their special needs met, and to graduate in the shortest possible time. External constituencies (governing boards, legislatures, donors, and accrediting agencies) expect satisfied students and efficient use of resources. Outcomes expected by central administrations who understand the importance of advising are higher retention and graduation rates, students with a shorter time to graduation, students who make better academic decisions, and satisfied students. Outcomes expected by advising administrators include few advising mistakes, student satisfaction with the process, and an advising process that accomplishes its goals. They further expect that advising will not cause problems for administration.

Advisor expectations about the advising outcomes include having an environment where their efforts are valued and important, student satisfaction, a working system, adequate support to do their jobs, feedback from referrals, student growth and development, and rewards for good work. Teaching faculty expect that students with the appropriate interest and ability levels will appear in their classes and that these students will be satisfied with their advising. Staff in student, administrative, and fiscal affairs expect that students will be referred appropriately, that advisors know the available services and extracurricular activities, that students will use such services and will meet published deadlines. Students expect such outcomes as satisfaction with the advising relationship; proper guidance in course and major selection; assistance in meeting personal needs through such services as financial aid, housing, counseling; correct information about institutional rules and regulations; available advisors who know them; accurate advising records; and courteous and respectful treatment.

Special populations. Special populations also have expectations about advising. Special populations include athletes, commuters, concurrently enrolled high school students, displaced workers, students of ethnic or cultural minorities, gay and lesbian students, honors students, international students, single parents, special needs students, students from rural backgrounds, students from urban backgrounds, students with substance abuse problems, underprepared students, undecided or undeclared students, and students with needs unique to a specific campus. Some students are members of more than one special population.

External constituencies expect that the special populations served by individual campuses will be advised without prejudice or stigma. Family, parents, and students expect that the needs of students will be met with sensitivity and confidentiality. Central administration expects that all populations will be served and that all needs will be met. Advising administrators expect that faculty advisors will use available training to better serve special students and that they will work to become aware of their own prejudices and move beyond them. Teaching faculty expect that students' special needs will be identified and met so that students function well in their classrooms. Staff in student, fiscal, and administrative affairs expect that an effective system is in place to serve students with special needs, that everyone on campus understands the system, that advisors will work well with the various offices that serve special needs students and will respect students' confidentiality. Faculty advisors expect that they will be given campus demographics to determine what special needs exist, that they will receive training for advising special needs students that such students will self-identify, and that there are offices or people on campus to serve the special needs students who need to be referred to them.

Advisor-training expectations. Advisor-training expectations also vary among the different stakeholders. External constituencies, teaching faculty, parents, family, and students often do not have specific expectations in regard to training other than that it exists, that faculty advisors use it, and that it have positive outcomes. If the institution is aware of the importance of advising, the central administration usually expects the training to be aligned with the institutional and advising mission statements, to be cost-effective, regular, and in line with accreditation standards.

Examples of such mission statements are given further in this chapter. Advising administrators—who plan and often deliver the training—expect faculty advisors to attend and benefit from it, although they often fear that those who need it the most will not attend. Faculty advisors have expectations that the training will address their specific needs, will supply skills they need in order to serve special populations, will be available on demand or at least be offered when they can attend, and will not be boring.

Expectations of advising evaluation. A variety of expectations surround the process of evaluation, or assessment, of advising. Ideally, advisors, advising processes, advising centers, and advising systems all should be evaluated regularly. Evaluation can be either formative or summative, and it can focus on outcomes or on process. There is an overall expectation that if assessment is done, its purpose is to improve advising; that the data collected will be used; and that there will be some comparative aspect to it. Parents, families, and external constituencies share the expectation that the advising process is continually reviewed to improve service to students. Students expect that they will have input into the evaluation of their advisors and that their input will be listened to. Students further expect that evaluation will identify good and bad advisors and that bad advisors will be required to correct deficiencies.

The enrollment management units within student, fiscal, and administrative affairs expect to have assessment data provided to them to enable them to determine the effectiveness of the advising process and its role in carrying out the institutional mission; they expect data to demonstrate that advising is a good investment of time and resources. Student affairs professionals expect that the information from advising assessment will facilitate improving the quality of student life and show the effectiveness of their own area as it relates to advising, and they expect to participate in the process of evaluation. Depending on the way the campus views advising, teaching faculty may have few to no expectations of advising evaluations, or they may expect to be involved in the evaluation process, to benefit from the changes made as a result of assessment, and to analyze results for possible departmental or institution-wide application. If they understand the importance of advising, people in the central administration expect that evaluation will be done.

Advising administrators with the responsibility to create a coherent evaluation system expect that the evaluation will identify successful processes and good advisors and will indicate areas needing improvement, that they will receive cooperation from all parties involved in assessment, and that assessment results will be used to bring about improvements. Advisors have expectations that the evaluation process will be fair, will not take a lot of time, will not be intrusive, will be tied to reward and training, and—on a few campuses—will lead to possible opportunities to do research and publish or present at conferences. They further expect that they will be involved in the process of creating an evaluation system and that the results of that system will be clearly communicated to them.

Expectations about rewards for advising. Expectations concerning rewards also vary among the stakeholders. Students, family, and parents expect to have quality advisors who are paid accordingly. External constituencies expect the reward system for advisors to be reasonable and comparable to that for other professionals at the institution. Central administration expects that the reward system will fit the culture and history of the institution. Faculty who do not advise expect a reward system that does not lower their own rewards and that is proportional to the value placed on advising by an institution. Staff in student, administrative, and fiscal affairs expect to have input into a reward system, that the reward system will show a return on investment, that it will be fair, and that the rewards will be competitive enough to attract quality people to advising. Advising administrators expect that the reward system will be fair and competitive, be based on quality advising, and be good enough to maintain the services of top advisors. Advisors expect that the reward system will recognize quality performance, that they will have input into the creation of the system, that they will clearly understand it, that it will be fair, and that it will provide incentives and opportunities for professional development. A good reward system indicates the importance an institution places on advising.

Rights and Responsibilities of Advisors and Advisees

Ideas about rights and responsibilities grow out of the general expectations discussed above. Often they are reciprocal of each other: the right of the student is a responsibility of the advisor. Thus, the student's right to confidentiality implies the advisor's responsibility to use confidential information correctly.

FIGURE 4.1

ADVISOR AND ADVISEE RIGHTS AND RESPONSIBILITIES

Rights of Student Advisees	**Responsibilities of Advisors**
• Access to accurate information • Being treated with respect • Needs addressed seriously and with confidentiality • Accurate records of progress at the institution • Assistance from advisors in decision making • Referral to appropriate support services • Obligation to make the final decision	• Provision of accurate information • Treating students with respect • Address student needs seriously and with confidentiality • Keep accurate records of student progress at the institution • Assist student in decision-making • Refer students to appropriate support services • Allow the student to make the final decision
Rights of Advisors • Advisees actively participate in the advising process • Advisees are responsible for their own actions • Advisees are on time for appointments • Advisees come prepared • Advisees are willing to discuss problems and challenges • Advisees respect advisors	**Responsibilities of Student Advisees** • Actively participate in the advising process • Responsible for their own actions • Be on time for appointments • Be prepared • Be willing to discuss problems and challenges • Respect advisors

To create a commonly held vision of advisor and advisee rights and responsibilities requires participation from all parts of the campus community through surveys, focus groups, advisory committees, and benchmarking against similar institutions.

HOW TO ELEVATE THE STATUS OF ADVISING

For many faculty members, advising is regarded as a low-status activity or as an add-on to a faculty load already full with the obligations of teaching, research, and service. There are, however, many things that can be done to elevate its status on a campus. The advising mission statement could be included in the important documents that establish the values, rules, and regulations of an institution—the strategic plan, catalog, schedule of classes, and university web site. Advising itself could be mentioned in the university's mission statement. The institution could conduct the necessary research and share with faculty and staff the impact of good advising on students and the institution: improved retention and graduation rates, the fiscal impact of retention, fewer drop/adds, improved student and faculty satisfaction with advising, shorter time to graduation, increased institutional cooperation, and an enhanced reputation for the institution.

Advising administrators might give faculty advisors structured opportunities to reflect on their contribution to student growth and development. Advising should be seen as a developmental activity, not just as an exercise in class scheduling. Advisors should see themselves as assisting students to become self-actualized adults with improved decision-making and goal-setting skills and the ability to use support services effectively. Focusing on advising as teaching, as discussed in Chapter 1, and emphasizing the mentoring aspects of advising could also raise its status. Administrators could encourage faculty to conduct research on advising for conferences and publication. The legitimacy of this research would need to be recognized in the promotion and tenure process. Attendance at advising conferences could be funded. Influential senior faculty might be asked to present at advisor-training sessions.

Elevate advising to a total-campus issue. Advising administrators could encourage the president and vice presidents to attend advising events, to mention advising in addresses to the faculty, and to recognize master advisors. The central administration could devote visible campus resources to support advising. An annual lecture series that focuses on important campus advising issues could be established. Outstanding-advisor awards established at the campus level could be accorded status equal to that of outstanding teaching, research, and service awards. Results of advising or assessment could be shared with all campus constituencies on a regular basis. A summary of advising accomplishments could be presented on an annual basis to the governing board or board of regents.

Including advising as a major factor in the merit pay, promotion, and the tenure process is probably the most potent way to elevate the status of advising, since most people directly associate rewards with importance.

ESTABLISHING CLEAR EXPECTATIONS FOR ADVISING

If good advising is to be considered in the faculty-reward process, clearly defined expectations must be in place. Ideally, such expectations need to established and reviewed by the major participants in the process: faculty, the staff supporting advising, and students. They need to be included in the faculty handbook and available on the institutional web site. The most basic statement of expectation should be found in an institutional advising mission statement. Mission statements vary by the kind, type, history, and culture of an institution. The following examples show the similarities and differences among mission statements for a number of different schools.

Aims Community College offers the following institutional philosophy statement and accompanying institutional goals for academic advising:

> Academic advising exists to help students gain the maximum educational and personal benefits from Aims Community College. The advisor facilitates the development of these benefits by knowing the resources of the institution, by understanding the needs and goals of individuals, and by bringing these elements together in the development of meaningful educational plans.

Institutional Goals of Advising

1) To assist students in their consideration and clarification of educational goals.
2) To assist students in developing an educational plan, college program, and selection of courses consistent with the student's goals and objectives.
3) To provide accurate information about institutional policies, procedures, resources, and programs.
4) To assist students in evaluation or re-evaluation of progress toward established goals and educational plans.
5) To involve all faculty in student advising.
6) To make referrals to resources within and out of the college as appropriate.
7) To empower and encourage students to be self-directed learners. (Aims Community College, 2002)

Hamilton College, a liberal arts college, defines expectations for advising in the following language:

> Academic advising is one of the many ways in which students engage with faculty on an individual basis. Advisors and advisees work together to craft a unique, individual academic plan based upon each student's strengths, weaknesses, and goals. The College views the advising relationship as an on-going conversation that transcends mere course selection and attempts to assist students as they explore the breadth of the liberal arts curriculum, experience college life, focus on a major concentration, and prepare for life after college. (Hamilton College, 2002)

Syracuse University, a research institution, has the following expectations in regard to advising:

> Academic advising is an essential part of a Syracuse University education. The University is committed to providing the individual advice and assistance that students need at every step throughout their degree programs. A successful system of academic advising is highly dependent upon a shared commitment of students, faculty and staff to the process and the availability of

timely, accurate information. (Syracuse University, 2002)

The final example is from Western New Mexico University, a four-year, public, comprehensive institution. A faculty committee crafted the mission statement and definition of advising which they then shared with the faculty as a whole to offer them a chance to comment and react.

Academic Advising Mission Statement

The mission of academic advising is to assist students in relating their needs, values, abilities, and goals to the educational programs of the University. In support of the University's mission statement, academic advising recognizes the need to address the diverse cultural and academic background of its students, while promoting academic excellence. Successful advising contributes to a significant goal of a college education—developing mature and self-directed students, capable of thinking, judging, and making appropriate decisions.

Definition of Successful Advising

Academic advising goes beyond the clerical functions of scheduling classes and preparing degree plans. Good academic advising assists students in clarifying personal and career goals, developing consistent educational goals, and evaluating their progress toward established goals. Academic advising utilizes the resources of the University and refers students to the appropriate academic support services. It is a decision-making process in which the sharing of information between student and advisor promotes responsible and appropriate choices and facilitates a successful academic experience. (Western New Mexico University, 2002c)

For advising to be considered a major factor in the promotion, tenure, and merit pay process, it should be accorded a weight equal to that given to teaching or research. Requirements for documenting advising success will vary according to the history and culture of the institution. But the expectations should be stated as clearly as possible so that advising administrators can construct training that will enable faculty advisors to meet them.

The following example of an attempt to clarify expectations for promotion and tenure comes from Western New Mexico University. At this institution, the annual faculty evaluation process includes various elements. Every spring each academic department establishes goals and objectives for the next year within the context of the school's goals and objectives. Early each fall, faculty members establish goals and objectives in five areas: teaching, advising, scholarly and creative activity, professional contributions, and personal relationships. Then the chair meet twice that year with faculty to review progress toward meeting these goals. This evaluation process includes a discussion of progress toward tenure and promotion for untenured faculty members.

A group of faculty met and brainstormed the following expectations for faculty in relation to tenure and promotion. This list, shared broadly with faculty through email and the institutional intranet, is discussed and refined annually. The guiding purpose of this activity was to help faculty see how expectations increase and roles change with different ranks and years of service and to establish a minimum expectation for attaining tenure. The expectations for tenure and for assistant professor should be viewed together since most faculty are hired as assistant professors. The expectations listed for assistant, associate, and full professors assume that earlier expectations continue, so only new expectations are given.

Expectations for Tenure

- Know advisees both personally and in terms of institutional demographics.
- Understand the kinds of challenges and problems faced by these students.
- Keep good advising records.
- Know how to use the student information system for advising.
- Demonstrate basic knowledge of general-education and major requirements.
- Demonstrate knowledge of all majors within the department.
- Establish a track record of successful advising.
- Demonstrate awareness of the professional qualities graduates need for success in the field.

- Make progress toward mastery of advising as demonstrated in the annual evaluation process.

Expectations for Assistant Professor Rank

- Demonstrate an interest in mentoring students.
- Establish rapport with students.
- Be active in retention efforts.
- Attend advisor-training sessions.
- Advise undergraduate students.
- Direct students into majors appropriately.
- Follow all university policies and procedures in regard to advising.
- Understand the emerging needs of the field and communicate them to advisees.
- Be knowledgeable about and use campus support services.

Expectations for Associate Professor Rank

- Demonstrate more experience and maturity in mentoring.
- Attend advisor-training sessions and help deliver training.
- Advise students on issues after graduation—work or graduate school.
- Effectively facilitate student decision making.
- Create degree plans focusing on student needs.

Expectations for Professor Rank

- Demonstrate mastery of mentoring process.
- Work toward building collaboration among students in the major.
- Conduct advisor-training session, help organizing training, attend training sessions.
- Demonstrate competence in helping students reach their goals.
- Exhibit few advising errors.
- Share expertise with junior faculty.
- Be actively involved in advising both students and faculty.
- Identify improvements needed to departmental and institutional policies and procedures.

- Direct graduate programs.
- Demonstrate knowledge of degree plans across departments.
- Answer colleagues' questions on advising issues.
- Assist with difficult advising situations.
- Know the major and work to shape it appropriately.
- Look to the future and imagine.

(Western New Mexico University, 2002d)

Clearly delineating expectations for faculty at different stages in their tenure track will help faculty and administrators set benchmarks and goals for faculty advising.

TRAINING

With a widely shared mission statement and a clear understanding of advising expectations on a particular campus, advising administrators are ready to begin planning for advisor training or development.

Shaping Expectations: Training Constituencies Other Than Faculty

Addressing the expectations of all those with an interest in advising is often crucial to the success of an advising program. As stated at the beginning of this chapter, various constituencies may bring with them negative expectations of advising based on prior experience. Still others will have little or no experience or few expectations, and the advising administrator will want to develop or shape their expectations. While the process of shaping expectations is not often considered as training and cannot be addressed directly in advisor training sessions, it is nevertheless important to consider.

Parent and family expectations can be shaped through information provided in recruitment material and through the orientation experience they share with their student. Advising administrators might consider developing a handout that describes the advising system on the campus and what the family or parental role could be in the advising process; that provides appropriate contact information; and that discusses the regulations imposed on a campus by the Family Educational Rights to Privacy Act (FERPA). This information is especially crucial when students are first-generation college students.

External constituencies such as members of governing boards may have negative expectations based on student complaints or personal experience. Care must be taken to address any complaints in a timely and thorough fashion. Annual reports to the board are a venue in which to shape expectations. An initial report could share the advising plan or system at a very general level; subsequent reports could show success in implementing the plan. This report could include statistics such as retention and graduation rates, student success stories, and any news stories about advisors and advising.

Expectations of central administration can be shaped by national and institutional research reports, white papers, and annual reports. The advising plan or system as well as updates documenting successful implementation need to be shared with this group. Teaching faculty, central administration, and the student, administrative, and fiscal affairs staff would be interested in information on the impact of advising on retention and graduation and in the numbers and kinds of advising sessions, student satisfaction with advising, and the advising process. Campus-wide communication vehicles that mention advising activities, papers, publications, advising reminders, and attendance at advising conferences should be shared with them.

Student expectations can be shaped by the information included in the catalog, by the schedule of classes, and by experiences at orientation. Initial interviews with advisors after the start of classes could focus on the rights and responsibilities of advisors and advisees and further shape expectations. Conducting student evaluations of individual advisors and evaluations such as ACT advising assessments or the Noel Levitz Student Survey and sharing the results will educate students about the success of the advising program and the issues with which advisors grapple.

An advising administrator should establish a consistent and comprehensive plan to shape the expectations of these groups in ways that enhance the ongoing development or training plan for faculty advisors.

Faculty-Advisor Training or Development

Faculty advisor training or development should grow out of the expectations of a particular institution and be unique to that campus. The program should be based on the needs of the faculty. The most well-structured training program possible will still not be successful if it does not provide the information or skills that advisors need to do their job well. But good advisor-development programs have some characteristics in common. Factors to be considered when creating a comprehensive training program are the time and place of training, how the sessions will be advertised, the mode of presentation, audience analysis, handouts and other training support materials, content of the sessions, and evaluation of the individual sessions and the entire program.

Needs assessment. Needs assessments can be conducted in a variety of ways—through surveys, focus groups, structured interviews, threaded discussions of advising topics on institutional web pages, and results of student evaluations of advising. Asking faculty advisors to help structure the content of development programs allows them to buy in to the process and can yield benefits of greater attendance when training sessions are offered.

Time and place. Once the perceived needs have been established, the trainer should consider the times and places for the various sessions. Offering multiple times for faculty to attend sessions is recommended, since a faculty member's teaching, research, or service schedule may preclude attendance at a one-time-only session. The venue chosen should be comfortable and convenient, yet separated enough from offices and departments to help faculty concentrate on the session and not be interrupted. Refreshments are helpful in getting faculty to relax and participate.

Advertising the program. How can the advisor training program or sessions be advertised or marketed? Examples of effective campus communication vehicles include flyers, announcements at faculty meetings, and notices on the faculty listserv or advisor training web page. Special invitations by phone or email or in person are often needed to get the attendance desired. Distributing a list of training sessions at the beginning of the academic year or semester allows faculty members to plan ahead and fit the training into their schedules. One useful strategy is to send a thank-you note to the faculty member at the end of the session and send a copy to the chair of the department.

Mode of presentation. The mode of presentation should be carefully considered. Faculty are adult learners and respond best to training sessions in which they are treated as such. Sessions need to accommodate different learning styles. For example, if an audiotape is used to illustrate a point or convey information, the transcription should be available so the listeners can follow along. If videos are used, they should be closed-captioned. Training sessions should employ a variety of tools and formats. These could include faculty-advisor or student panels, role playing, video vignettes, audiotapes, brainstorming, case studies, games, discussions, workshop exercises, reflective writing, as well as lectures and presentations. The advising administrator responsible for the training program should also consider who would best present the training: an external consultant, a respected senior advisor, or an expert on the faculty.

A number of advisor-training video resources are available, including one developed by NACADA that consists of a series of vignettes that follow the development of a new faculty advisor and her undecided freshman advisee over the course of a year. Two stand-alone vignettes present advising sessions with older, nontraditional students. Commentary on advising issues addressed in the vignettes is provided by experts in the advising field. There is also a comprehensive facilitator's manual. Syracuse University and Noel Levitz both offer other advisor-training videos.

Audience analysis. A certain amount of audience analysis is also called for. Who will attend the sessions? What is their skill level or level of expertise? Will there be multiple skill levels or levels of expertise in the same session, or do there need to be separate sessions? How willing are the faculty advisors to participate actively in the training session? Will they be asked to do reading or other preparation before attending the sessions?

Training materials. Consideration should also be given to providing asynchronous training materials. If faculty members are too busy to attend a face-to-face advisor training session, they may be willing to use materials in a self-guided, web-based process. Still another option is to offer a web course to a group of advisors who can participate asynchronously but still get the benefit of interacting. Almost all aspects of face-to-face training lend themselves to being videotaped and shared from a web page by video streaming or on CD. The trainer in that case will need the support of an instructional designer, a technician skilled in video production, as well as some student workers to create a useful web course.

Content of advisor-training sessions. The content of advisor-training sessions needs to be responsive to the perceived needs of faculty advisors for routine activities like class scheduling. But, like classroom teachers, advising administrators may possess a broader vision of what students need to learn than do the students. This vision needs to be informed by research in the field, requiring administrators to remain as current as they would be in any other academic discipline. Advising administrators should consider developing a long-range, comprehensive training plan that will both address immediate needs and look at the more complex issues of advising.

Content for advisor-training programs can be divided into three areas: conceptual content, informational content, and relational content. The conceptual elements of advisor training are those concepts that a good advisor must understand. The informational elements are the facts and resources that an advisor needs to know or know how to use. The relational elements are skills an advisor must exhibit or demonstrate.

Training on the conceptual elements can include, but is not limited to, the relationship between the institutional mission and the advising mission statements, the definition of advising for the specific campus, developmental versus prescriptive advising, intrusive advising, expectations of the various groups involved in advising, the relationship between advising and retention, legal and ethical issues in advising, the rights and responsibilities of faculty advisors and their advisees, models and theories of student development and how to use them in advising specific students.

Student-development models include Terry O'Banion's (1972) description of the five stages of developmental advising: exploring life goals, exploring vocational goals, facilitating program choice, facilitating course choice, and facilitating scheduling choice (O'Banion, 1972). Victoria McGillin (1996) in the NACADA Faculty Advising Training Facilitator's Manual discusses a number of student-development theories: psychosocial theories, such as those by Erickson, Chickering, and Kenniston, in which an individual develops through a series of stages that constitute a life cycle; cognitive theories, such as those of Perry, Kohlberg, and Piaget, in which development is viewed as "a series of irreversible shifts in the process by which individuals perceive and reason about their world" (p. 18); maturity models, such as that of D. Heath, which focus on the "simultaneous development of thinking, valuating, relating, and inquiring skills" (p. 18); and typology models, such as those of R. Heath and K. P. Cross, which focus on "persistent individual differences such as cognitive style, temperament, or ethnic background, which interact with development" (p. 18). Laura Rendon's (1994) validation model is also powerful in working with Hispanic, Native American, and African-American students.

Training in informational elements includes but is not limited to student demographic information for the specific campus; general-education and major degree requirements; institutional policies, procedures, and deadlines; student support services' hours, location, and scope of operation; student clubs and organizations; appropriate use of advising tools such as the schedule of classes, catalog, degree plan, placement-test results, and interest and ability inventories; using the student information system to access data, and teaching advisees to access their own data; employment projections; and career selection information.

Relational elements of training include but are not limited to verbal and nonverbal communication skills such as active listening, paraphrasing, and closed, involving, and clarifying questions; rapport building; referral skills; advocacy and intervention skills; intrusiveness skills; skills in challenging and confronting students; goal-setting and problem-solving strategies; validation strategies; and creation and maintenance of good advising records.

Evaluation. Finally, a good faculty-advisor training program has a plan for evaluation built in from the beginning. Individual training sessions as well as the overall program should be evaluated. The evaluation needs to grow from the specific objectives of the session and the program and to provide information to enable outcomes to be measured and improvements made the next time the session is offered. Objectives should be SMART—that is, specific, measurable, achievable, realistic, and tangible. For example, an objective for a training session on referral skills might be "To improve the effectiveness of the referral process by increasing the number of completed referrals to student support services by 10%."

Sample Advisor Training Session

Creating a training program is often a process of becoming increasingly more specific about goals of training and, therefore, planning and evaluation processes. An example is given in the description of the process below. By answering the following questions, advising administrators in the hypothetical example can focus in on more specific outcomes.

1) *What is the expectation that needs to be met?* Students expect faculty advisors to have access to reliable, accurate information concerning student records and institutional policies and procedures and to know how to use them.
2) *Who is involved?* In this case, two primary groups are involved. First are the staff who create, change, and update the student records and the policies and procedures; they include staff in admissions, the registrar's office, financial aid, and the faculty curriculum committee. The other group consists of the faculty advisors who use the information in advising sessions. For the purposes of this example, the faculty advisor group will be the focus.
3) *What competencies do faculty need in order to use the information well?* They need to know where to find the information and how to interpret it, how to deal with exceptions, how to report errors in the data, how to facilitate changes in policies and procedures that have an adverse and unfair impact on advisees. And they need to understand the applications of FERPA.
4) *How will the training be structured to enable faculty to attain these competencies?* For this example, the focus will be on a training session for faculty who will advise new freshmen and transfer students in a summer orientation program. The first two objectives stated above will be emphasized.
5) *How is the context of the training defined?* The training will need to be done in one session that will take place late in the spring semester. The school is an open enrollment, four-year, public comprehensive with programs ranging from associate degrees through

master's degrees. Its ethnic breakdown is 52% Caucasian, 43% Hispanic, 3% Native American, and 2% African-American. Approximately 70% of the incoming freshmen will need developmental classes. The average age of the incoming class is 26.

6) *How is the audience defined?* Those attending the training will be full-time faculty. Many of them have advised for more than 20 years. A few are new to campus and new to the field of advising. Thus there will be a mixture of abilities and expertise. Although they are paid a stipend to advise during the summer, their departments are required to choose one faculty member who will advise at each orientation session. Faculty advisors must attend training to advise.
7) *How will the session be evaluated?* An evaluation form will be distributed at the end of the session that will ask questions in the areas of process, content, and relevance. After the first orientation, a follow-up evaluation will be sent to faculty advisors to find out what they actually used from the training session. Students will also be asked to evaluate the advising they received at orientation.
8) *How will the session be structured?* Appendix 4.1 contains is the agenda for the training session, which addresses the issues of content, handouts, media, and timing. Appendix 4.2 is an evaluation form that will be given to attendees.

This example has focused on one advisor training session, for a specific situation, to meet a finite objective. At the other end of the continuum of advisor training is an entire advisor training program or course such as that offered by Aims Community College in Colorado. This school requires as a condition of continued employment that faculty members complete a two-credit-hour, pass/fail advising course called Introduction to the Process and Techniques of Academic Advising. The syllabus from that course is included Appendix 4.3

CONCLUSION

Many stakeholders possess expectations in regard to advising: students, parents, faculty, staff, administration, governing boards, and legislators. Expectations from all the participants in the advising process have an impact on the success of the process. Expectations vary according to the type of institution, the institutional history and culture, and the specific experience of the participants in the advising process. Areas of expectation include support for advising in terms of staffing, budget, and facilities; collaboration and communication; organization of advising; technology; time spent in advising; advisor qualifications; special populations; advisor training; accountability and evaluation; and rewards. An institution needs to establish a list of rights and responsibilities of advisors and advisees that grow out of its specific set of expectations. In considering how to elevate the status of advising, advising administrators need to realize that it is a total-campus issue and that all stakeholders need to be involved.

Once expectations are clearly expressed and understood by all parties, then an appropriate training program can be created. The expectations of all stakeholders in regard to advising can be shaped by advising administrators. In developing a successful training program for faculty advisors, administrators should consider the advising mission, needs assessment, time, place, duration, modality of training, training content, and evaluation.

The samples of advisor training programs in this chapter can be used as benchmarks, but each institution's advisor training program needs to grow out of its unique history and context and be responsive to the particular expectations of its stakeholders. Clearly articulated and understood expectations and training are crucial to the success of faculty advising.

REFERENCES

Aims Community College. (2002a). Aims Community College academic advising institutional philosophy statement. In *Academic advising summer institute 2002 session guide* (pp. 139–146). Manhattan, KS: National Academic Advising Association.

Aims Community College. (2002b). Edu 206a: Introduction to the process and techniques of academic advising. In *Academic advising summer institute 2002 session guide* (pp. 139–146).

Manhattan, KS: National Academic Advising Association.

Hamilton College. (2002). *Academic advising at Hamilton College.* Handout at the American Association for Higher Education Conference on Faculty Roles and Rewards, Phoenix, AZ.

McGillin, V. (1996). A theory base for developmental advising. In J. Burton, B. Crow, W. Habley, V. McGillin, F. N. Vowell, & T. Kerr (Eds.), *NACADA faculty advising training facilitator's manual* (pp. 18–21). Manhattan, KS: National Association for Academic Advising.

O'Banion, T. (1972). An academic advising model. *Junior College Journal, 42* (6), 66–69.

Rendon, L. (1994). Validating culturally diverse students: Toward a new model of learning and student development. *Innovative Higher Education, 19,* (1) 33–50.

Syracuse University. (2002). *Syracuse University statement on academic advising.* Handout at the American Association for Higher Education Conference on Faculty Roles and Rewards, Phoenix, AZ.

Western New Mexico University. (2002c). *Western New Mexico University academic advising mission statement.* Handout at the American Association for Higher Education Conference on Faculty Roles and Rewards, Phoenix, AZ.

Western New Mexico University. (2002a). *Advisor training for orientation.* Internal document.

Western New Mexico University. (2002b). *Training session for faculty advising in orientation.* Internal document.

Western New Mexico University. (2002d). *Western New Mexico University expectations for promotion and tenure.* Handout at the American Association for Higher Education Conference on Faculty Roles and Rewards, Phoenix, AZ.

APPENDIX 4.1

Training Session for Faculty Advising in Orientation
Western New Mexico University
Student Memorial Building Seminar Room
Friday, 12 April 2002
1:30 p.m. to 4:30 p.m.

Overview of University Goals and Special Initiatives (10 min.)
There will be an overview of Learning Communities (Title V Grant) and the Academic Quality Improvement Project Goal on Advising.

Demographic Information (20 min.)
A profile will be presented of last year's freshman class, including gender, average age, ethnicity, number receiving financial aid, enrollment in developmental classes, full- and part-time status, and non-traditional and single-parent status. (This will be presented using PowerPoint, a handout, questions and answers, and asking advisors to share strategies for advising special-needs groups in an orientation situation.)

How Will the Orientation Be Structured? (10 min.)
A handout of the activities for the day will be distributed so that advisors can understand how advising fits into the whole scheme and where students need to go after the advising session. Advisors will also learn the dates of orientations and the times they need to advise.

What Information Will Be in the Advising Folder? (15 min.)
There will be an overview of the contents of the folder: application form, test scores, high school transcript, college transcripts (and transcript evaluation if appropriate), AP or CLEP scores, and intended major. Discussion will focus on how to read the placement-test scores. (The sample folders will give hypothetical information on students that will be used later in the session.)

Break with Refreshments (10 min.)

What Other Materials Will Be Available? (30 min.)
Samples of the following information will be available: class schedule, open and closed class lists, catalog, general-education

handout, degree plans for all majors, advising forms, anecdotal entry form, grid used to schedule classes, and learning-community handout. (The focus here will be on becoming familiar with the information in these advising tools and on the importance of good record keeping. Faculty from the various departments will be asked to share expert tips for advising in their particular area or discipline.)

What Information Do Advisors Need to Obtain from Students? (25 min.)
What are the student's career and educational goals? What concerns does the student have? Does the student attend full- or part-time, work, have special family obligations, commute, have an athletic scholarship, or have special needs? (Advisors will be placed in groups of three and asked to role-play a hypothetical student situation. One will be the student, one the advisor, and one the observer. After 20 minutes, the observer will report back to the entire group on the specific strategies employed in establishing an initial rapport with students and eliciting necessary information.)

Application (20 min.)
Advisors will observe a sample advising session. (They will be asked to note the instances where information and strategies presented in the session were applied. After the simulation, they will share what they observed. They will also be asked to write a sample anecdotal advising entry. Volunteers will be asked to share what they wrote.)

Evaluation (5 min.)

(Western New Mexico University, 2002b)

APPENDIX 4.2

Advisor Training for Orientation
Western New Mexico University

Date: ___________

	Agree				Disagree
1) The information presented was relevant.	1	2	3	4	5
2) The handouts were effective.	1	2	3	4	5
3) The presenters were organized.	1	2	3	4	5
4) The time was used effectively.	1	2	3	4	5

5) What I liked best was ______________________________

____

____

6) The following should be changed:______________________

____

____

7) The following should be added: ______________________

____

____

(Western New Mexico University, 2002a)

APPENDIX 4.3

Aims Community College
EDU 206A: Introduction to the Process and Techniques of Academic Advising

2 Credit Hours Tuesdays, 3:15–5:00 p.m. (April 4–June 6)
S/U Grade Room 758—College Center
Instructor: Dr. Debra Bell Baker, Program Director, Advising

Course Description

Student growth, persistence and campus vitality—all are related to academic advising and influenced by programs and policies that academic advisors deliver. Research on student persistence and advising has linked successful academic advising programs to the opportunity for advisors to participate in professional development activities. The overall goal of this course is to support and enhance the role of faculty advisors.

The topics will be organized to include three content areas: Conceptual Skills, Information Skills, and Relational Skills.

Course Objectives:

By the end of the course, students will be able to

1) understand the processes and tasks involved in academic advising.
2) comprehend the principles involved in college student development and apply these principles in advising process.
3) explain the career-development process and the factors involved in educational and vocational decision-making.
4) form a solid knowledge based with respect to the nature and patterns of organizational functioning of (a) Aims College programs and services, (b) major transfer program from other community colleges and universities in our service area, and (c) the utilization of resources necessary to academic advisement.
5) utilize the skills associated with interpersonal dynamics of the advising process.

Course Format

A combination of lecture, group discussion and experiential activities, as well as presentations by course consultants will be used.

Course Materials

The instructor will provide reading material, activities, and research studies. Folder/notebook needed for organization of materials.

Evaluation

S/U grade based on

1) Participation in all activities and discussions. It is assumed that students complete all reading and other assignments prior to each class.
2) Keeping an integration journal. The purpose of the journal is to provide a forum for your thoughts, impressions, and concerns about class topics and issues. The journal should expand on
   - What you have learned.
   - What you believe or feel.
   - How you apply what you have learned to your role as advisor.

This journal will be turned in on a weekly basis and will be reviewed by the instructor. Journal entries may be submitted via email to dbell@aims.edu.

3) Complete Discover (Career Guidance System) Modules 1–5; turn in review/feedback paper to instructor (2 pages).
4) Participate in 3 advising shadowing experiences with a core advisor/or instructor. One of the advising sessions should be with a new student advisee and one with a returning student advisee. Students will receive a schedule during the week of May 20th–June 6th. Students are expected to complete and return to me the Advising Evaluation Survey and a 1–2 page evaluation of each advising session. What did you learn about actual advising?

SESSION	DATE	TOPIC
Session 1	Wednesday, April 4, 2001 3:15–5:00 p.m. College Center/Room 758	• Introduction & Objectives • Defining Advising • Impact of Academic Advising on Retention • Student Expectations • Role of Faculty Advisor
Session 2	Wednesday, April 11, 2001 3:15–5:00 p.m. College Center/Room 758	• Developmental Advising Model • Student Development Theory • Aims Advising System Policies & Procedures • Transfer Advising—Part I
Session 3	Wednesday, April 18, 2001 3:15–5:00 p.m. College Center/Room 758	• Legal & Ethical Issues—Academic Dean, BSES • Ethics of Advising
Session 4	Wednesday, April 25, 2001 3:15–5:00 p.m. College Center/Room 758	• Role of Aims Assessment: Interpretation & Placement Program Director, Assessment
Session 5	Wednesday, May 2, 2001 3:15–5:00 p.m. Career Resource Center Room 258—General Services Building	• Career Advising Model—Program Director, Career & Placement Services • Discover—Computer Resources Guidance Tools, Career Education
Session 6	Wednesday, May 9, 2001 3:15–5:00 p.m. College Center/Room 758	• Admission and Registration Policies and Procedures • Registrar
Session 7	Wednesday, May 16, 2001 3:15–5:00 p.m. College Center/Room 758	• Transfer Advising Issues —Aims Faculty Role —Core Curriculum —Major Transfer Programs • What faculty advisors need to know about Financial Aid • Director, Student Financial Assistance
Session 8	Wednesday, May 23, 2001 3:15–5:00 p.m. College Center/Room 758	• Developmental & Remedial Education: Purpose & course • Sequencing-advising issues —advising case studies
Session 9	Wednesday, May 30, 2001 3:15–5:00 p.m. College Center/Room 758	• Transfer Advising, continued • Advising case studies • Relationships of advising to teaching
Session 10	Wednesday, June 6, 2001 3:15–5:00 p.m. College Center/Room 758	• Student-Centered Service /Welcoming our students • 3–4 p.m.—Student Rights & Responsibilities: What faculty/advisors need to know—Kim Black, Program Coordinator, Academic & Student Affairs • 4–5 p.m.—Orientation & Student Life Program Coordinator, Orientation & Student Activities • Wrap up activities

5 THE ROLE OF EVALUATION AND REWARD IN FACULTY ADVISING

Victoria A. McGillin

Academic advising is the single most important relationship offered to students by an institution of higher education. It is through this relationship that students will engage in a critical narrative process that will give shape and meaning to their curricular and life choices and through which they come to understand the interconnections of knowledge and the curricula. Students arrive on our campuses ready to be changed by the experience of higher education. They embrace change as a primary function of a college education and perceive this change as both the reward for their efforts and a measure of the rewards to come.

Faculty also arrive on our campuses expecting to be changed, whether as new faculty hoping to learn the entirety of what it means to be a professor, or as senior faculty seeking to adapt to their new institution or to a new curriculum. While many faculty find themselves drawn to the "meaning-making" interactions with students that form the core of advising, few actually seek out opportunities to develop as advisors, given an institutional reward structure erected predominantly on scholarly activity. What will promote faculty involvement in opportunities to improve themselves as advisors? The answer most frequently put forward is that faculty will seek out opportunities to advance as advisors if and when that activity is significantly recognized, evaluated, and rewarded.

Nationally, less than one-third of faculty advisors receive any evaluation, much less any recognition or reward (Habley & Morales, 1998). Those considering the introduction or refinement of a faculty-advisor reward system must first consider the following questions: What do you hope to accomplish and what use will you make of the results? In what way do you hope assessment and reward systems will change faculty advisors? Deans, department chairs, and division heads need a fundamental understanding of what motivates people to change, what is involved in the process of change, and what will promote more change to take place. In what way is the professorate different from other workforces, and are there principles of change unique to this population? How effective are our current measures of faculty development? Finally, those considering a new assessment and reward system need to understand the current modes of faculty advisor assessment, recognition, and reward.

HUMAN CHANGE

"On several levels, of course, we are all seeking—and achieving—some form of change every moment of our lives" (Mahoney, 1991, p. 5). Change, however, will be balanced against forces for stability. Mahoney affirms that humans can change, but that change is rarely smooth, rapid, or easy. We humans are not infinitely plastic in our potential to change, nor are we as constrained in our potential for adult change, as some psychodynamic thinkers would have us believe.

Altering what Mahoney calls the "core processes" of reality (one's sense of order), self (one's personal identity), values (the valence or importance attached to something), and power (one's sense of personal control) will meet with greater resistance (Mahoney, 1991). Consider the many ways in which these processes go to the heart of an advising encounter. First, faculty-student advising relationships are inherently about the core themes of power and influence. Second, while faculty members' advising expertise may not "matter" as much as their disciplinary expertise, the quality of advisors' interpersonal communication skills (listening, responding) reflect a core element of their sense of self. By altering those very personal dimensions, well-intentioned efforts to develop faculty as advisors have the potential to elicit self-protective resistance (Mahoney, 1991). As a result, in any effort to develop faculty potential as advisors, a dynamic balancing change and stability should be expected.

Stages of Change

Change, by definition, implies something happening over time. Prochaska and his colleagues (Prochaska & DiClemente, 1983;

Prochaska, DiClemente, & Norcross, 1992; Prochaska & Velicer, 1997) have proposed a five-stage transtheoretical model of intentional change that engages the key elements of emotions, cognitions, and behavior. This model was designed as a "recruitment" model that assumed individuals were not ready for change. It has proven particularly helpful in retaining people on a path of change, matching individual needs to specific programs of change. An advisor initially introduced to a faculty-development program of advisor workshops and skills assessments may actually have no interest in changing in the near future. In the developmental process of change, individuals in the earliest stages of change may avoid reading, thinking, or talking about their problematic behavior. Targeting assessment data or rewards at this population is unlikely to be successful. Advisors who do intend to change at some point in the future are usually stuck in the stage of "behavioral procrastination" (Velicer, Prochaska, Fava, Norman, & Redding, 1998). They do respond to evaluation feedback, which raises their awareness of the need to change, but they are not ready for action-oriented models of change (for example, "Do this now"). While they know they should improve as advisors (they have assessment data pointing to areas they should change and they understand why improved advising makes sense), they are also aware of the "costs" of such change (such as moving from a research to a teaching track and time on one's own scholarship versus time with students).

Advisors in the middle stages of change will develop a plan for change (for example, attend additional workshops; consult mentors) and are good candidates for action-oriented faculty development programs. As they begin to take action (for example, agreeing to teach a first-year seminar or to take on major advising responsibilities), they move to a new level of performance. This is the point where relapse to an earlier stage is most possible. Recognition and reward can reinforce the change already accomplished. Finally, advisors in the last stage of change will engage in activities that establish this new status quo and are less tempted to slide back (they might agree to mentor a new advisor or host a workshop about advising).

Prochaska and colleagues found that unless the processes employed to promote change are matched to the stage of the individual, change would not occur. Faculty-development programs must be more finely tuned to the faculty. Rather than "across the board" programs, or programs for individual departments, Prochaska's data suggest the need to identify faculty at comparable stages and invite them to programs specifically targeted to their stage of change (Velicer et al., 1998). "Experiential" processes (such as performance feedback, testimonials, documentary films on advising, facilitating a workshop for other advisors, and reflection on the changes one has made) are most effective with advisors in the earliest stages of change, while "behavioral" processes (such as joining a support group, mentoring a younger advisor, countering peer pressure, receiving recognition for advising, and taking a leadership role in changing advising on one's campus) work best with advisors in later stages of change.

Following this model, it becomes evident that evaluation of faculty advisors can prove crucial at different stages than recognition and reward activities. Evaluation (feedback on one's own and others' behavior) can play an important role in the early stages of change. Feedback about how one is doing as a faculty advisor, instruction on what good faculty advising looks like, and campaigns to help faculty interpret those discrepancies are key to increasing awareness for change and beginning the change process. Recognition and reward will support changes that have been made and promote continuation of one's growth as an advisor. Prochaska's model also suggests that effective systems of assessment and reward need to be very sensitive to the timing of evaluations and recognition or reward.

FACULTY AND CHANGE

The Evolving Institutional Mission

Your institutional mission *should* provide the framework upon which all-important initiatives are built. During the latter part of the 20th century there have been a series of disconnects between institutions' missions and values and their assessment and reward systems (Atkinson & Tuzin, 1992). Formal changes in assessment and reward systems have lagged behind the national shifts in mission by a decade or more. For example, from the 1950s through the 1970s, the phenomenal growth in higher education and in grants to support (primarily) scientific research pushed many institutional missions towards the "Scholarship of Discovery" (Boyer, 1990), the production of primary research. By the 1970s, the assessment of and reward for research and publication had replaced most attention to other faculty work, even at many teaching institutions. A second shift occurred in the 1980s and 1990s. As institutional bottom lines became critical, higher education began to focus on who actually paid the bills, the individual student or the state legislature. Critiques of teaching and learning and concerns about accountability to the state resulted in renewed, mission-driven attention to the "Scholarship of Teaching" (which includes advising), the "Scholarship of Integration" (giving new meaning to existing knowledge), and the "Scholarship of Application" (integration of theory and practice) (Boyer, 1990). Existing evaluation and reward systems have only just begun to take note of this shift (Kaun, 1984). Assessment, training, and reward of faculty advisors must be tied to an institution's current mission and strategic goals. This guarantees that support exists from the "top down" and that meaningful institutional resources will be in place to help achieve faculty-advising goals.

> ***Recommendation 1:*** *Determine how and where advising can be woven into your institutional mission and goals, if it is not yet explicitly in place. Engage a powerful group of your faculty in the task of using those goals to construct the critical elements of the evaluation and reward systems.*

The disconnection between what is "valued" and what is actually rewarded is even more troubling to faculty when they feel that they have had no voice in establishing the mission or reward emphasis at their institutions. While securing sufficient resources for faculty-advisor development comes from the top down, the specifics of any faculty development program must come from the bottom up—from the faculty themselves. On your campus, what role have faculty played in shaping the goals and mission of your institution? The willingness of faculty to commit to change is often a direct reflection of their participation in the development of and identification with new missions and goals (Glotzbach, 2001). Additionally, you may need to consider to what extent your faculty see the institutional mission and goals as nothing more than a public relations campaign for external audiences that leaves core processes untouched; as some passing administrative fad that can be waited out by a patient professorate; or as faculty-determined goals, to which they can make a firm commitment.

> ***Recommendation 2:*** *Determine to what extent your faculty have participated in constructing any institutional mission statements or goals that address faculty advising. Engage them in the process, if possible.*

The Changing American Professorate

Before constructing an evaluation and reward system, it is critical to determine what percentage of the faculty on your campus will retire and be replaced in the next ten years. We are facing the largest turnover in faculty since the Baby Boom–influenced hiring drive of the 1960s (Burgan, Weisbuch, & Lowry, 1999; Trower, Austin, & Sorcinelli, 2001). Collie and Chronister (2001) reported that in 1998 more than 44% of all tenured faculty were 55 or older and were facing retirement within the next ten years. Who will replace these faculty? While this will vary dramatically by institutional type and mission, it is important to review the national trends in hiring.

According to Finkelstein and Schuster (2001), new faculty are more likely to be female, more likely to be part of an ethnic minority, and more likely to be "off track" than the faculty they replace. That is, our population of mostly white, mostly tenured, mostly male faculty are being replaced by a population both increasingly diverse and increasingly on part-time or term appointments. In fact, in the 1990s, the majority of all full-time faculty appointments were off the tenure track. According to Finkelstein and Schuster (2001), "Non-tenurable term appointments—essentially non-existent three decades ago—have become the norm, the modal type of faculty appointment" (p. 5). These authors also report that faculty in term appointments and part-time faculty are nearly twice as likely to spend no time with students outside the classroom. Examine your faculty contracts covering part-time and nontenure- track faculty. Are they able to advise? Are they allowed to advise? Are they invited to advise? Fewer than 12% of part-time faculty contracts specify noninstructional responsibilities (Rhoades, 1996). The new American professorate, substantially composed of temporary faculty, may be unwilling or unable to do the work of a permanent faculty (Burgan, Weisbuch, & Lowry, 1999).

A final area of concern derives from the new faculty hired into those fewer tenure-track positions. Trower, Austin, and Sorcinelli (2001) report that these faculty are arriving on our campuses looking for learning communities and contact with scholars and students. Their research indicates that these new young professors are being advised by their senior colleagues to avoid students and teaching or face losing the rare tenure-track slot they now inhabit. The pool of faculty who are able and willing to advise may be shrinking precipitously.

> ***Recommendation 3:*** *Consult with your academic vice president's office to determine the retirement and replacement hiring plans anticipated over the next ten years. Determine who will be responsible for advising students in your evolving system. Determine to what extent your part-time or term appointment faculty are expected, allowed, and invited to advise as part of their contract. If you are losing tenure-track faculty advisors, and term or part-time appointment contracts do not include advising as a compensated activity, you are approaching an institutional advising crisis. Ensure that this analysis is provided to those responsible for your institutional strategic plan.*

Once you have determined where advising fits within your institutional goals and mission and who your faculty are and will be, you are in a position to consider why and how to evaluate and reward advising as a valued activity among the faculty.

FACULTY EVALUATION AND REWARD SYSTEMS

A number of authors have begun to give voice to the "culture wars" taking place on American campuses—wars between the cultures of administration and of faculty. Jerry Berberet (1999) described the corporate, or managerial, culture of the administration, "which conceives its power source, ultimately, in a top down hierarchy beginning with the president and the board of trustees" (p. 35). Faculty believe that the "ennobling" nature of academic work provides them with "a special status in society that transcends their localized institutions" (Berberet, 1999, p. 35). The former values a more "corporate" tradition of outcomes, competition, and strategy; the latter places highest value on the process of discovery, independence, and thoughtful reflection and tends to resist administrative control (Ferren, Kennan, & Lerch, 2001; Gumport, 2001). Nowhere is this clash of cultures more evident than in the campus debates around the evaluation and reward of faculty. Models of evaluation and reward developed within hierarchical systems of administration may prove antithetical to the faculty.

> ***Recommendation 4:*** *Determine the extent of faculty participation in the development of the current faculty-evaluation and -reward systems on your campus. To what extent are "top-down" versus "bottom-up" debates on governance rife? The answers should determine how you structure the faculty group that will explore and develop your advising assessment and reward system. Respect your current campus culture, but remember that faculty "buy in" to your system of assessment and reward will depend upon their sense of active participation in its development (Strada, 2001; Wergin, 2001).*

Problems With Current Faculty Evaluation and Reward Systems

Several problems hamper current efforts to evaluate and reward faculty advising. These include conflicting purposes for assessment and reward; inconsistent evaluation; problematic performance criteria; disconnections among assessment, development, and reward; and lack of attention by the institution.

Conflicting purposes for assessment and reward. There are two categories of assessment—formative and summative. They are directly related to the two dimensions of rewards—control of behavior and information (Deci & Porac, 1978). Formative evaluation involves a continual stream of information on performance and, for the purpose of faculty development, is used to provide ongoing feedback to faculty, allowing for their continuing development as advisors (Creamer & Scott, 2000; Nelsen, 1981; Seagren, Creswell, & Wheeler, 1993). Formative data is usually placed under the control of the faculty member. This data can help advisors to identify areas for improvement and to set personal goals (Creamer & Scott, 2000; Seagren, Creswell, & Wheeler, 1993). The goal of a formative assessment for advising is on information delivery to the faculty member and the development of that individual advisor.

Summative evaluations usually occur less frequently and are used for personnel decisions, such as salary review, merit review, reappointment, or tenure (Nelsen, 1981; Seagren, Creswell, & Wheeler, 1993). They are also used for comparative purposes, such as awarding top-advisor awards (Creamer & Scott, 2000). Information passes from the control of the faculty advisor to a source of evaluation, where departmental or institutional decisions are made. The goal of summative assessment is to arrive at a personnel-related outcome.

While early studies (Nelsen, 1981) found most faculty in agreement that some system of assessment and reward or recognition was necessary, more recent surveys report that only a minority of faculty are supportive of assessment (Peterson & Augustine, 2000). This decline in faculty acceptance of evaluation and reward systems became dramatic during the "assessment decade" of the 1990s, when the preponderance of assessment efforts shifted from process (formative) to outcome (summative) (Haskell, 1997a; Neal, 1995; Strada, 2001). This was also reflected in a shift in reward systems from those that promoted individual development and the intrinsic motivation to teach and advise (for example, grants to attend an advising conference) to those that served as extrinsic rewards in a comparative competition (such as a decision on tenure, and winning or not winning an Outstanding Advisor award).

> ***Recommendation 5:*** *Determine the purpose of your faculty-advisor evaluation system and your relative balance between formative and summative evaluation needs.*

Inconsistent evaluation. Inconsistent or episodically employed assessment and reward systems cause problems for institutions (Nelsen, 1981). Annual advising evaluations within only one college of a university may rightly result in faculty questions about this discrepancy. Implementing assessment and reward systems some years and not others, without clear rationales for the episodic appearances and disappearances, can also undermine their credibility. To be effective, assessment and reward systems must apply to all faculty, not just those in one program or department or those who are coming up for tenure in one year.

One significant discrepancy in who encounters assessment and reward systems has been across faculty rank. While faculty might continue to be evaluated after tenure, the underlying premise is that this has little serious impact, given that tenured faculty employment is secure. The advent of post-tenure review has raised the possibility of consistently applying the connection between reward and evaluation across all faculty ranks (Licata & Morreale, 2001).

> ***Recommendation 6:*** *Determine if your evaluation and reward system will be applied to all faculty, faculty in rank, or only faculty within one unit of the institution. Consider working for across-the-board implementation of any proposed system. Determine whether or not you have institutional and faculty commitment to implement advising assessment and advising reward systems on an ongoing, formal basis.*

Problematic performance criteria. Even when expectations for advising were clear and the faculty had a meaningful role in articulating those expectations, faculty evaluation and reward systems have still been hampered by a lack of concurrence on the criteria for assessment and reward (Nelsen, 1981; Seagren, Creswell, & Wheeler, 1993). Rarely do the systems in place reflect predetermined performance criteria (Beattie, 1995; Bond, 1996) for good teaching, much less for good advising. For example, Leslie, Harvey, and Leslie (1998) found that most academic vice presidents in their study used research publication counts as a criterion for the determination of faculty teaching skills. Your criteria should be tailored to the performance in question and should be evaluated in a qualitative or quantitative manner appropriate to the data. Faculty evaluation and reward systems have also been faulted for overreliance on quantitative (usually survey) modes of assessment (Mittler & Bers, 1994; Nelsen, 1981; Seagren, Creswell, & Wheeler, 1993; Strada, 2001). Surveys allow for quick, summative judgments, but do not provide the rich texture of data collected using a qualitative method.

There has been particular concern with the overreliance on student evaluations (Haskell, 1997b; Prus & Johnson, 1994) to the exclusion of all other sources of data. Bias is the most frequently voiced faculty complaint. For example, a recent study of student perceptions of course and teaching quality reported that student ratings of instructors varied as a function of their prior beliefs about the reputation of the faculty member (Griffin, 2001). Reliance on single sources of data reduces the validity and reliability of any assessment (Haskell, 1997b). Critical alternative sources could include peer or colleague evaluations, self-assessments and personal statements, supervisor evaluations, assessments by alumni and others (Creamer & Scott, 2000; Seagren, Creswell, & Wheeler, 1993).

> ***Recommendation 7:*** *Determine with your faculty committee the multiple criteria by which faculty advisors will be evaluated and rewarded. Determine your needs for qualitative and quantitative assessments.*

Disconnections among assessment, development, and reward. Work goals can be seen as either intrinsically motivated (pleasurable in and of themselves) or extrinsically motivated (undertaken for an external reward) (Spence & Helmreich, 1983). Motivational research has well documented the ability of extrinsic rewards (such as money) to increase measurable performance of routine tasks (Deci, 1978). However, advising is (or should be) a complex, open-ended, and interesting task. Research on faculty work has consistently found that the primary sources of job satisfaction are intrinsic to the work itself (Bergquist & Phillips, 1977), and that satisfaction is mostly centered on one's role as teacher (Diamond, 1993). In fact, there is solid evidence that extrinsic rewards actually decrease intrinsic motivation for doing interesting and open-ended tasks (Deci, 1978). Could we endanger the good work our faculty are doing by implementing a potentially damaging reward system?

Few faculty are satisfied with the current systems to reward or recognize faculty work (Berberet, 1999). As noted earlier, there has been a failure to tie faculty development and rewards to the institutional mission. The present system of faculty rewards and recognition for scholarly research tie faculty more closely to their disciplines than to their campus or department (Collie & Chronister, 2001). Numerous authors have called for reform in the assessment and reward system (Arnstein, 1978; Astin, 1985; Atkinson & Tuzin, 1992; Chopp, Frost, & Jean, 2001; Licata & Moreale, 2001).

Common forms of external reward for faculty included job security (tenure), promotion, merit increases to base pay, temporary "bonuses" to salaries, grants to underwrite faculty research, reimbursement for scholarly activities, space and equipment, student workers, prizes or awards and recognition by others (Diamond & Adam, 1995). Extrinsic rewards (such as money) are useful only to control and motivate behavior when a task is dull or unchallenging (Deci, 1978). If advising on your campus means nothing more than rote degree-requirement checking and registration-card signing, extrinsic motivators may well be necessary. However, rewards that carry information about the person's competence or self-determination (such as awards) emphasize feedback and can maintain intrinsic motivation in more challenging tasks, such as advising (Deci, 1978).

Wergin (2001) has proposed that faculty are motivated by autonomy (for example, support to conduct their research, release time for research, and support for disciplinary meetings or their labs), recognition (for example, awards for excellence and "write-ups" in campus publications), and efficacy (for example, invitations to join important committees or task force groups that are involved in important work, and opportunities to develop new programs). Given the nature of these listed motivations, it is not surprising that male faculty have reported greater satisfaction with the current assessment and award system than female faculty (Blix, Cruise, Mitchell, & Blix, 1994).

Faculty also join higher education in search of a community of scholars but often find tremendous isolation (Trower, Austin, & Sorcinelli, 2001). Faculty with stronger "affiliative" needs may find themselves drawn into teaching and advising because those needs are better served through these tasks than through their roles as autonomous scholars (Bergquist & Phillips, 1977). Reward systems should be sufficiently diverse to offer incentives that fill affiliative needs as well. For example, recognizing faculty by appointing them to groups that are working on interdisciplinary engagement in challenging and interesting tasks might be superior to release time for research.

The prevalence of available awards is also crucial. If the number of awards is so small that the likelihood of any one individual receiving one is minimal (for example, one advising award for an entire university faculty of 1,000), the award loses meaning for faculty. They are quick to discount the validity of both the assessment and the recognition. In one study, teaching awards were not found to motivate faculty (Ruedrich, Cavey, Katz, & Grush, 1992). Those less likely to win such an award attributed their failure to factors outside their control, while faculty who believed themselves likely to win a teaching award attributed this to personal qualities or accomplishments (Ruedrich, Reid, & Chu, 1986).

> ***Recommendation 8:*** *Determine what rewards are valued by your faculty (intrinsic versus extrinsic rewards, autonomy versus affiliative rewards). Secure sufficient rewards to have an impact beyond the award winners.*

Lack of attention by the institution. In three national surveys over a ten-year period, evaluation and reward of academic advising were ranked least effective of the 11 areas for effective advising assessed (Habley & Morales, 1998). This was consistent across institutional type and mission. Moreover, these ineffective ratings resulted from data generated by the less than one-third of all schools surveyed—those schools that employed any sort of evaluation or reward system. What rewards there were mostly came from departments and department chairs (Larson & Brown, 1983).

Why has there been so little attention to evaluation and reward systems for faculty advising? Creamer and Scott (2000) attributed this to the lack of time, resources, and expertise available to assess advising, as well as the diversity of delivery systems and the paucity of rewards available. Advising also taps into themes of power and self-concept, the intimate, core processes discussed earlier (Mahoney, 1991). Individuals are much less likely to expose those core parts of themselves to an external evaluation. Weak evaluation and reward systems may also be the result of the poor training higher education provides to faculty. It is hypocritical to structure an assessment and reward system when you have never offered an opportunity to those faculty to first develop needed skills. To effectively assess an advisor means to evaluate that faculty member on the most personal themes of effective communication and interpersonal power. To assess advising means to measure faculty performance on something for which we rarely provide effective opportunities to first develop skills. Moreover, to assess advising means opening the doors of faculty offices and rendering the invisible, visible.

The cultural climate of higher education is changing, at least, in the domain of teaching. No longer can a faculty member (easily) get away with "blowing off" classes, coming unprepared to a class, or lecturing ad nauseum. With renewed national attention on the scholarship of teaching, critical encounters between faculty and students have begun to move to the fore. Those faculty who would maintain that this preeminence is fine for teaching but does not apply to advising should attend to the messages from their own disciplinary organizations. In their two publications, summarizing what should be rewarded in faculty work, Diamond and Adam (1995, 2000) reported that the overwhelming majority of disciplinary organizations (for example, the American Historical Association, the American Psychological Association, Joint Policy Board for Mathematics) listed advising as part of the teaching role of faculty. They have followed the lead of Ernest Boyer (1990) who, in his seminal work on scholarship reconsidered, placed advising within the scholarship of teaching. He, in turn, followed the National Academic Advising Association, which hosted a conference on academic advising as teaching in 1984.

> ***Recommendation 9:*** *Determine the campus climate for faculty advising. Ensure that decision makers are aware of the degree of disciplinary support for advising as teaching.*

What have we learned from the history of faculty evaluation and reward systems in higher education? What must we consider when embarking on a new system to assess and recognize faculty advising?

EVALUATION AND REWARD OF FACULTY ADVISING

Having reviewed the issues facing department chairs, deans, and directors of advising, we will now explore how you might implement the recommendations developed previously and investigate specific practices in the evaluation and reward of faculty advising.

Stage One: Create Your Advising Assessment and Reward Committee

To implement recommendations 1 through 6, you must bring your faculty and institutional leadership into the process from the start. Strategically consider who should be invited to be part of this planning group. It is strongly recommended that you invite senior faculty who have power and leadership roles on your campus, as well as junior faculty who are widely seen as part of the vibrant new faculty community. This will ensure that the two most potent power bases are participants in the process.

Engage these faculty and campus leaders in an exploration of the institutional mission as it applies to academic advising. Determine your institutional purpose for implementing an assessment and reward system for advising, balancing the personal skill-development needs of faculty (formative systems) with your institution's need to make critical personnel decisions (summative systems).

Stage Two: Define Good Academic Advising on Your Campus

Each campus must determine for itself what good faculty advising should be. The nature of advising relationships can vary by institutional culture, disciplinary culture, and role expectations. Science advisors, working with students in laboratories, may advise very differently from humanities advisors who meet students in their offices. Advisors of adult students or graduate students may assume greater levels of "authorship" in their students. Advisors of students in prescribed professional programs, almost fully determined once the initial major choice is made, will have very different relationships with their students than will advisors of students in a traditional arts and sciences major, who are capable of still pursuing a range of choices.

The following definition of advising is offered to set the context for this discussion. Good advising is nothing more nor less than the most important narrative relationship a student can have in college. Richard Light (2001) has described advising as the "single most underestimated characteristic of a successful college experience" (p. 81). On too many college campuses, what is defined as advising is the boring, unchallenging, and repetitive activity of degree and credit checking, combined with a personal identification number (PIN) or signature delivery. Sitting in one's office for the required number of hours each semester to complete this sort of rote activity would certainly require an extrinsic reward, as there is nothing intrinsically appealing about those tasks.

Good academic advising, however, engages student and advisor in a systemic transaction through which each has an impact on the other. The impact is felt most keenly by the student, as the act of entering college marks the student as an individual anticipating change. With traditional-aged (and some nontraditional) students, college may mark the first time that they have actively experienced themselves as "authors" of their own lives, making choices (writing a life script) with significant consequences. Through genuine encounters with a faculty advisor, students and advisors engage in a "co-construction" of the students' unfolding life narrative. A student will enter the relationship with years of experience in which some other person "wrote the story of their life." Through the advisor and advisor referrals, students are introduced to a range of "storylines" open for them to explore. Testing out their identities as prelaw "lawyers," medical technicians, criminal justice agents, or history scholars allows them to experience this authorship with their advisors. It is through trial and error or directed explorations of these identities that students can make the transition to full authorship, consulting with their advisor as needed on later choices.

At the same time, the advisor is also the sole individual placed by the institution into the center of students' experience, prepared to help them engage in making meaning of their curricular and cocurricular experiences. Faculty are the experts on the curriculum, capable of helping students understand the interconnections of the disciplines and of the many elements of their major. This distinctly academic meaning making also links the curriculum and the learning that is taking place inside the classroom to the learning that occurs outside the classroom. Good advising calls for a commitment to mastering a considerable body of information, to an ethical and genuine relationship with a student, and to a transformational relationship, designed to facilitate another's intellectual, academic, and personal development. The selection of classes is just the outcome of a longer, richer process. Such encounters are challenging, open-ended, and complex, the kind of activities least likely to respond to external forms of motivation.

Stage Three: Construct Your Evaluation System

If you accept the above definition of academic advising, who, what, and how you evaluate advising should reflect this definition. If academic advising is a dynamic transactional system, then a comprehensive assessment would evaluate what both parties bring to the advising encounter, the process by which they interact with one another, and the outcomes that result from those interactions.

Advising input. Advisors and students both bring a great deal to the advising encounter. Both bring their availability and willingness to meet, their belief systems about what ought to occur, and varying strengths in knowledge and information about the curriculum, the majors, the institution, careers, and life. If advising includes teaching advisees about what is expected, then faculty also play a pivotal role in their advisees' "input."

Advising process. What happens in an advising encounter is, without question, a function of what both the advisor and student bring to that interaction. Communication skills (listening, understanding, speaking, and questioning), as well as openness to whatever the other has to offer, are core components of the interaction. Given their power in the interaction, advisors set the tone for the original encounters—how and what they are open to discuss lays down the parameters for the interaction. Beyond basic communication skills, the advisors' ability and the students' willingness to explore meanings and to understand connections (among curricular offerings, courses and careers, and life issues and major decisions), move the advising encounters beyond course selection into "life narrative" development.

Advising outcomes. The best preparation or knowledge base and the most enlightened of interactions have little meaning if neither advisor nor advisee leave an interaction prepared to take steps that will bring more meaning into their lives. Whether and how well a student follows through on an advising encounter (resulting in satisfaction, skills developed, errors in registration, or changing advisors) are both critical measures of what has happened. Similarly, the advisor also leaves an interaction changed and prepared to take action (resulting in satisfaction, commitment to change campus-advising policy, development of advising materials, research on advising). Those outcomes are also a crucial source of data on the advisor.

Stage Four: Select Your Evaluation Methods

Ideally, you want to evaluate advisors and their students through an assessment of their perceptions, behaviors, and outcomes.

Realistically, your committee will need to make choices from the available options. At this point, you must begin to ask tough questions: Are you more interested in how advisors conceive of their role in advising (input) or with the quality of students' decisions after the interaction (outcome)? Are you more concerned with a faculty members' actual knowledge base (input) or how well it is communicated and perceived by students (process)? Are you more concerned with how advisors and students interact (process) or with students' satisfaction and advisors' development of new advising materials as a function of that interaction (outcome)? The answers to these questions, combined with your decisions concerning summative or formative evaluations and your institutional definition of advising will determine which methods you select. Table 5.1 presents a conceptual organization of the assessment methods to be discussed next.

There is near universal agreement that a good evaluation must use multiple methods of data collection (Creamer & Scott, 2000; Habley & Morales, 1998; Lynch, 2000; Tharp, Hensley, & Meadows, 1996). Ideally, these are combined into a faculty advising portfolio. Just as portfolios are emerging as a preferred model for both summative and formative evaluation of college teaching (Reece, Pearce, Melillo, & Beaudry, 2001), they hold great promise for reconceptualizing advising evaluation as a serious process. The primary categories of materials in a full assessment process include self-assessment, assessment by others, behavioral evaluation, and analysis of materials or outcomes.

TABLE 5.1

INPUT, PROCESS, AND OUTPUT CONCEPTUAL ORGANIZATION OF ADVISING ASSESSMENT METHODS FOR ADVISORS AND ADVISEES

Stage	Advisor Measures	Advisee Measures
Input	Statement of advising philosophy (S) Assessment of knowledge /information (S): • Department and major courses/ requirements • College courses/ requirements • Curriculum as a whole • Career expectations and information • Institutional regulations and resources • Familiarity with student file • Good advisor practices	Statement of advising expectations (S) Assessment of knowledge /information (S): • Department and major courses/ requirements • College courses/ requirements • Curriculum as a whole • Career expectations and information • Institutional regulations and resources • Familiarity with own record • Good advisee practices
	Number of advisees or advisee contacts/week (B)	Assessment of advisor availability (B)
	Number of hours available /week for advising (B)	Number of times sets up appointment (B)
	Number of appointments advisor missed (B)	Number of appointments student missed (B)
Process	Behavioral checklist after each encounter (B) • (behaviors shown by advisor/by advisee) • Listening/responding behavior • Probing behavior • Clarity of communication • Helping behavior • Referral behavior • "Narrative development" skills	Behavioral checklist after each encounter (B) • (what behavior shown by advisee/by advisor) • Listening/responding behavior • Openness to probing • Clarity of communication • Help-seeking behavior • Follow-through behavior • Openness to narrative development

Note: (S) = Self-assessments; (O) = Assessments by others; (B) = Behavioral measures; and (M) = Material/activity assessment

Stage	Advisor Measures	Advisee Measures
Process, cont'd	Skilled observation of live or video interaction (B) (behaviors shown by advisor) • Listening/responding behavior • Probing behavior • Clarity of communication • Helping behavior • Referral behavior • "Narrative development" skills	Skilled observation of live or video interaction (B) (what behavior shown by advisee) • Listening/responding behavior • Openness to probing • Clarity of communication • Help-seeking behavior • Follow-through behavior • Openness to narrative development
	Focus group of advisees or alumni (O) • Advisor knowledge, interpersonal skills, "narrative development" skills	Focus group of advisees or alumni (S) • Advisee knowledge, interpersonal skills, • openness to narrative development
Output	Philosophical statement on outcomes expected (S) Perception of effectiveness/ student change (S)	Statement on outcomes expected (S) Perception of effectiveness/ change (S)
	Perception of skills developed by student (S)	Assessment (B) or perception (S) of skills developed
	Satisfaction with encounter and with own advising (S)	Satisfaction with encounter and advisor in general (S)
	Number of follow-up appointments scheduled (B)	Number of repeat appointments (B)
	Focus group of advisees or alumni (O) • Outcomes and satisfaction with	Focus group of advisees or alumni (S) • Outcomes and satisfaction with self
	Number of advisees (B): • Returning for follow-up meetings, requesting to change advisors, who change majors, retained and retained to	Assessment of own follow-up to advisor (B): • Referrals, recommendations, suggestions

Note: (S) = Self-assessments; (O) = Assessments by others; (B) = Behavioral measures; and (M) = Material/activity assessment

Stage	Advisor Measures	Advisee Measures
Output, cont'd	graduation, graduating on time Number of courses dropped by advisees (B) Number of petitions for academic exception citing "advisor error" (B) Solicited or unsolicited letters of complaint or commendation (S) Student, peer, supervisor, expert evaluation of (M): • Advising publications, handouts, training materials, Web pages Supervisor, peer evaluation of advising activities (M): • Campus and departmental committees, system-wide groups, mentoring advisors, training and workshops attended or developed, departmental and campus reports written, advising conferences attended Supervisor and expert evaluation of advising professional activity (M): • Local, regional, or conference presentations • Refereed scholarly publications • Keynote addresses or chapters	

Note: (S) = Self-assessments; (O) = Assessments by others; (B) = Behavioral measures; and (M) = Material/activity assessment

Self-assessments. Faculty self-assessments are most frequently used as part of a summative, promotion, tenure, merit, or annual-review process. However, they can also prove very helpful in a formative evaluation. Self-assessments can take the form of a philosophical statement of advising or completion of a survey questionnaire. Srebnik (1988) identified five published surveys with complementary advisor and student versions, and five questionnaires developed just for advisor self-assessment. Self-evaluations are subjective and nonverifiable but do provide insights into motivation and may serve as accurate descriptions of an advisor's actual behaviors (Daller, Creamer, & Creamer, 1997). Towson State University and West Carolina State University require or suggest a narrative self-evaluation as part of the tenure process, while Concordia University utilizes an advisor checklist.

Student self-assessments, while exceptionally valuable sources of information concerning students' contributions to the advising process (Pennsylvania State University, University Advising Council, 2002), are rarely used. A few notable exceptions are instruments in use at the University of West Alabama, Pennsylvania State University (Eberly College of Science), and Wheaton College in Massachusetts. While students are rarely asked to espouse their own philosophy of advising, increasingly a number of institutions are employing an entering-student advising survey to elicit the students' expectations for the advising process.

Assessments by others. Assessment by others is the method most commonly employed in advisor evaluation. Advisors are evaluated by their advisees and graduates, their colleagues, and their supervisors. Peer and supervisor evaluations are least likely to be used in advisor evaluations (Habley & Morales, 1998) but may be perceived by advisors as a more acceptable source of feedback than student evaluations (Creamer & Scott, 2000). According to Habley and Morales (1998), only 2% of evaluations are conducted by peers and 12% by supervisors. Peer and supervisor assessments can prove helpful for both formative and summative purposes. Supervisor and colleague evaluations most often take the form of narrative, summary impressions of the other. One exception is a survey, developed at Middle Tennessee State University, which can be used by a peer or supervisor to assess a faculty advisor.

Student evaluations of advisors are the tools most often employed in any evaluation process. They can take the form of an interview, a focus group, or the more common survey. While students or alumni may feel less intimidated by a focus group than by an individual interview (Creamer & Scott, 2000), both interview and focus groups allow for a careful and richly nuanced exploration of the advising process. Using open-ended questions and probing follow-up questions, a skilled interviewer can elicit information about advisees' feelings, their experiences, their thoughts, and perceptions (Creamer & Scott, 2000; Tharp, Hensley, & Meadows, 1996).

Student or alumni surveys are ubiquitous in advising-evaluation systems. Too often, surveys provide little more information than an assessment of the informant's satisfaction with advising (Creamer & Scott, 2000). While some authors have found a degree of agreement between advisor and advisee evaluations (McAnulty, O'Connor, & Sklare, 1987), others have found student assessments to vary systematically by prior experience (Alexitch, 1997), gender (Bardovi-Harlig & Hartford, 1993), nationality or culture (Hartford & Bardovi-Harlig, 1992), and characteristics of the relationship, particularly the power structure (Dreisbach, 1990). Students, however, are the "consumers" of the advising relationship and are uniquely placed to report on the behaviors of others and on changes personally experienced (Scriven, 1995).

Given the systematic sources of variation in evaluations, committees developing an assessment and reward system must pay close attention to the validity and reliability of their measures. Surveys selected or developed must be held to high standards of validity—that they measure what they purport to measure—and reliability—that they consistently measure those same dimensions. Do you develop your own survey or select one with documented reliability and validity (Sun & Valega, 1997)? Developing an instrument on your own campus increases the likelihood of "fit" with your assessment goals but may be limited in validity and reliability, having poor or misleading questions, being either too long or too short, and asking global (such as, "Are you satisfied?") or inappropriately comparative questions (such as, "Compared to other advisors . . . ") (Scriven, 1995).

If your committee selects an available instrument with documented validity and reliability, such as the Academic Advising Inventory (Winston & Sander, 1985) or the ACT Survey of Academic Advising, it will benefit from an established measure with national norms for comparison. Each of these instruments contains one section that asks students about their advisor. The Academic Advising Inventory is limited by its reliance on a simplistic, bipolar model of advising as either prescriptive or developmental (when subsequent research has documented that both behaviors coexist). The latter is a longer, more broadly focused satisfaction survey, limited (as are most instruments) by assessing only the students' perceptions of their advisors. However, while nationally normed instruments may allow you to ask "campus-specific" questions, your assessment process loses the ability to ask only the crucial questions, potentially limiting the validity of the results.

There are a considerable number of advisor-evaluation instruments available in published form (Srebnik, 1988) or on the web (for example, Pennsylvania State University, Eberly College of Science; Walla Walla College; and Michigan State University, College of Natural Science). Srebnik's review of 19 instruments for students and ten surveys for advisors found that very few questionnaires had established either reliability or validity. As the web instruments on the are published for ease of student download or interactive completion, an interested advising-assessment committee would need to contact the sponsoring institution directly to determine if they have completed a formal item analysis and have established validity and reliability.

For purposes of this discussion, the author completed a content analysis of the student instruments reviewed by Srebnik (1988) and 21 web-based questionnaires or assessment tools. This analysis revealed considerable variability in length (as few as two items on an East Carolina State University web survey to 30 items on the Claremont Graduate School of Religion web questionnaire). Questionnaire length is critical, regardless of whether it is administered on paper, over the web, or by telephone. If there are too few items, little information of value will be collected. Too long a questionnaire reduces compliance. In contrast to the variability in length, the content analysis of instruments revealed relative consistency in content.

The vast majority of instruments reviewed asked students to share a perception ("seemed interested") or general evaluation ("was knowledgeable") of the advisor. Only two surveys (Survey of Advisor Traits and Advisor Effectiveness, Polson, 1981; Advisor Information Form, Kramer & Gardner, 1983) asked students to assess some of their personal outcomes after an advising encounter (for example, increased comfort in decision making or increased confidence about academic choices). All surveys reviewed contained items that could be categorized into one of five areas: 1) knowledge or information about curriculum, careers or campus resources; 2) interpersonal communication and relational skills; 3) skills that facilitated the student's growth or development; 4) availability (either in person or electronically) and preparation; and 5) satisfaction with the advisor. All but one questionnaire asked students to rate their advisors on information or knowledge, while more than half (11) eschewed the use of a "satisfaction" measure. Only two questionnaires (Advisor Information Form, Kramer & Gardner, 1983; Advising Satisfaction Questionnaire, Grites, 1985) asked students to assess behaviors in the advising encounter (for example, "advisor was rushed" or "advisor challenged me to higher academic performance").

The method of survey administration can introduce bias as well as influence compliance. If students are free to choose whether to complete an instrument on their own (whether on the web, on paper, or over the phone), compliance will be weaker. (In social science research, a 30% response rate is considered good.) In those cases respondents are most likely to represent the two ends of the continuum, those happiest and those most disappointed with their encounters. To increase compliance and decrease bias, some schools have used incentives (one free transcript, a chance for a gift certificate, and so on). Others have made completion of an assessment compulsory (for example, students cannot receive their registration PIN until they submit their advisor evaluation or the web-based form is a mandatory screen that must be completed prior to finishing one's registration online). At Iowa State University (Department of Industrial and Manufacturing Systems Engineering), students cannot get a registration number until they hand in their advisor evaluation. At Syracuse University (School of Human Development), advisor-evaluation forms are distributed and collected in classes right after the advising period.

Letters submitted by students, whether solicited or not, are potentially helpful for formative purposes, but the lack of consistency in who writes a letter to applaud or condemn a faculty advisor render them problematic for summative purposes. Most advising award competitions welcome some letters of support, but faculty are free to invite those submissions.

Behavioral measures. Behavioral evaluations have the fewest standards for comparison. Observation or videotaping of advising encounters provide the most accurate, direct source of information about advising interactions but could raise serious questions about confidentiality. Further, unless advisors are taped or observed during all (or a significant subset) of their advising encounters, the potential for selective bias in the observations is raised. The lack of any standardized observational system (what to look for in an advising encounter) also reduces the reliability of any summary comments. Observation and feedback by a colleague or supervisor could provide valuable formative information. For summative purposes, a sample videotape is, at best, illustrative. At present, no institutions identified have included formal observations or videotape reviews as part of their assessment process, but, given increased use of such reviews in teaching assessment, this may begin to change.

Simple behavioral counts of appointments kept, average time per appointment, number of requests for advisor changes, dropped courses, petitions for exception based on "advisor error," students retained to graduation, and students graduated on time pose fewer problems with reliability or validity. West Carolina University has recommended and the University of South Carolina–Union has implemented audits of student files and transcripts. In contrast, the Geology Department of Kansas State University evaluates the ease with which students have achieved graduation requirements. Arizona State University (English/philosophy department), in turn, includes a review of student requests for change in advisor in their review.

Assessment of materials and activities. Peer, supervisor, or expert evaluations of materials developed by an advisor (for example, web pages, handbooks, requirement checklists, and scholarly research) are comparable to peer reviews of publications.

Familiarity with the advisor in question can introduce bias. For formative purposes, collegial feedback on such materials would be very helpful. For summative judgments, "blind" reviews are best. Materials developed for a specific department, college, campus, or system clearly must be evaluated by those with expertise within that system, as they will have the necessary familiarity with the needs and goals of those populations. Similarly, involvement in local or campus advising councils or advising initiatives are best assessed locally, while engagement with regional or national advising organizations warrant external review. Requests for submission of such materials as part of "outstanding advisor" recognition processes are very common (for example, at Iowa State University, Monroe Community College, and the University of Connecticut).

Stage Five: Construct a Meaningful Reward System

As mentioned previously, reward systems are as poorly established as are evaluation systems. Less than one-third of all institutions surveyed offered some form of recognition or reward for faculty advisors (Habley & Morales, 1998). Further, the significance of the rewards employed has decreased since 1992. In 1992, advising was considered a major factor in promotion and tenure considerations for 23% of campuses surveyed and a minor factor for 54%. By the time of the fifth American College Testing (ACT) survey of advising, the advising activities of faculty had dropped, both in consideration as a major and a minor factor in tenure (to 7% and 14%, respectively) (Habley & Morales, 1998).

Most colleges offer no recognition or reward for advising (Lunneborg & Baker, 1986), and faculty have expressed deep dissatisfaction with this status (Biggs, Brodie, & Barnhartt, 1975; Kelly, 1995). Advising was often categorized as "service," traditionally the weakest element of institutional reward model (research, teaching, service). Increasingly, however, advising is being reformulated as teaching (in the faculty disciplinary organizations, in national dialogues on teaching and learning, and on campuses), while teaching is emerging as a far more significant factor in reward at all but the most unyielding research institutions. As a crucial teaching function of the faculty, faculty advisors themselves will increasingly demand serious consideration for their advising activities. In one recent study (Dillon & Fisher, 2000), faculty from each college of one university were asked about advising rewards. Nearly all (91%) felt that advising should count in promotion and tenure, given the time demands of good advising. Nearly one-third of the faculty surveyed agreed that the importance of advising should warrant its inclusion in faculty reward.

A Taxonomy of Reward Systems

There are four major categories of recognition and reward in higher education: merit, promotion, and tenure; stipend or pay considerations; workload and release time; and recognition or award programs. As we have seen from the higher-education and human-change literature, rewards are best introduced once change has already taken place, as they serve best in a reinforcing role. We have also seen that faculty are much more likely to be motivated by intrinsic desires for autonomy or affiliation, challenge, efficacy, or accomplishment than by external rewards. If used, extrinsic rewards work best when they convey information about the competence of the faculty member.

Awards that are given annually to a tiny portion of the population are problematic, but popular. As mentioned earlier, while they certainly convey information about the competence of the recipient, they are unlikely to change the behavior of the recipient or of others. Do the winners of outstanding faculty advisor awards improve their advising after winning such an award? Change by the award winner is unlikely. Other faculty are unlikely to change their behavior as a result of a colleague receiving an award, given their belief that nothing they could do would result in winning (Ruedrich, Cavey, Katz, & Grush, 1992). Awards, however, remain popular since they are usually inexpensive (rarely above $2,000), they rely on voluntary assessment of the faculty advisors, and they can be "added on" to existing systems, not demanding a change in the underlying structure of campus rewards. A web search found more than 200 entries on higher education web pages for the combined terms "faculty advisor" and "advisor award." Some notable examples are the University of South Carolina Ada B. Thomas Outstanding Advisor Award, the Virginia Tech Excellence in Academic Advising Award, Stanford University School of

Engineering Distinguished Advisor Award, and Kansas University's J. Michael Young Academic Advisor Award. The National Academic Advising Association, in conjunction with ACT, sponsors an annual competition (Kerr, 2000) to which many campuses nominate their campus winner.

One exception to the single-award model, with potential to influence other faculty, can be found at the University of Illinois (School of Engineering), where the top 10% of all advisors are recognized annually. Another model, proposed but not implemented, called for recognition of the entire department having the highest average advising evaluations (McGillin & Kornfeld, 1998). Such systems do have the potential to influence larger numbers of faculty because they increase the likelihood of being recognized. Departmental awards may also induce collegial peer pressure to change one's advising behavior.

In another form of recognition, institutions provide certificates or award a title, such as "master advisor" (and send accompanying letters to deans, department chairs, and academic vice presidents), once faculty complete specified training programs (such as Southwest Missouri State University's much-copied "Master Advisor" program). Given in larger numbers, such recognitions could have an impact far beyond the individual advisor receiving the certificate.

Stipends for advising are problematic as they do not always serve as an incentive. As we have seen from the motivational literature, pay for inherently interesting work may be counterproductive. Faculty identify the bureaucratic aspects of advising as the least attractive part of the experience (Kelly, 1995). Technology is increasingly freeing faculty advisors from degree-checking and requirement-monitoring activities. However, if those elements still dominate your campus advising process, stipends or pay make sense. Examples include the University of Georgia (Franklin College) and Ohio University (Kerr, 2000). One university (Clark University) offered a very small stipend to first-year advisors, which they could use toward travel, research, or journal purchases. This tied the award to research activities valued by the faculty.

Time is often described as faculty's most valued commodity. It is not surprising that faculty with larger advising loads express less satisfaction with their institutional system than those with lower loads (Biggs, Brodie, & Barnhartt, 1975). Rossman (1968) also found that this carried over into student satisfaction. Faculty who were granted release time to advise had advisees who were more satisfied with their advising experience than did faculty who advised as an overload. While faculty do feel that advising should be factored significantly into their workload as part of the reward system (Berdahl, 1995), an early review of collective-bargaining contracts found little evidence of advising in load consideration (Teague & Grites, 1980).

Examples of workload consideration for advising are numerous. Some schools offer release time for faculty to advise in a centralized advising center (for example, Temple University offers one course release for eight hours per week of advising) (Kerr, 2000). Other schools compute a direct exchange, such as three semester hours of teaching load for 50 advisees, as reported at Cloud County Community College (Kerr, 2000). Some schools are considering (for example, the University of Idaho) or have implemented (Syracuse University, Arts and Sciences/Religion Department) the ability to rewrite job descriptions or adjust the merit weighting to enable those advising more students to be so recognized.

In the culture of faculty, however, merit, promotion, and tenure are the preeminent modes of both recognition and reward. As tenure-track positions are fewer, the award of tenure becomes that much more significant. No faculty member is likely to receive tenure or to be promoted based on good advising alone. However, a number of institutions are clearly articulating the position that bad teaching and advising could work to the detriment of one's career. Some examples of institutions that have implemented advising as part of their teaching merit, promotion, and tenure review include University of Wisconsin–Whitewater, Towson University, Temple University, Syracuse University, Arizona State University, and Pennsylvania State University–Altoona.

Will rewarding or recognizing academic advising actually change faculty behavior? Some indirect evidence for this does exist. Johnson and Pinkney (1980) paid an experimental group of faculty to attend an advising workshop while not rewarding a control group of faculty who also attended. Six months later, those who had been paid to attend were more likely to have implement ed changes, based on the workshop, than the control group. Faculty do report that advising contributes to their professional development. Unfortunately, those with fewer advisees see it as more likely to interfere with scholarly productivity (Mahoney, Borgard, & Hornbuckle, 1978). As research-driven, tenure-track positions become fewer, faculty anxiety about a balance between advising and scholarly productivity (Kramer, 1986) will remain high. The only way that this anxiety can be directly addressed will be to follow the recommendations laid out here and move faculty advising into the mainstream of institutional assessment and reward systems.

CONCLUSION

Faculty advisors are engaged in complex behaviors for change, both their own personal change and the transformation of their students. As the culture of higher education moves further away from the metaphor of a community of scholars, the changing face of the professorate reflects a faculty increasing in size but decreasing in the contractual commitments to their college. These changes are taking place simultaneously with national movements to engage faculty more directly in meaningful learning encounters with their students. Academic advising is one such meaningful engagement. If your institutional missions are shifting toward increased recognition of teaching, they must also recognize faculty advising.

REFERENCES

Alexitch, L. (1997). Students' educational orientation and preferences for advising from university professors. *Journal of College Student Development, 38,* 333–343.

Arnstein, D. (1978). Improving instruction: Reform the institution, not the faculty. *Liberal Education, 64,* 266–277.

Astin, H. (1985). Providing incentives for teaching underprepared students. *Educational Record, 66,* 26–29.

Atkinson, R., & Tuzin, D. (1992). Equilibrium in the research university. *Change, 24,* 21–31.

Bardovi-Harlig, K., & Hartford, B. (1993). The language of co-membership. *Research on Language and Social Interaction, 26* (2), 227–257.

Beattie, J. (1995). Assessment in higher education. *Higher Education Management, 7,* 281–296.

Berberet, J. (1999). The professoriate and institutional citizenship. *Liberal Education, 85,* 32–39.

Berdahl, R. (1995). Educating the whole person. *New Directions for Teaching and Learning, 62,* 5–11.

Bergquist, W., & Phillips, S. (1977). *A handbook for faculty development* (Vol. 2). Washington, DC: Council for the Advancement of Small Colleges.

Biggs, D., Brodie, J., & Barnhartt, W. (1975). The dynamics of undergraduate academic advising. *Research in Higher Education, 3,* 345–357.

Blix, A., Cruise, R., Mitchell, B., & Blix, G. (1994). Occupational stress among university teachers. *Educational Research, 36,* 157–169.

Bond, L. (1996). Norm- and criterion-referenced testing. *Practical Assessment, Research and Evaluation, 5.* Retrieved August 2002, from ericae.net/pare/getvn.asp

Boyer, E. (1990). *Scholarship reconsidered: Priorities of the professoriate.* Princeton, NJ: The Carnegie Foundation for the Advancement of Teaching.

Burgan, M., Weisbuch, R., & Lowry, S. (1999). A profession in difficult times: The future of faculty. *Liberal Education, 85,* 6–15.

Chopp, R., Frost, S., & Jean, P. (2001). What's old is new again: Alternative strategies for supporting faculty. *Change, 33,* 43–46.

Collie, S., & Chronister, J. (2001). In search of the next generation of faculty leaders. AAC&U *Peer Review, 3,* 22–23.

Creamer, E., & Scott, D. (2000). Assessing individual advisor effectiveness. In V. Gordon & W. Habley (Eds.), *Academic advising: A comprehensive handbook* (pp. 339–348). San Francisco, CA: Jossey-Bass.

Daller, M., Creamer, E., & Creamer, D. (1997). Advising styles observable in practice: Counselor, scheduler and teacher. *NACADA Journal, 17,* 31–38.

Deci, E. (1978). Applications of research on the effects of rewards. In M. Lepper & D. Greene (Eds.), *The hidden costs of reward: New perspectives on the psychology of human motivation* (pp. 193–204). Hillsdale, NJ: Lawrence Erlbaum.

Deci, E., & Porac, J. (1978). Cognitive evaluation theory and the study of human motivation. In M. Lepper & D. Greene (Eds.), *The hidden costs of reward: New perspectives on the psychology of human motivation* (pp. 149–176). Hillsdale, NJ: Lawrence Erlbaum.

Diamond, R. (1993). Changing priorities and the faculty reward system. In R. Diamond & B. Adam (Eds.), *Recognizing faculty work: Reward systems for the year 2000* (pp. 5–12). New Directions for Higher Education, No. 81. San Francisco, CA: Jossey-Bass.

Diamond, R., & Adam, B. (1995). *The disciplines speak: Rewarding the scholarly, professional and creative work of faculty.* Washington, DC: American Association for Higher Education.

Diamond, R., & Adam, B. (2000). *The disciplines speak II: More statements on rewarding the scholarly, professional and creative work of faculty.* Washington, DC: American Association for Higher Education.

Dillon, R., & Fisher, B. (2000). Faculty as part of the advising equation: An inquiry into faculty viewpoints on advising. *NACADA Journal, 20,* 16–23.

Dreisbach, C. (1990). Retention and advising: Paternalism, agency, and contract. Paper presented at the Noel-Levitz Conference on Student Retention, Washington, DC. (ERIC Document Reproduction Service No. ED 331 412)

Ferren, A., Kennan, W., & Lerch, S. (2001). Reconciling corporate and academic cultures. *AAC&U Peer Review, 3,* 9–11.

Finkelstein, M., & Schuster, J. (2001). Assessing the silent revolution. *AAHE Bulletin, 54,* 3–7.

Glotzbach, P. (2001). Conditions of collaboration: A dean's list of do's and don'ts. *Academe, 87.* Retrieved August 2002, from www.aaup.org/publications/Academe/01mj/mj01glot.htm

Griffin, B. (2001). Instructor reputation and student ratings of instruction. *Contemporary Educational Psychology, 26,* 534–552.

Grites, T. (1985). Advising satisfaction questionnaire. Unpublished manuscript, Stockton State College, Pomona, NJ.

Gumport, P. (2001). Divided we govern. *AAC&U Peer Review, 3,* 14–17.

Habley, W. R., & Morales, R. H. (1998). *Current practices in academic advising: Final report on ACT's fifth national survey of academic advising* (Monograph Series No. 6). Manhattan, KS: National Academic Advising Association.

Hartford, B., & Bardovi-Harlig, K. (1992). Closing the conversation: Evidence from the academic advising session. *Discourse Processes, 15,* 93–116.

Haskell, R. (1997a). Academic freedom, tenure and student evaluation of faculty: Galloping polls in the 21st century. *Education Policy Analysis Archives, 5.* Retrieved August 2002, from http://epaa.asu.edu/epaa/v5n6.html

Haskell, R. (1997b). Academic freedom, promotion, reappointment, tenure and the administrative use of student evaluations of faculty: Views from the court. *Education Policy Analysis Archives, 5.* Retrieved August 2002, from http://epaa.asu.edu/epaa/vol5.html

Johnson, C., & Pinkney, J. (1980). Outreach: Counseling science impacts on faculty advising of students. *Journal of College Student Personnel, 21,* 80–84.

Kaun, D. (1984). Faculty advancement in a non-traditional university environment. *Industrial and Labor Relations Review, 37,* 592–606.

Kelly, J. (1995). Faculty speak to advising. *New Directions for Teaching and Learning, 62,* 13–24.

Kerr, T. (2000). Recognition and reward for excellence in advising. In V. Gordon & W. Habley (Eds.), *Academic advising: A comprehensive handbook* (pp. 349–362). San Francisco, CA: Jossey-Bass.

Kramer, H. (1986). Faculty development: The advising coordinator's changing scene. *NACADA Journal, 6,* 31–42.

Kramer, H., & Gardner, R. (1983). Advising by faculty. Washington, DC: National Education Association. (ERIC Document Reproduction Service No. ED 235 742)

Larson, M., & Brown, B. (1983). Rewards for academic advising: An evaluation. *NACADA Journal, 3,* 55–60.

Leslie, P., Harvey, P., & Leslie, G. (1998). Chief academic officers' perceptions of the relationship between faculty research and undergraduate teaching. *Sociological Spectrum, 18,* 185–199.

Licata, C., & Morreale, J. (2001). Implementing post-tenure review. *AAHE Bulletin, 54,* 3–5.

Light, R. (2001). *Making the most of college: Students speak their minds.* Cambridge, MA: Harvard University Press.

Lunneborg, P., & Baker, E. (1986). Advising undergraduates in psychology: Exploring the neglected dimension. *Teaching of Psychology, 13,* 181–185.

Lynch, M. (2000). Assessing the effectiveness of the advising program. In V. Gordon & W. Habley (Eds.), *Academic advising: A comprehensive handbook* (pp. 324–338). San Francisco, CA: Jossey-Bass.

Mahoney, J., Borgard, J., & Hornbuckle, P. (1978). The relationship of faculty experience and advising load to perceptions of academic advising. *Journal of College Student Personnel, 19,* 28–32.

Mahoney, M. (1991). *Human change process.* New York, NY: Basic Books.

McAnulty, B., O'Connor, C., & Sklare, L. (1987). Analysis of student and faculty opinion of academic advising service. *NACADA Journal, 7,* 49–61.

McGillin, V., & Kornfeld, M. (1998). Advisor recognition and reward. Paper presented at the National Academic Advising Association national conference, San Diego, CA.

Mittler, M., & Bers, T. (1994). Qualitative assessment: An institutional reality check. *New Directions for Community Colleges, 22,* 61–67.

Neal, J. (1995). Overview of policy and practice: Differences and similarities in developing higher education accountability. *New Directions for Higher Education, 91,* 5–10.

Nelsen, W. (1981). *Renewal of the teacher scholar: Faculty development in the liberal arts college.* Washington, DC: Association of American Colleges.

Pennsylvania State University, University Advising Council. (2002). *UAC assessment guidelines.* Retrieved August 2002, from http://www.psu.edu/dus/uac/aseval.htm

Peterson, M., & Augustine, C. (2000). Organizational practices enhancing the influence of student assessment information in academic decisions. *Research in Higher Education, 41,* 21–52.

Polson, C. (1981). The impact of advising skills upon the effectiveness of the departmental academic advising center. *NACADA Journal, 1,* 47–55.

Prochaska, J., & DiClemente, C. (1983). Stages and processes of self-change of smoking: Toward an integrative model of change. *Journal of Consulting and Clinical Psychology, 51,* 390–395.

Prochaska, J., DiClemente, C., & Norcross, J. (1992). In search of how people change: Applications to addictive behavior. *American Psychologist, 47,* 1102–1114.

Prochaska, J., & Velicer, W. (1997). The transtheoretical model of health behavior change. *American Journal of Health Promotion, 12,* 38–48.

Prus, J., & Johnson, R. (1994). A critical review of student assessment options. *New Directions for Community Colleges, 22,* 69–83.

Reece, S., Pearce, C., Melillo, K., & Beaudry, M. (2001). The faculty portfolio: Documenting the scholarship of teaching. *Journal of Professional Nursing, 17,* 180–186.

Rhoades, G. (1996). Reorganizing the faculty workforce for flexibility; Part-time professional labor. *Journal of Higher Education, 67,* 627–659.

Rossman, J. (1968). Released time for faculty advising: The impact on freshmen. *Personnel and Guidance Journal, 47,* 358–363.

Ruedrich, S. L., Cavey, C., Katz, K., & Grush, L. (1992). Recognition of teaching excellence through the use of teaching awards: A faculty perspective. *Academic Psychiatry, 16,* 10–13.

Ruedrich, S. L., Reid, W. H., & Chu, C. (1986). Rewarding teaching excellence with cash: A faculty response. *Psychiatric Annals, 16* (6), 370–373.

Scriven, M. (1995). Student ratings offer useful input to teacher evaluations. *Practical Assessment, Research and Evaluation, 4.* Retrieved August 2002, from ericae.net/pare/getvn.asp?v=4&n=7

Seagren, A., Creswell, J., & Wheeler, D. (1993). *The department chair: New roles, responsibilities and challenges* (ASHE-ERIC Higher Education Report No. 1). Washington, DC: The George Washington University, School of Education and Human Development.

Spence, J., & Helmreich, R. (1983). Achievement-related motives and behaviors. In J. Spence (Ed.), *Achievement and achievement Motives: Psychological and sociological approaches* (pp. 7–74). San Francisco, CA: W. H. Freeman and Associates.

Srebnik, D. (1988). Academic advising evaluation: A review of assessment instruments. *NACADA Journal, 8* (1), 52–62.

Strada, M. (2001). Assessing the assessment decade. *Liberal Education, 87*, 42–49.

Sun, A., & Valega, M. (1997). *Assessing reliability of student ratings of advisors: A comparison of univariate and multivariate generalizability approaches.* Paper presented at the annual meeting of the American Educational Research Association, Chicago, IL. (ERIC Document Reproduction Service No. ED 411 262)

Teague, G., & Grites, T. (1980). Faculty contracts and academic advising. *Journal of College Student Personnel, 41*, 40–44.

Tharp, T., Hensley, B., & Meadows, D. (1996). *Current trends in the evaluation of academic counselors.* Retrieved August 2002, from www.nade.net/documents/SCP96/SCP96.20.pdf

Trower, C., Austin, A., & Sorcinelli, M. (2001). Paradise lost: How the academy converts enthusiastic recruits into early-career doubters. *AAHE Bulletin, 53*, 3–6.

Velicer, W., Prochaska, J., Fava, J., Norman, G., & Redding, C. (1998). *Detailed overview of the transtheoretical model.* Retrieved August 2002, from www.uri.edu/research/cprc/TTM/detailed overview. htm

Wergin, J. (2001). Beyond carrots and sticks: What really motivates faculty. *Liberal education, 87*, 50–53.

Winston, R., & Sander, J. (1985). *Academic advising inventory and advising conference record.* Athens, GA: Student Development Associates.

6 ORGANIZATIONAL MODELS AND DELIVERY SYSTEMS FOR FACULTY ADVISING

Margaret C. King

The way advising services are organized and delivered on college campuses varies from institution to institution, yet closer inspection reveals many similarities, particularly in the involvement of faculty. As indicated in Chapter 2, the fifth national survey on academic advising, conducted by the American College Testing Program (ACT), shows that on 48% of the campuses responding to the survey, faculty are the sole providers of academic advising services for students. On many other campuses faculty share advising responsibilities with others.

This chapter will focus on seven organizational models of academic advising identified in research by Habley (1983), Habley and McCauley (1987), and ACT, and will discuss the role of faculty in each. It will also consider other groups on campus that can provide effective advising in partnership with faculty, as well as those factors essential to any successful advising program. It will conclude with a discussion of the importance of viewing and structuring academic advising as a system with shared responsibility.

FACTORS INFLUENCING THE ORGANIZATION AND DELIVERY OF ADVISING SERVICES

Before discussing specific organizational models and delivery systems, it is important to look at those factors that greatly influence the way in which advising services are organized and delivered. These factors include the institutional mission, the student population, the role of faculty, institutional programs and policies, budget, facilities, and organizational structure.

Institutional Mission

The institutional mission includes control (whether the institution is public, private, or proprietary), the level of educational offerings (associate, baccalaureate, or graduate), the nature of the educational offerings (liberal arts versus professional versus vocational or technical), and selectivity (open door versus highly selective). Advising services may need to be organized differently at a public, open-door, community college offering liberal arts or vocational-technical degree programs than they would at a highly selective four-year private university.

Student Population

The student population will definitely influence how advising services are organized and delivered. An institution with students who are predominantly first generation, underprepared, nontraditional, exploratory, socioeconomically diverse, and commuters needs a more centralized and intrusive advising system than an institution where students fall at the other end of the spectrum.

The Role of Faculty

Faculty also have a definite impact on the organization of academic advising. The extent of that impact will depend on their interest in advising, their awareness of existing problems related to advising, and their willingness to address those problems and to accept training. Faculty interest and willingness may be affected by other responsibilities such as research, publication, curriculum development, committee work, and the like. It may also be affected by the priority the administration places on advising, the extent to which academic advising is evaluated, recognized, and rewarded, and the existence of any faculty contracts or collective bargaining agreements.

Institutional Programs and Policies

The complexity of institutional programs, policies, and procedures influence academic advising services. This factor includes such things as the sequencing of courses, the scope of the general education requirement, the complexity of graduation requirements, and the degree to which the advisor must approve a variety of academic transactions. As complexity increases, the need for highly skilled advisors working in a well-defined advising organization increases.

Budget

The institutional budget will affect how advising services are organized and delivered. As will be discussed later in this chapter, there are four other common systems for delivery of advising, but all of them cost additional money. With faculty advisors, advising is typically part of their overall teaching responsibility and therefore does not cost the institution additional funds.

Facilities

Different organizational structures for academic advising require different space and facilities. If campus space is limited, there will be less opportunity to create an advising center, and it will be more likely that faculty advisors will work out of their offices.

Organizational Structure

The organizational structure of the institution will influence the organization and delivery of advising services, particularly in terms of where the responsibility for advising lies. If the vice president or dean of academic affairs has ultimate responsibility, an advising center staffed by student-affairs staff will be less likely to exist and advising will more likely be a faculty responsibility.

ORGANIZATIONAL MODELS

Research by Habley (1983) and Habley and McCauley (1987) first identified seven organizational models of academic advising. That research was expanded in ACT's five national surveys on academic advising (Habley, 1988, 1993; Habley & Morales, 1998). With one exception, all models utilize faculty to provide all of or some advising services on college campuses. Those models can be grouped into three categories: 1) decentralized, where advising services are provided by faculty and staff in their academic departments, and, while overall coordination may be centralized, advisors are accountable to their respective departments; 2) centralized, where all advising takes place in an administrative unit, usually an advising or counseling center, with a director and staff generally housed in one location; and 3) shared, where advising services are shared between a central administrative unit and faculty or staff in academic departments (Pardee, 2000). Data from the ACT surveys has shown a continued movement from highly centralized and decentralized models toward those models where responsibility for advising is shared (Habley & Morales, 1998).

It is important to note that all the decentralized and shared models can use faculty very effectively. And all models can work very effectively in all institutional types. In fact, even the one centralized model, while most commonly found in community colleges and which often does not utilize faculty, can be used in other institutional types and, if designed appropriately, can include faculty advisors. Unfortunately, little research has been done to show the overall effectiveness of one model over another.

Decentralized–Faculty Only

The faculty-only model of advising is the only one where organizational model and delivery system are the same. In this model each student is assigned to a specific faculty member for advising, generally someone in the student's program of study. Undecided students may be assigned to faculty at large, to liberal arts faculty, to faculty who volunteer to advise them, or to faculty with lighter advising loads. This model was used by 28% of the institutions surveyed by ACT, a decrease from ACT's fourth national survey. It is the most popular model of advising found in private four-year institutions and the second most popular in two-year private institutions. Strengths and weaknesses of this model will be discussed in the section on advising delivery systems. This model may or may not have a campus-wide coordinator of advising; however, supervision of advisors is generally decentralized in the academic subunit.

Beloit College (Wisconsin) provides one example of a faculty-only model. First- and second-year students are advised by the faculty member who teaches their first-year seminar. Once they declare a major, students are assigned a faculty academic advisor, usually of their choice, from their academic department. At Beloit, advising is one of the four parts of the tenure decision process, along with teaching, scholarship, and service to the college. A director of academic advising provides overall coordination, which includes advising assignments, advisor training, an advising handbook, and producing materials for students. The director also serves as a resource for faculty and for students dealing with a variety of issues.

Decentralized–Satellite

The satellite model is sometimes referred to as the multiversity model because advising offices are maintained and controlled within the academic subunits (schools, colleges). Undecided students are generally advised in a separate satellite office that has responsibility for overall campus coordination of advising and for providing support to all advisors. Faculty may or may not have responsibility for advising in the academic subunits, and it is not uncommon for advising responsibilities to shift from an advising office to specific faculty. This model of advising was found in 6% of the institutions surveyed by ACT, a slight increase from the fourth national survey, and is more common in public universities. The overall coordination of advising may be an issue in this model, as well as the need to provide careful assistance in helping transition students who declare or change majors, and assisting students with special needs.

Pennsylvania State University has adopted this model. Students with declared majors are advised in their respective school or college, while the Division of Undergraduate Studies advises exploratory students and students on probation. That division also provides campus-wide coordination for academic-advising services. That coordination includes assigning a programs coordinator as a liaison with each college, providing a university-wide advising handbook online, producing a book called the Penn State Advisor designed to help faculty be better advisors, maintaining a web site—the Center for Excellence in Academic Advising—which contains information to help faculty in their advising roles, and providing academic orientation for all new students. While the satellite model is the overall advising model for the university, individual colleges use different models, ranging from a faculty-only model from first year to senior year, to an advising-center model with professional advisors for the first two years and then a faculty model when the students enter the major, to a system with professional advisors who share advising responsibilities with faculty, allowing faculty to serve more as mentors while the professional advisors handle curriculum, schedule planning, and other administrative functions.

Centralized–Self-Contained Model

This is the only model that generally doesn't utilize faculty. In this model all advising from orientation to departure takes place in a centralized unit (advising center or counseling center) administered by a dean or director who has responsibility for all advising functions on the campus. This model was found in 12% of the institutions surveyed by ACT, a decrease from 16% in the fourth national survey. It is a popular model in public two-year colleges, where the counseling center typically has responsibility for all advising. In this model a trained group of advisors have advising as a priority, are generally housed in a central location, and are easily accessible to students. The major weaknesses of this model are that, unless faculty are part of the advising staff and work part-time in the advising or counseling center, advising doesn't take advantage of faculty expertise and doesn't promote faculty-student interaction.

Johnson County Community College (JCCC), a large suburban institution in Kansas, uses this model. Traditionally, all academic advising was provided through the Counseling Center. JCCC recently introduced their Student Success Center, staffed by trained and accessible generalists, to provide a first stop for entering students. The Student Success Center operates in conjunction with the Counseling Center, to which students are referred for more in-depth advising and counseling. Recently recognized as a "Best Practice" by IBM and the Society for College and University Planning (Beede & Burnett, 1999), the JCCC model "moves beyond the traditional concept of 'one-stop shopping,' which views enrollment as the end product. Rather, it focuses on the facilitation of each student's growth and development, encouraging learning and promoting achievement of individual goals" (p. 116).

Tarrant County College Southeast Campus also uses a self-contained model. In their model, however, while faculty do not advise students, they do take an active role as student mentors.

Shared–Supplementary Model

In this model faculty serve as advisors for all students, yet there is an advising office with a part-time coordinator who assists faculty but has no original jurisdiction for approving academic transactions. Such a coordinator could assist faculty by creating and maintaining a faculty handbook, conducting advisor training, updating information systems, and being a referral resource and an information clearinghouse. This model was found in 20% of the institutions surveyed by ACT, a slight increase from the previous survey, and is the most popular model for two-year private institutions. The major strength of this model is that there is an office that provides overall coordination and support for advising. Weaknesses might include the cost involved and the credibility of the advising office with faculty.

Richard Stockton College of New Jersey provides an example of the supplementary model. All faculty are required to advise students, but there is an advising office, which analyzes transcripts, assigns advisors, maintains the advising handbook, performs graduation clearance for general-education requirements, and meets with all students whose grade point average falls below a 2.0 prior to registration.

Wartburg College (Iowa) is another example of this model. At Wartburg, all faculty advise students. Advising is coordinated by the director of the Pathways Center, which provides faculty development in advising, serves as a supplemental advising service for students on probation and others in academic difficulty, and provides career services, personal counseling, testing services, supplemental instruction, a writing/reading/speaking lab, and the first- and second-year experience programs.

Linfield College (Oregon) takes a different approach to this model with its Freshman Colloquium, a one-credit course required of all freshmen in which a group of faculty advisors works with groups of freshmen advisees in their anticipated areas of concentration. Linfield's program is coordinated by a director of academic advising who is a half-time administrator and half-time instructor.

Shared–Split Model

In this model the initial advising of students is split between faculty members in academic subunits and the staff of an advising office. The advising office has original jurisdiction for advising a specific group of students (for example, exploratory or underprepared students or athletes). Once specific conditions have been met, such as declaring a major or completing developmental coursework, students are assigned to advisors in their respective academic subunits. Those subunits may utilize full-time advisors, faculty on a part-time basis, or peer advisors. The advising office has a coordinator or director and may have campus-wide coordination responsibility. The office may also serve as a referral resource for students assigned to advisors in the academic subunits. This model was found in 27% of the institutions surveyed by ACT, an increase from the previous survey. It is the most popular model in two- and four-year public institutions. Strengths of this model include the utilization of both faculty and advisors who have the specialized skills necessary to advise higher-risk students. In this model, however, it is important that there be close coordination between the advising office and the academic units and that careful attention be paid to students transitioning from one to the other.

Schenectady County Community College uses a split model of advising. Staff of the Academic Advisement Center serve as the assigned advisors for all students who are part-time or admitted to the 24 Credit Hour Program, a program for students who have not graduated from high school or earned a GED. Full-time matriculated students are assigned to full-time faculty advisors. When part-time students change status and become full-time, they then are assigned to full-time faculty advisors, as are 24 Credit Hour students once they complete the 24 credits required for their GED.

Shared–Dual Model

In this model, students have two advisors. While faculty members provide advising related to the student's program of study, advisors in an advising office provide advising related to academic policies, registration procedures, general-education requirements, and the like. The advising office also generally advises undecided students and typically has a coordinator with campus-wide coordination responsibilities. This model was utilized by 3% of the institutions surveyed by ACT, a slight decrease from the fourth national survey. This model has the advantages of two delivery systems with the strengths of each. However, with this model it is imperative that the responsibility of each advisor be clearly articulated so that students know whom to see for what.

Fox Valley Technical College in Wisconsin uses a modified dual advising model. Counselors in student services have primary responsibility for working with students in specific assigned programs from the time the student applies through the first semester of enrollment. Students are then assigned a faculty advisor, but the counselor remains as a consultant and a referral source. This model was a NACADA award winner.

Oklahoma City Community College is in the process of moving to a dual model. In the past, the Center for Student Development provided all of the initial advising for students. Now, some students are assigned a faculty advisor in addition to receiving advisement from student-development counselors in the center.

Shared–Total-Intake Model

In this model all initial advising of students is done by a core group of advisors, generally working out of an advising office, until institutionally predetermined conditions have been met. Examples of such conditions could be completion of the initial registration, completing the first semester, or earning a specific number of credits. At that time students may be assigned to faculty in their academic subunits. A director or dean of the advising office may have responsibility for campus-wide coordination of advising. The office may also have responsibility for the development and administration of curriculum and instruction, and the development and enforcement of policies and procedures. This model has the advantage of front-loading the system with trained advisors who want to advise (preferably a combination of faculty, professional advisors, and peers or paraprofessionals) and who are prepared to work with all students (those who are underprepared, exploratory, and so on); yet it also maintains the benefits of a faculty-based advising program, assigning students to faculty advisors when they are more settled in their major and better able to take advantage of faculty expertise. This model was utilized by 5% of the institutions surveyed by ACT, a number that has stayed consistent more than ten years. In this model it is important that attention be paid to transitioning students from one advisor to another.

The University of Central Arkansas utilizes the total-intake model. The Academic Advising Center (ACC) was created as a collaborative effort between the six academic colleges and the Division of Undergraduate Studies. In this model each college assigns a faculty member to advise freshman majors in the ACC, and there are three full-time advisors for exploratory students. In addition, a continuing education faculty member works with evening students. The ACC advises all freshmen, all undeclared students, and all pre-education majors. Students are then assigned to faculty within academic departments. This model was a NACADA award winner.

Ball State University (Indiana) also uses a total-intake model. All entering students are advised through the Freshman Advising Center, where the advising staff includes professional advisors as well as faculty. Ball State also has created advising resource centers strategically located throughout the campus. These have responsibility for the transition of students from the Freshman Advising Center to the discipline-based faculty-advising program for sophomores, juniors, and seniors. The advising center coordinators have responsibility for faculty-advisor training, informational updates, transfer-student intake, dealing with major-changers, and handling requests for changes of advisor.

At Lansing Community College, faculty and professional advisors are utilized in the Advising Center, a center that is part of a much larger, one-stop shop, where students can enroll, be assessed, advised, or registered, make payments or receive financial aid, and obtain a student ID. All students receive their initial advisement there and then move to a program advisor once their goal is cleared.

Organizational Models at the College, Campus, and Department Levels

It is important to note that each of the organizational models described above at the institutional level may exist on a smaller scale at the college, campus, or department level. It is not uncommon to have, for example, the satellite model at the institutional level yet have any of the other models utilized within each college or department. As one example, the College of Letters and Sciences at the University of Wisconsin–Whitewater moved from a faculty-only model of advising to a supplementary model when they incorporated a three-quarters-time position for a coordinator of advising (combined with a one-quarter-time academic staff faculty position). The coordinator developed a program for undeclared students and provided information and training for the faculty advisors. The college also formed a "Master Advisors" group, made up of advising experts from each department in the college who are responsible for sharing information and being an advocate for advising within their departments. This model was a NACADA award recipient.

DELIVERY OF EFFECTIVE ACADEMIC ADVISING

Faculty can very effectively provide academic advising. However, academic advising approached as a developmental process has become a complex activity due, in part, to the increasing diversity of student populations and the complexities of curricula. Because of that, faculty shouldn't be expected to do it alone. Several other groups on campus can provide very effective advising services, which, when combined with faculty advising, can greatly enhance the advising process for students. They include full-time professional advisors, counselors, paraprofessionals, and peers. Each group has strengths and weaknesses, which is why most effective advising programs utilize more than one delivery system. In determining which group or groups to utilize, it is important to consider the importance of each of the following criteria: 1) accessibility and availability of the advisor to students; 2) priority placed on advising by the advisor; 3) the advisor's knowledge of his or her major field of study; 4) the advisor's knowledge of student-development theory; 5) the amount of training required; 6) cost; and 7) credibility with faculty and staff (King, 1993).

As stated earlier in this chapter, faculty have sole responsibility for academic advising in 48% of the institutions surveyed by ACT. When viewed according to the above criteria, strengths of using faculty would include advisors' knowledge of the academic discipline and field (which is very important in helping students understand the content of courses and the relationship of the courses to the world of work), credibility with faculty and staff, and, in institutions where all faculty are required to advise, cost.

Weaknesses might include accessibility to students (although this would not be the case in situations where the faculty member has the student in class), the priority placed on advising, and advisors' knowledge of student-development theory (which is of particular importance when working with exploratory or underprepared students or students with other special needs). If faculty are required to work with these special populations, advisor training becomes extremely important in order for them to be effective.

Full-time, professional advisors bring different strengths to an advising system. Used by 67% of institutions surveyed that had an advising office, they are typically more accessible and available to students since they are generally housed in a central location, advising is their priority, and they have good knowledge of student-development theory, which makes them more effective in working with special populations. Appropriate training gives them broad-based knowledge of all programs of study, so when working with first-year students they are able to advise across all program areas. However, professional advisors don't have the in-depth knowledge of the academic disciplines that faculty have, nor do they have the knowledge of the world of work for each discipline. They are also a much more expensive delivery system and they may not have credibility with faculty. Counselors, used by 7% of the institutions surveyed, would be similar.

Paraprofessionals, used by 13% of the institutions surveyed by ACT, and peers, used by 10% of the institutions surveyed, can be wonderful supplements to an advising system if carefully selected, trained, and supervised. They bring enthusiasm to the job and can provide basic advising services for students, thus freeing the faculty or professional advisor to provide more in-depth advising.

COMPONENTS OF SUCCESSFUL FACULTY ADVISING PROGRAMS

The most effective faculty advising programs have the following components: 1) an advising program mission statement that guides the advising activities, 2) a specific individual designated by the institution to coordinate or direct advising activities, 3) a systematic training program for all advisors, 4) evaluation of both the advising program and individual advisors, and 5) recognition and reward for exemplary advising.

Mission Statement

An advising program mission statement should provide a clear statement of philosophy to guide advising activities, and should be built on goals and objectives that are integrally tied to the institution's mission statement. The statement should identify the purpose and goals of advising (for example, "to assist students in the development and implementation of their educational plans") and should include information on the nature of the advising program, the organizational structure, a statement of beliefs about students, and expectations of advisors and advisees (White, 2000).

Coordination

It is critical that advising programs have a director or coordinator, someone who devotes concentrated time to that activity. Responsibilities of the coordinator could include creation and maintenance of an advising handbook, providing the necessary training for advisors, being a resource for advisors, coordinating the assessment of advising services, providing recognition and reward for effective advising, and addressing issues related to online advising and advising for distance learners.

Based on responses to the ACT survey, the most common titles of the person in the role of overseeing faculty advising programs are director or coordinator, vice president or dean of academic affairs, and assistant vice president or dean of academic affairs. It is far more common to have academic advising reported through academic affairs, although in many community colleges, reporting lines through student affairs are not out of the ordinary.

Advisor Training

Academic advising has evolved from a course scheduling activity to a complex process requiring comprehensive knowledge and skills. Consequently, advisor training is critical to the success of an advising program. Yet, results from ACT's fifth national survey on academic advising indicate that comprehensive training is not in place at many institutions. Of those schools responding to the survey, only 34% of their academic departments provided training, and that was generally a single workshop of one day or less that had information and facts as its focus (Habley & Morales, 1998).

To be effective, a training program should have objectives that are realistic, specific, and measurable. The content and format of the program must be designed specifically for faculty, and coordinators should consider the skills of the faculty advisors, the experience they have in advising, and their willingness to participate in the training program. The format and techniques used for the training should also be designed with the audience in mind. Formats could range from a single workshop of one day or less to the preferred model of a series of workshops held throughout the year. Formats could include a presentation, panel discussions, brainstorming, role playing, case studies, or advisor-training videos.

A faculty-advisor-training program should include conceptual, informational, and relational components. Conceptual components include those basic concepts in advising such as a definition of advising, student expectations of advising, the relationship between advising and student retention, and the rights and responsibilities of both advisors and advisees. Informational components include the basic information advisors need to know such as programs and course offerings, referral resources, and institutional rules and regulations. Relational components include behaviors the advisor needs to demonstrate, such as good listening skills, asking questions that invite the student's involvement in the discussion, and providing a welcoming environment. As Habley (1995) states, "Without understanding (conceptual elements), there is no context for the delivery of services. Without information, there is no substance to advising. And without interpersonal skills (relational), the quality of the advisee/advisor interaction is left to chance" (p. 76).

Assessment and Evaluation

Assessment and evaluation of academic advising is important, not only to improve the advising program but also to determine if the advising program is producing the desired results, to address the demands for accountability, and to justify budget expenditures. Assessment and evaluation efforts should be planned by a committee that includes faculty, because they will likely be affected by the results. The committee should be clear about the mission, goals, and objectives of the advising program. It is particularly important that members agree to the purpose of the evaluation and to how the results are to be used. The committee will need to determine the questions to be answered by the evaluation, to define the focus of the evaluation (individual faculty advisors or the overall advising program), to identify data to be collected, and to determine the sources that can provide the data and the methods to be used for collecting that data. A review of assessment instruments can be found in the 1988 *NACADA Journal.*

ACT's fifth national survey showed that of the institutions responding, 51% indicated that they regularly evaluated the overall effectiveness of their advising program. Of those, 29% indicated that they evaluated advisors in the academic departments while 66% evaluated advising staff in advising offices. Program evaluation is clearly the easier of the two since it is less threatening to individual advisors. If there is agreement to evaluate individual advisors, it is important to determine in advance whether those results will be used in a formative way (for improvement of performance) or in a summative way (for personnel decisions such as promotion and tenure). Overall, evaluation results may enhance advising services, promote increased institutional support, support staffing changes and salaries, and help identify areas for increased advisor training.

Advising program assessment is also important in terms of providing data that can document the impact academic advising services have on student satisfaction, success, and persistence, as well as show what models and methods work best. A key challenge is "providing evidence that advising on your campus does indeed make a difference not only in the lives of your students but also in the success of your college" (Habley & Morales, 1998, p. 66).

Recognition and Reward

For many faculty advisors, particularly those who view advising as teaching, the intrinsic rewards they receive from assisting students and watching them grow and develop are enough reward for their efforts. However, as Habley (2000) states, "the function of advising is too critical to be left solely to those who intrinsically cherish it." Recognition and reward for both individual advisors and for the institution are important because they can help improve the quality of service for students, and they also provide evidence that the institution values advising. Recognition and reward for faculty can be provided through consideration in promotion and tenure, release time, stipends, support for travel to conferences, annual campus awards, and external recognition such as a NACADA Outstanding Advisor Award.

EFFECTIVE ACADEMIC ADVISING: A SHARED RESPONSIBILITY

Because academic advising has evolved from a course scheduling process to a complex system requiring specialized knowledge and skills and because it is almost impossible for one advisor to be all things to all students, most successful advising programs view advising as a shared responsibility and use more than one delivery system. Susan Frost (1991), in her publication *Academic Advising for Student Success: A System of Shared Responsibility,* notes that when advising is viewed this way, there are many positive outcomes for students.

Looking back at the shared organizational models, one can see how they allow institutions to utilize advisors with the appropriate skills for the appropriate student populations. For example, in the total-intake model, an institution could put together a core group of trained advisors to provide all initial advising of students. This group could include faculty who would advise students who are certain of their major, full-time advisors to advise those who are exploratory or who need developmental coursework, and peers or paraprofessionals to assist with scheduling. In that model, those students who remain undecided could retain their full-time advisor, who would have the training and background to help them explore options as well as provide the knowledge of support systems on campus where those students could go for additional assistance. However, once the student is set in a major, he or she would work with a faculty advisor who would be better able to assist with course and program content and with career and transfer information related to the student's major.

Richard Light (2001), in his book *Making the Most of College,* discusses the importance of academic advising, particularly faculty academic advising, noting, "Advisors play a critical role. They can ask a broad array of questions, and make a few suggestions, that can affect students in a profound and continuing way" (p. 84). He goes on to discuss the importance of human relationships in a college education and notes that "one set of such relationships should, ideally, develop between each student and one or several faculty members" (p. 85). Describing his conversations with students, he states, "And then I share with them the single most important bit of advice I can possibly give to new advisees: 'your job is to get to know one faculty member reasonably well this semester, and also have that faculty member get to know you reasonably well'" (p. 86).

As stated earlier in this chapter, there is very little research that documents the effectiveness of any given model over the others. And with the possible exception of the self-contained model, all models can utilize faculty very effectively. However, if this author were to select a model she believed would be most effective, it would be the total-intake model. This model allows an institution to front-load the advising system, providing well-trained advisors who have advising as their priority to advise students initially and to continue to work with students who are exploring majors. This model allows faculty to focus their energies on students who are more settled in a major and who can take advantage of faculty expertise and knowledge of their field. If this faculty advisor assignment is made at the end of students' first or second year, students may have identified a faculty member whom they would like to have as their advisor. Light talks about the importance of providing opportunities for students to work one-on-one with a faculty member in a mentored research project. If faculty can focus their energies on advisees who have a sense of where they want to go with their education and careers, there is more opportunity for this kind of interaction. To be effective, this model would have a director of advising who would coordinate advisor training, maintain an advising handbook, coordinate the evaluation of advising, coordinate online advising, and provide recognition and reward for exemplary advising.

CONCLUSION

Faculty advisors are a critical link in helping students achieve their goals, and when that occurs, the institution is achieving its goals as well. But faculty should not have to do it alone. As Susan Frost

(1991) recommends, institutions should consider advising as an institution-wide system centered around student involvement and positive college outcomes, and should promote concepts of shared responsibility for both students and the institution (pp. 71–72). When that occurs, students are being well served and the contributions of faculty advisors are maximized.

REFERENCES

Beede, M., & Burnett, D. (1999). *Planning for student services: Best practices for the 21st century.* Ann Arbor, MI: Society for College and University Planning.

Frost, S. H. (1991). *Academic advising for student success: A system of shared responsibility* (ASHE-ERIC Higher Education Report No. 3). Washington, DC: ERIC Clearinghouse on Higher Education, George Washington University.

Habley, W. R. (1983). Organizational structures for academic advising: Models and implications. *Journal of College Student Personnel, 26* (6), 535–540.

Habley, W. R. (Ed.). (1988). *The status and future of academic advising.* Iowa City, IA: The American College Testing Program.

Habley, W. R. (1993). *Fulfilling the promise?* Iowa City, IA: The American College Testing Program.

Habley, W. R. (1995). Advisor training in the context of a teaching enhancement center. In R. E. Glennen & F. N. Vowell (Eds.), *Academic advising as a comprehensive campus process* (pp. 75–79) (Monograph Series No. 2). Manhattan, KS: National Academic Advising Association.

Habley, W. R. (2000). *Critical topics in assessing and rewarding faculty advisors.* National Academic Advising Association's Summer Institute on Academic Advising.

Habley, W. R., & McCauley, M. E. (1987). The relationship between institutional characteristics and the organization of advising services. *NACADA Journal, 7* (1), 27–39.

Habley, W. R., & Morales, R. H. (1998). *Current practices in academic advising: Final report on ACT's fifth national survey of academic advising* (Monograph Series No. 6). Manhattan, KS: National Academic Advising Association.

King, M. C. (Ed.). (1993). Academic advising: Organizing and delivering services for student success. *New Directions for Community Colleges, No. 82.* San Francisco, CA: Jossey-Bass.

Light, R. (2001). *Making the most of college: Students speak their minds.* Cambridge, MA: Harvard University Press.

Pardee, C. F. (2000). Organizational models for academic advising. In V. N. Gordon, W. R. Habley, & Associates (Eds.), *Academic advising: A comprehensive handbook* (pp. 192–209). San Francisco, CA: Jossey-Bass.

Srebnik, D. (1988). Academic advising evaluation: A review of assessment instruments. *NACADA Journal, 8* (1), 52–62.

White, E. R. (2000). Developing mission, goals and objectives for the advising program. In V. N. Gordon, W. R. Habley, & Associates (Eds.), *Academic advising: A comprehensive handbook* (pp. 180–191). San Francisco, CA: Jossey-Bass.

7

MANAGING AND LEADING FACULTY ADVISING TO PROMOTE SUCCESS

David H. Goldenberg and Steve B. Permuth

Flipping through an in-flight magazine, your eyes will invariably light on the myriad of advertisements by incentive organizations. They take single words—like "Teamwork" or "Effort"—and use a photo and a quotation to epitomize its meaning. The message of one on "Quality" has particular relevance: "Quality is never an accident. It is always the result of high intention, sincere effort, intelligent direction and skillful execution. It represents the wise choice of many alternatives" (Corporate Impressions, 1998).

Perhaps this is the most appropriate place to begin a chapter about managing and leading change to promote success. Student success ought to be an effort that is not arrived at by accident. Faculty, department chairs, and deans ought to be able to point to the philosophy, planning, roles, relationships, choices, activities, and challenges that brought about student success. And so, an addendum to the in-flight magazine might indicate that quality in higher education brings together many stakeholders, which is accomplished through the power of process.

Success in managing and leading faculty toward a quality institutional program of academic advising requires a strategic planning model that focuses upon student learning, faculty understanding of the roles played, and organizational resources to support both. Such a plan is best laid out in the collaborative model of leadership in higher education. Throughout this chapter, we highlight case studies in leadership. These are studies identified as (NAW)—NACADA Award Winners—and can be retrieved on the Internet at www.nacada.ksu.edu/Awards/archives2.html.

There would be no need for this text if there were unanimity from faculty, deans, vice presidents, and presidents about the role that faculty should play in the advisement process. At some universities and colleges advisement is a formalized process, while at others the roles are less formal. At some universities there is a mismatch between what key administrators expect and reward and how those priorities are communicated to individual faculty members at the departmental level. At some universities and colleges, advisement is seen as an "extra," whereas at other institutions it is considered integral to the student experience.

Management is often thought of as "getting the job done." Do the advisement folders get to the place they ought to be in a timely manner? Are students assigned an advisor? Are there faculty development seminars to assist new and continuing faculty with changes in curriculum and their impact on advising? These are the nuts and bolts that must get done. Leadership, on the other hand, requires one or more members of the organization to envision a different, and better, manner of achieving student success through academic advising. Individuals must be able to articulate a vision, but the vision requires broad-based support to be effective.

THE COLLABORATIVE MODEL

Colleges and universities, which operate under a shared governance model, are unlike most other kinds of organizations. Significant changes, whether to personnel, curriculum, student life, or general administration, come out of a system that utilizes committees composed of both faculty and administration. The shared governance model often moves cautiously and with reflection on the past. Leadership in this system, therefore, comes from many sources and is most effective when using a collaborative model of change.

A 1985 landmark study by Bennis and Nanus examined organizations to determine the characteristics that make some more effective than others. Out of this came the paradigm that a collaborative model of leadership must do three things: develop a vision, develop commitment and trust, and facilitate organizational learning. Each of these elements has particular bearing on building an effective advising model and leading faculty toward institutional quality.

Organizations need to articulate a vision that is believable and can be shared. The vision within an organization must find common ground so that all stakeholders will feel connected to it. This is true at the institutional level, by the president, as well at the advising level, by deans, department chairs, and directors. As Bennis and Nanus note, when President John F. Kennedy established the goal of "putting a man on the moon by 1970," he also put the power and the resources of the presidency behind it.

Commitment and trust come from the experience we have with our leaders. Do we have confidence that they can follow through? Much of commitment and trust comes from the perceived expertise of our leaders. When we search for leaders as department chairs, deans, provosts, and presidents, do we project the importance of advising? And, when those individuals go forth and hire faculty, do they reflect that same importance of advising? In other words, leading faculty means helping all members of the group subscribe to creating certain organizational aims. But it really isn't "leading" faculty if all members of the organization believe this is their natural role, no less important than teaching a class.

Organizational learning is the ethos of the new millennium. Rules and regulations change, new theories of developmental learning emerge, and our understandings of the roles we play in higher education evolve over time. Organizational learning requires that leaders facilitate learning more so than training. What kind of outcomes do we want from advising? Do we want students to take greater responsibility, as posited by Frost (1991)? How do we work with faculty to achieve that end?

Advising in higher education organizations fails when the institution espouses the importance of advising but then does not recognize it in the reward structures. In practice, effectiveness in scholarship often overshadows the additional roles of teaching and service. How often are faculty denied tenure or promotion because they misadvised students? And, even if effectiveness in advising is included among the list of positive attributes desired in a tenured faculty member, it is often an afterthought. Leaders interested in change must consider, in this collaborative model, new perspectives for faculty and the shared governance system so that new and revised roles can be debated and, hopefully, embraced.

One positive case study is the Hartford College for Women. It had a long history of serving traditionally aged women with what could best be described as a traditional curriculum. By the late 1990s the college found that its student body was now almost exclusively comprised of nontraditionally aged women. These women had a different set of advising needs than did the students of a decade earlier.

It was not enough for the administration and faculty to articulate a revised vision to respond to the particular needs of these students. The vision statement was created through the involvement of stakeholders, who were asked the question "What shall we become to best meet the needs of the community?" The school also had to adjust its curriculum and services. The faculty and staff, meeting with stakeholders, explored how the student body had changed. Faculty developed new delivery models that would make it possible for women to meet the many and varied demands in their lives.

This organizational learning process was focused upon understanding how this different student body could best be served. Today new curriculum reflects the needs of adult women, and the career services focus on retooling skills and recognizing the experiences of women at different stages of their lives. Throughout it all, the dean—responsible for advising—asked questions about how these students are advised. This dean provided the leadership initiative that made the end product—a reinvented institution—possible.

Another study in leadership can be found at Wheaton College in Massachusetts, where teams of faculty advisors, student peer advisors, and student-life professionals engage in the Preceptor Program (NAW). These advising teams focus on the needs of entering students through the first-year student seminars. But the impact of initiating such teams goes much farther. Wheaton College reports that the collaborative model creates faculty, staff, and students who are well informed on issues facing the college. Consequently, these advising teams have become a powerful force on campus and are consistently sought out for counsel before any major institutional initiative is undertaken. Here, leadership isn't knowing all the right answers. Rather, it is an empowering of many groups to focus on what is best in advising and then on the greater institution for the purpose of creating a learned community.

A CHANGING DEMOGRAPHY

Thomas Jefferson, in *Notes on Virginia*, and John Adams, at the Second Constitutional Convention of Massachusetts, urged the nation to consider the advanced education of our populace as a way of preserving democracy. By the beginning of the 20th century, American higher education served approximately 240,000 students. These students were principally white, upper-class males. Although there were exceptions, economic and political station in life generally made it possible to study at the universities (Snyder, 1993).

Shortly after the close of World War II, more than 2,400,000—a tenfold increase—were now enrolled in postsecondary education. The shift reflected the rise of the American middle class and the power of public policy, through the GI Bill, to mold public thinking about the importance of higher education and, as Jefferson wrote, "the common good" created by advanced study. Within a 40-year period, an entirely different type of student had enrolled in higher education, but the roles of faculty had not shifted dramatically.

With the creation and expansion of community colleges in every state the student population had grown to eight million by 1969. New demographics of gender, race, and economic background were taking hold as a result, again, of public policy that supported financially needy students. While some authors suggested that higher education would begin a downward slide in enrollments, visionaries such as Howard Bowen predicted that continued education would lead the nation to self-improvement (Bowen, 1980). People would seek advanced education throughout their lives rather than during a single four-year period. As the very core mission of American higher education was changing, minimal effort was made to determine how the roles of faculty might change and how advisement by faculty might be integrated into this process. It was not until the creation of the National Academic Advising Association (NACADA) that faculty had a forum in which to discuss these changes.

At the start of the new millennium more than 15 million students were enrolled in American higher education. The new demography of age, predicted by Bowen, was taking hold. Further, social public policy, as exhibited by the Hope Scholarships, once again molded public opinion, this time about the importance of lifelong learning.

In addition to public policy initiatives, long-term economic prosperity has been a key lever identified with higher education. A study done at the end of 1997 indicated that males with only a high school diploma had a median income of $27,005, whereas college graduates with a bachelor's degree had a median income of $41,579. The same study indicated that women with only a high school diploma had a median income of $16,225, whereas women with a bachelor's degree had a median income of $28,328.

And so, while 100 years ago the fabric of American higher education was rather homogeneous, the student body of today creates a coat of many colors. Every classroom in America reflects diversity of gender, race, age, and economic position.

Faculty work in a system of higher education that reflects social, economic, and cultural changes. In 1910 just 24% of the bachelor's degrees in the United States were granted to women. With the passage of legislation giving women the right to vote, that figure jumped to 34% by 1920. By the end of the 20th century, the majority of bachelor's degrees, 53%, were being awarded to women, who make up 51% of the total population of this nation. This change has been consistent and gradual over the 100-year period.

Changes in gender balance in higher education have led to new programs and services. There is scarcely a college or university that has not responded with gender studies curricula. Virtually all colleges and universities have women's centers, specialized women's health services, and referral services. But have ways in which faculty advisors know and understand the nature of issues facing women been examined? Do faculty advisors truly understand what it is like to be, for instance, a single mother who is attempting to hold down a job, attend college, and care for a family? How does that perspective affect managing and leading faculty?

In 1931, 29% of the faculty in institutions of higher education were women. By 1960, the figure had actually dropped to 22%. At the end of the 20th century the number had risen to 42%.

William Gray, III, president and CEO of the United Negro College Fund (UNCF), writes about changes over the past century with respect to African-American attendance in colleges and universities. In 1900 only 1,700 African-Americans attended college. At the close of World War II, that number had risen to 40,000. Statistics for 1970 indicate that there were more than 522,000 African-American students in college, and that number had risen to more than 1.5 million by the end of the century (1997).

The dramatic rise in numbers of African-American students has not been matched by corresponding numbers of African-American faculty. Although the faculty of today, principally educated in the 1960s, 1970s and 1980s, were in the middle of incredible change taking place in the demography of college and university attendance, they themselves were generally not trained by diverse faculty. Their ideas, experiences, and perspectives have been based in white Western culture. In 1975 according to the Digest of Educational Statistics (U.S. Department of Education, 1995), the number of African-Americans who already had a bachelor's degree was only 6.1% of the African-American population.

Statistics on the educational attainment of persons of Hispanic origin provide a clear pattern. Data collected in 1993 showed that 53.1% of the Hispanic population had earned a high school diploma. This was up from 36.5% in 1974. Over the same period of time, the percentage who had completed college degrees increased from 5.5% to 9.0%.

The extraordinary changes in gender, race, education, economic background, and age in higher education have been matched over the past 100 years with an extraordinary rise in the types of institutions that serve American higher education. After World War II, there were just 242 public two-year colleges in the United States. By 1974, that number had increased to 760. During the same period of time, the number of private two-year colleges remained the same. In the last quarter of the 20th century, the number of public two-year colleges—including branch campuses that serve as feeders to large public universities—had increased to 1,000 campuses. In some cases, the rise in the 1970s can be tracked to such systems as Penn State University, with its elaborate 25-campus system that serves the general populace of Pennsylvania. In other cases, such as Florida, systems were created whereby campuses were designated as "senior," serving principally upper-division learning, while the public community colleges educated students during the first two years.

During all these changes, the role of academic advising and the ways in which faculty met that responsibility remained fairly consistent until the last decade, when faculty and staff had the opportunity to move in new directions. Harvard professor Richard Light provided some interesting insights on the role of advising as he looked back on his career and on discussions with students.

MORE THAN THE CLASSROOM

In his book *Making The Most of College: Students Speak Their Minds,* Light (2001) notes nine findings that helped him understand the student of the new millennium. Specifically, Light comments that he had wrongly assumed that learning inside the classroom was most important to students. Instead, he writes, learning outside the classroom, particularly in the residential environment and in extracurricular activities, was vital. In fact, 80% of students, in picking the most important moment of their college experience, selected an experience outside of the classroom. Similarly, he found that students desired group learning outside of class. He found himself making out-of-class assignments so complex that students naturally formed groups to divide up the tasks. It was in these groups that students learned teamwork.

Mentoring internships were also of value to students, and those who engaged in some out-of-class assignment with a faculty member were the most successful. Similarly, students wanted the academic advising function to grow and take place outside of the classroom.

Light's research builds upon the already existing studies by Crookston (1972) and Frost (1991, 1993). Crookston identified three aspects of effective advising that should be understood by faculty and used as the foundation of the advising experience with students: 1) demonstrating awareness of the relationship between education and life, 2) demonstrating the ability to set realistic goals for academic and career aspirations, and 3) demonstrating awareness of life beyond college.

In addition to the research from Light, premises about the hierarchy of student needs defined by O'Banion (1972) and refined in the 1980s are an expansion of Crookston's work. It still holds true. That is, students may initially define their "advising" needs as the selection of sections of courses for the next semester. Faculty have tended to support this model, which makes filling out a schedule the primary advising event. But if the institutional vision defines advising as effectiveness in selecting classes, then it falls short of truly helping students. In O'Banion's hierarchical pyramid, the activity of choosing sections is at the bottom. Above it is the choice of courses to be taken. Why should a student take a particular set of classes beyond their being a "requirement to graduate"?

Above that on the pyramid is the exploration of the academic major. Why did the student select this particular major over others? With so many majors to choose from, what was intriguing about this one that matched up with the student's competencies and interests? Above the major is the exploration of college goals. What does the student wish to gain from the overall college experience? Closely associated with that is the exploration of career goals and their interrelationship to college goals and selection of a major.

Finally, the hierarchy of student needs indicates that advisement, at its best, enables the faculty member and the student to explore life goals together. What is important to this student in terms of the world we live in and the contribution that the student might make over a lifetime?

With each advising session there is the need to do the mundane of section selection, but O'Banion challenged faculty to utilize those moments to have the student explore these deeper choices. Frost (1991) built upon O'Banion's work to suggest that this relationship represents an alliance between the faculty member and the student. And paramount to that relationship is the willingness of the student to take responsibility for his or her own future. In taking responsibility for themselves, the students' need to ask questions and probe into their own personal development increases. And the need for the advising alliance also grows. Frost suggests that new advisement technologies open the door to continual faculty member and student interaction. In fact, through the use of email, instant messaging, advisement chat rooms, and the like, seeking the counsel of an advisor is often no longer a face-to-face matter and has developed into a 24-hours-a-day, seven-days-a-week opportunity.

An example of leadership through the implementation of new technologies is the work done at the University of Wisconsin–Eau Claire (NAW). At UWEC, faculty advisors received special training in the use of email in advising. New students were told to expect advising messages from faculty every two weeks. Faculty reported knowing advisees far better, and new students felt immediately connected to the university. Students said that the email strategy resulted in timely information in a format with which they were comfortable.

Gordon and Habley (2000) show that developmental advising is a process. The role of the advisor as mentor is enhanced when the faculty member uses sessions to ask open-ended questions. These questions require the student to take ownership of the process but allow the faculty member to help the student as a guide. This point is reiterated in Light's (2001) work, where he writes about meetings with students following generic discussions of goals at college. He leads students to think about the relationships of courses to goals. He writes, "We discuss what courses the student will take in this first year, and how those may lead to future courses. My special effort is to encourage students to reflect on what courses, taken in that critical first year, will most help them to make wise, informed choices in the following three years. I warn students against simply choosing random classes that sound interesting, with no real idea of how taking certain classes may help them make decisions about future courses and even about their major or area of concentration" (pp. 85–86).

The development models of O'Banion, Light, Frost, and Gordon and Habley engage the faculty member to mentor the student. Therefore, faculty and administrative leadership of the college or university must focus upon the development of faculty. Astin (1997) noted that the number of hours of teaching and advising were inconsequential in student satisfaction compared to the quality of the time spent. To focus upon quality suggests that faculty development seminars must stress not only the accuracy of information faculty have to share but their communicative skills, which show students that advising is integral to the institutional experience and part of an overall mentoring relationship.

ORGANIZING ADVISING FUNCTIONS

Fieldler's (1967) work on situational analysis suggests that differences between organizations and variables in the situations they face make it impossible to establish a single "best" answer to solve problems through an organizational structure. Since there are 3,400 different institutions of higher education in the United States, there are probably as many different ways of organizing the advising function. Nevertheless, there are three major ways in which the advising function is managed.

Departmentally Based System

The departmentally based, decentralized system places the responsibility for advising in the hands of faculty. Although supported by data from the registrar's office, faculty depend upon their own resources to guide and direct students.

The strength of this system is that the faculty advisors' academic expertise matches the field of study of the student. In that regard, the faculty member is well versed in the content of departmental coursework and can address specific questions. He or she is familiar with the transition students make after graduation toward either employment or graduate study. Further, the faculty member is familiar with graduates of the department and their successes. The faculty member is also knowledgeable of resources within the department for everything from tutoring to academic honor societies.

One weakness of this system is that students do not experience the institution from a departmental basis alone. A study done as part of a faculty development program at a Midwestern university demonstrated that only 16% of faculty were aware that the career development office had moved or what building it had moved to! Further, the same study indicated that most faculty were not aware of the content of general education courses. The accuracy of information provided was marginal.

Another major weakness of the departmentally based system is the handling of students classified as "undecided." Such students are the most prone to attrition in higher education. If a faculty member is well versed solely in departmental matters, the exploration of these students' major, career, and life goals becomes increasing difficult. A deficiency in these skills can be overcome with a strong faculty development program, but this area of advising in general has been the source of dissatisfaction among students advised under the departmentally based model.

Centrally Supported System

A more common model is the departmentally based system supported by a strong central university advising office. The department and its faculty take charge of the students who are in the major. When students have career questions, they are generally about the success of alumni and the paths taken to reach those positions. This model includes an office of advising that is either independent or, often, integrated with other university responsibilities such as orientation, registration, and retention.

The University of Central Arkansas (NAW) had experienced inconsistent results with a purely departmentally based advising system. The provost created the Academic Advising Center with a director and support staff to assist the six academic colleges. The leadership decided to have the central office handle all first-year and all undecided students. After the first year, students would migrate to their chosen college for advisement. The director was able to demonstrate to academic departments the value of centralized support in aiding students in clarifying their educational and career goals. Consequently, students entering specific majors were better informed of the expectations, and the retention rate improved.

With so many advisees seeking assistance in a centralized office, new technologies became important. Online support has been created to handle frequently asked questions (FAQs) for students, faculty, alumni, parents, and others in the community. The centralized advising office monitors these cyberspace questions and provides a physical place for students and others to go for a variety of academic exploration activities. Often, the office of advising is the place students should go when they are uncertain or having second thoughts about their current major. It might be a place where students can go to get answers to questions about the general education requirements of the college or university. At some institutions it is a place where, through computer modeling, students can not only do a degree audit for the major they are currently enrolled in at the university, but can also explore the effects of changing majors on the choice of classes taken to date.

The strength of this model is that it takes the best of faculty advisors and matches it with university resources to assist all students and faculty. Most important, with the right leadership, the centralized function can promote organizational learning about the importance of academic advising and enhancement of skills to achieve improvements.

Another strength to this system is that it can handle the many needs of undecided students. The office can make certain that students are directed toward the major appropriate for them. In some cases, they can serve as a reality check for students. For example, a student with a 2.3 overall grade point average wishing to change into premedical studies would most likely have a conversation with personnel in the centralized office who might redirect the student's interests to a field of study in which success would be more likely.

A weakness of this model can be how the central advising office is perceived by faculty. If the office establishes a record of facilitating faculty needs, the area will enjoy a positive review. However, if the office creates paper shuffling or barriers that are not positively viewed by faculty, success will be less likely. In addition, if the office does not have the resources to achieve its goals and to see results, then the function will be ineffective. Often, a major weakness of the system is the lack of regular feedback to faculty to inform them of the value of the service provided. Success is more likely if the office of advising is created out of a collaborative process with faculty, has goals that are reached jointly with the faculty leadership, and has feedback systems to monitor its mission against outcomes.

Another example of leadership in this area is Bradley University (NAW) with its Division of Educational Development. This broader view of advising to embrace orientation, advising, counseling, diagnostic assessment, and retention was an emerging model in 1978. Today, the division continues to offer strong leadership through collaboration between the administrative roles played by the central office and the advising done by faculty.

University-Managed System

The university-managed system seeks to centralize the advising function within an office with faculty and professional advisors.

As a centralized system, students generally seek advising information at a prescribed location on campus. This model enables the university to monitor quality control over the movement and progression of students in the institution. Oftentimes a division of undergraduate studies will manage and lead this effort.

This model can be highly effective when it is used with students in the first two years of higher education. At the end of sophomore year, students are "transferred" to the appropriate academic department of their major for the final two years of work.

In this model, professional advisors aid departments by ensuring that students have taken the right prerequisite classes, mastered work, and prepared for the advanced stages of academic inquiry found in upper-level studies. Faculty members who serve or volunteer in these offices ensure quality control by making the advising professionals aware of changes in curriculum as they happen and of the kinds of hurdles students will experience in particular classes.

One of the key examples of a successful advising program in this model is Penn State's Division of Undergraduate Studies (NAW). Its director, indicating a need to effectively reach 84,000 students across the commonwealth, created a sophisticated advising and testing program. The spring before enrollment, students take tests, from which a data analysis is completed to assist students with course selection and advisement during the summer orientation programs.

A common weakness of the model deals with the commitment of faculty to these centralized functions. In addition, because faculty may have sabbatical leaves or sponsored research that takes them away from the centralized advising system, there may be informational gaps.

Each of these three organizing systems requires collaboration between faculty and staff. Each system has strengths and weaknesses. But as Astin (1997) suggests, whatever approach is used must employ some mechanism that explores and measures quality. And looking at modern research, few names have more international notoriety in quality control than that of W. Edwards Deming.

QUALITY CONTROL

Many believe W. Edwards Deming to be the father of "Total Quality Management." His ideas were first adopted by the Japanese after World War II, and in the latter part of the 20th century, they became part of the American management process. Modifications and refinements of his theories have developed over the years, but his work *Out of the Crisis* (2000), originally published in 1985, still stands as a seminal work on organizations and people.

While Deming's (2000) "14 Points" focused on the manufacturing sector, they may provide great insight and application to American higher education:

1) Create constancy of purpose for improvement of service.
2) Adopt the new philosophy. We are in a new economic age.
3) Cease dependence on inspection to achieve quality.
4) End the practice of awarding business on the basis of price tag alone.
5) Improve constantly and forever every process.
6) Institute training on the job.
7) Adopt and institute leadership.
8) Drive out fear so that everyone can work effectively for the company.
9) Break down barriers between departments.
10) Eliminate slogans, exhortations, and targets for the work that ask for zero defects or new levels of productivity. They create adversarial relationships.
11) Eliminate quotas. Eliminate numerical goals. Substitute leadership.
12) Remove barriers that rob workers of pride in workmanship.
13) Institute a vigorous program of education and self-improvement
14) Put everybody in the company to work to accomplish transformation.

How do these points fit into the work of faculty? Are they applicable to academic advising and the work of higher education? Deming looked at a process that manufactured products you could hold in your hand. How then does a faculty advisor deal with something as intangible as student needs?

Constancy of Purpose

Faculty are often handed as their only advising tool a catalog or given a web address where the catalog can be found. How often do presidents, provosts, deans, and department chairs establish a set of principles that more clearly define the purpose of advising and the role that faculty play both in and out of the classroom? Instead of a constancy of purpose, there are often poorly defined tasks, such as helping students select classes for the following semester, aiding them in the adding and dropping of classes, and being a mentor. In the Deming model, leadership would take faculty beyond that task-oriented perspective.

Just as a course syllabus begins with a statement of the purpose of the course and what the student can expect, so too the advising process should have a clear statement of purpose and plan. Faculty ought to work out with every student a "syllabus" for advising each semester that outlines what the student will do over those months to sharpen his or her focus on the future.

Students are not used to such relationships. Their experiences in high school focused on selection of classes, so why should they expect anything different from the college advising relationship? Faculty advisors must initiate the process and change the nature of the relationship, by setting down the academic, personal, and career-related goals for the semester. In doing so, advising becomes the primary relationship between the student and the institution.

The New Philosophy

Quality-driven advising begins with a new philosophy. Organizational ethos cannot come from just one faculty member. It is something that draws upon the resources and experiences of the faculty and administration of the college at large. It is something that all levels of the institution must buy into. With a new, institution-wide philosophy, a faculty member can feel confident in referring a student to an office for assistance. Faculty understand what offices such as career development will provide students. Faculty are able to seek assistance from colleagues to assist a student. This new philosophy is one of teamwork and collaboration. It is understanding the institution rather than simply the courses one is teaching.

Eliminating Dependence on Inspection

Degree audits were created to give students and faculty clear information about progression toward a degree. It, however, has become a substitute for the development of a human relationship, and it has become a way of catching errors at the end of the process. Deming would say that the degree audit is a good tool if it is used every semester and forms the basis of continual improvement. That is, the degree audit needs to be a tool that continually posits the question for students: Am I getting the most out of my academic and personal experiences here at the college? The University of South Florida has initiated OASIS, an online degree audit that the student and advisor can access at any time, day or night. The leadership decision to make this information available is critical to enhancing advising effectiveness.

Quality Over Price

How many faculty have simply handed a student a signed advisement slip? With the new online registration processes, how many faculty give departmental secretaries the codes to give out to students? Poor advising is about the easiest way of moving the student out of your office. It requires the least amount of time, the least amount of effort, and the least amount of psychic satisfaction. Quality advising is about the time that is needed at all times of the year to discuss student progress toward the goals set forth at the beginning of the semester. The Deming model places the importance on the interaction of the student and the advisor, while being aided by the new technologies.

Improve Constantly

Imagine a class in modern history drawn up in 1989 and not changed since. There would be no interest in or record of the Berlin Wall coming down, nor the news of the disintegration of the Soviet Union, just for two examples. Such a class wouldn't make sense. Every faculty member works to make the content of each course timely and challenging. We enhance and update syllabi. We integrate new technologies into classroom teaching. Why wouldn't the same hold true for advising?

Constantly improving advising means developing faculty so that they will be aware of changes in the career center, curriculum, and general education. Constantly improving means periodically modifying the statement of purpose to reflect new thinking and new processes.

At Monroe Community College (NAW), the creation of an ongoing faculty workshop series has resulted in improvement in advising. Faculty identify emerging needs, whether they be in advisement skills, tools, information updates, or developmental theory. The Deming model suggests that, when effectively integrated, these are not one-time seminars but continuous quality improvement.

Training on the Job

Often, there are advising seminars for new faculty, but these tend to highlight general education and the rules necessary for students to graduate, and deal with philosophy and purpose only at a tertiary level. To complement such training, individual departments need to devote time in department meetings to discuss advising matters and ways to improve the experience of students. Department meetings might include inviting guests from within the institution to speak about issues related to advising. Further, to better understand the courses taken by students, department meetings might evolve into joint meetings between two departments to discuss matters of common interest.

At Clark College's Business Division (NAW), the chair initiated this role of ongoing "training" for the purpose of helping entering students as well as informing support departments of issues facing the business division. With a very limited budget, but a desire to improve the performance of students, Clark College created an environment of information, feedback, and success.

Adopt and Institute Leadership

Leadership is too often described as a charismatic leader and therefore limited to a few. Deming's philosophy would suggest that leadership comes from the ability to focus on teamwork. Within the advising relationship, leaders can use teamwork to branch out and do explorations in small groups. For example, five or six advisees can gather together with a faculty member to discuss an internship opportunity or talk about a course. What was gained from that course? What content was most intriguing? Similarly, students may have had work experiences or observations that can be shared. The students of the group begin to take responsibility for the outcome.

In the Deming model, all faculty have the capacity to lead and mentor. This is best exemplified by the University of Pittsburgh (UP) School of Engineering (NAW), which instituted leadership teams that included students and faculty. Evaluations indicate that students complete their studies feeling very confident about their future and the experience gained at UP.

Drive Out Fear to Promote Effectiveness

Students need to feel that the advising relationship is one of trust. Students ought to be able to speak with faculty or peers about their experiences. An academic peer-advisor program was initiated at Oral Roberts University (NAW) to meet this student need. New students meet with a peer advisor three times during the first semester to smooth out the rough edges of transition. When a trusting relationship has been created, referrals to the faculty advisor and campus services are more effective.

Break Down Barriers Between Departments

Most of what faculty do with students—advising, teaching, and scholarship—is done on their own. Some faculty who choose to team teach will often share that team-teaching requires an enormous amount of time and energy. Why do they do it? Because of the satisfaction that comes from working with colleagues, engaging in discussions, and considering new points of view. The same can be said of advising. Many students will double major or major in one field and minor in another. Such students are often shuffled off to multiple locations for advisement.

Deming would suggest that we ought to knock down the barriers in advisement in the same way we do with team teaching. If there is a concentration of students majoring and minoring in a particular area, the two departments should discuss issues that face them, and group advising.

Eliminate Slogans

Deming's theory would suggest that slogans do not improve student performance or satisfaction. The Deming approach would be to focus on the quality outcomes of an advising program. Faculty advisors, therefore, should focus on advising well rather than on putting a "spin" on what they are doing. Rather than confuse students and parents, effective leadership of the advising function comes from being able to articulate advising outcomes in a manner that engenders support and recognition.

Too often, according to Deming, the focus is on a catchy phrase for this year's model, or in the case of higher education, for this year's program.

Substitute Leadership for Quotas

Improved advisement has been shown to improve overall institutional retention rates. But this measure, retention, should not become the sole focus of attention. The quantitative measure of retention is merely an outcome of an improved connection between the student, the environment, and the faculty mentor. Institutional leadership focuses on enhanced student learning, which as a result, enhances satisfaction with the aims of the institution.

The same can be stated for advisement. When there is a focus on success as a quota, then advisement suffers. For example, institutions will often discuss the student-to-advisor ratio as if the number in and of itself is important. Or a director might claim that his or her center saw 2,500 students during the recently held registration period. The leadership function in advising calls on the director to identify how students were helped, student satisfaction with the processes, and the outcomes. As an example, the University of Nebraska at Lincoln (NAW) focused on academic success through the creation of residential learning communities. Working with the housing office, academic advisors in the Division of General Studies were able to establish a residential learning community. Spaces were reserved in courses to keep the learning community together throughout the experiment, and students shared in special events and experiences. Students' satisfaction with their education was very high and, as one might expect, so was the retention rate. In fact, this group exhibited a retention rate that was 6% higher than the rest of the student population.

Northwestern State University of Louisiana (NAW) implemented its EXCEL program, directed at first-year students who require multiple developmental courses in order to fulfill academic requirements. Enhanced tutoring, advising, learning labs, and the like resulted in a higher success rate for these students, who had been identified as being most likely to be dismissed.

Create Pride in Advising

Far too often the advisement process is haphazard and taken casually. Advising's profile needs to be raised so that students will take their full measure of responsibility for success, and faculty will take pride in their responsibility. Recognition for faculty doing extraordinary work in academic advising ought to be on the same level as recognition for teaching and scholarship.

Syracuse University (NAW) initiated an all-university program to strengthen academic advising. In this three-year effort, the school worked with students of all academic levels, with the faculty, and with staff in administrative offices. The school rewarded excellence in advising and made advising a portion of the tenure and promotion review process. In doing so, Syracuse University made advising a point of pride for all those involved in the advising program.

Institute a Vigorous Learning Program

Organizational learning is paramount to success in the advisement program. After all, academic rules change over time as new requirements are created and others modified. Organizational learning can focus upon the personal desires for growth and development of faculty as well as the organizational desires for outcomes that produce quality advising. All areas of the institution should initiate opportunities for learning and development.

Among those institutions that follow this Deming approach to continuous learning is the University of Texas at Arlington (NAW). The office of advising initiated five major programs to strengthen advising at the campus. Each of these, from enhancement of the personal counseling skills of faculty to database accuracy improvement, were built upon the premise that a learning organization is constantly improving its processes. And at the University of Texas at Arlington, a key component of constant improvement is continuous assessment.

Everybody Works Toward Positive Transformation

Institutional progress takes place when academic advising is embraced by every segment of the college or university as a positive, integral part of the student experience. Again, Syracuse University's (NAW) all-university program to strengthen academic advising offers a comprehensive approach. Leadership came from the very top of the organization, but it was felt throughout the university through skillful execution by the advising office.

In conclusion, a Total Quality Management approach to advising in higher education is possible. And it is particularly possible with respect to enhancing academic advising. A positive transformation in the organization can lead to effective faculty advising.

EFFECTIVE FACULTY ADVISING

As mentioned earlier, effective advising is more than just signing students' registration cards. It requires a personal relationship and an effort to help students reach their college, career, and life goals. Following are some ways to increase the effectiveness of faculty advising.

Continuous Learning

The learning organization, under Deming's philosophy, constantly strives to improve its current position by knowing more and applying that knowledge. At the center of this knowledge is an understanding of the mission of the institution. Why was this institution founded and whom does it serve? The mission statement tells faculty about the larger goals, which should be reflected in the courses taught, faculty recruited, and students admitted. When an institution regularly applies new knowledge, a culture of misadvisement cannot endure.

Part of an institution's mission is found in its general education requirements, or core curriculum. These represent the purpose of the institution and are far more than mere requirements to be taken in order to move on with a major. The general education or core curriculum is the heart and soul of an institution and should be clearly understood by advisors. To accomplish this goal, a director of advising must forge effective partnerships with academic units of the institution.

When faculty understand the role courses play in the mission of the institution, they are able to discuss the content and importance of courses with the student. But, the discussion ought to be much broader than what is written in the catalog. To move to the next level, the level of mentorship, faculty members must know about the work of colleagues across the institution.

This kind of knowledge is not impossible to obtain. Every semester, in a shared governance process, faculty aid the university in determining who will gain tenure and be promoted in rank. Faculty also submit syllabi for review. For most regional accrediting agencies, the syllabi of courses must be submitted to the office of the dean at the start of each semester. This isn't "public" information, but it could be made such to benefit advising.

With web sites for classes on the Internet and on intranets within institutions, access to deeper information about the goals and objectives of a course is at the fingertips of every student and faculty member. Exploring these with advisees can be part of the process of probing into a student's learning goals for a new semester.

Advising Sections

As institutions have come to recognize that advising is much more than simply meeting with the student once a semester to sign a registration slip, creative ways of interacting with students have emerged. This is particularly so since the introduction of Gardner's Freshman-Year Experience program (www.brevard.edu/fyc/) and the University 101 continuing orientation program (www.sc.edu/univ101/). These courses introduce and acclimate students to the rules, guidelines, and processes of universities and help students begin the process of career exploration. They are also responsible for changing the nature of faculty roles. Whereas 20 years ago faculty members would teach their own academic disciplines, these continuing orientation courses enable faculty members to interact with students on subjects generally distant from their research and scholarship. In doing so, students see their faculty, or "mentors"—as Richard Light describes them—in new ways.

At some institutions faculty have "advising sections." That is, rather than identify a University 101 type of class, faculty who teach first-year students agree that a particular section of their normal course load will include their advisees. In some cases, such as at the University of Hartford's Hillyer College, the number of minutes per week that the class meets is increased. Faculty, therefore, will see students two or three times per week. These sections enable faculty to interact with advisees on a continual basis. Working with professional staff in student affairs and other areas of the university, extended class time can be used to disseminate critical information and to probe into the questions that students face, particularly during the first year.

Learning Outside of Class

Light (2001) had first-year students fill out a time log that would track their use of time over several days. A time log, used in an advising section or with individual advisees, can be a source of conversation about how students spend their time.

The role of the mentor, according to Light, is to encourage students to engage in activities outside of class. Good mentoring, he says, assists students in becoming involved in one or more campus organizations. When this philosophy is adopted, it becomes a matter of policy that faculty should encourage students to find an activity to involve themselves in.

Of particular interest are the ways in which faculty encourage and mentor students to grow and develop through out-of-class experiences. For instance, artwork by Pablo Picasso was being exhibited in one city during a recent fall semester. Working with the faculty in the required English composition course, advisors assigned students to attend the exhibit. Students were asked to examine and describe their inner thoughts about Picasso's work. It was their first time in a museum for some students. Advisors also asked students what other kinds of experiences they would like to participate in as part of the semester. Art exhibits, music recitals, plays, and guest speakers at the university can all help students understand the world and become introduced to different cultures and diverse ideas. Light considered this a crucial element in helping students develop.

Tools and Resources

When it comes to resources, the watchword of the new millennium is the Internet. From the web comes access to information that was locked away just a decade ago. Increased access to information makes the process of self-advisement by students much easier.

This open access to information is the very reason why the human relationship between faculty member and student is so important to develop. These resources do not eliminate the need for faculty-student interaction; rather, they enable the face-to-face meetings to be more meaningful and to be based on a joint responsibility for collection and analysis of information.

Faculty should aid students in understanding how these online tools can be best utilized. First, however, offices like those of the registrar and of information technology can engage faculty in regular development seminars to teach them how to use information databases. These seminars should provide two-way communication, training faculty to use the tools but also providing feedback for administrative offices on the kinds of tools that would improve advising. With this training, faculty can in turn train advisees to use the databases.

A variety of institutions provide online guides to help students better understand their options. Among those are Azusa Pacific's online guide, "Academic Guides and Services." Using the guide, students who have not chosen an academic major can easily navigate their way through the institution's academic programs and the resources available. Institutions such as the University of South Florida have an elaborate FAQ used by students, faculty, parents, and prospective students.

Most colleges and universities now also have online tools to aid the student with information about career planning, internships, cooperative education, and placement. These resources often include information about companies seeking interns or employees and supply links to the corporate web site for students to explore more deeply.

Many institutions have incorporated a software program called "Blackboard" to synthesize information. This online resource is a secure intranet location where a faculty member can disseminate general information to a group of advisees, engage in chat-room like discussions about particular issues, and use its reminder feature as a way of communicating with students about critical approaching deadlines. Some faculty even have online "office hours" at various times during the day when they use instant messaging to advise students.

REWARDING ADVISING

Earlier in this chapter we posited the question, How many faculty have been denied tenure due to misadvisement of students? It is a serious question about what higher educational institutions value and the tendency to identify some variables and overlook others.

Although there are exceptions, tenure is a commitment by an institution to a lifetime contract with a faculty member. There is no decision more critical for the faculty member or the institution. Where should advising fall in this tenure review? At some institutions academic advising continues to be thought of as "a part of teaching." The traditional categories of teaching, scholarship, and service are set forth. And so, as there are subsets under service for campus service versus community service, so too there is a subset under teaching for advising load.

Tenure reviews should be based on four, not three, standards: contributions to teaching, scholarship, advising, and service. The effectiveness of a faculty member in the classroom is separate and distinct from successful advising. In fact, Light's initial observation was that the majority of student learning takes place outside the classroom and requires a mentor who will probe, question, and help the student develop through inquiry and exploration.

Promotion in rank ought to require advising as a contribution to the institution. Promotion, particularly to the rank of full professor, should be a statement about leadership in an institution more so than about years of service. Has the faculty member provided leadership through advising and mentoring students in and out of the classroom?

Institutions such as Penn State University have formalized a post-tenure review process in which faculty are asked to comment on their experiences in advising students. This review makes clear the totality of the faculty member's contributions to the institution.

Performance measures that might be used in tenure, promotion, and post-tenure reviews include any or all of the following:

- Results of formal advising evaluation instruments. Such instruments usually explore the faculty member's competency in providing students with accurate, useful information.
- Narrative review of advising by the faculty member.
- Letters from colleagues and current and former students.
- Examination of student performance (for example, the percentage of advisees who continue on to a bachelor's degree after completing an associate's degree).

It is most appropriate for presidents, vice presidents, and deans to recognize the importance of advising through compensation review, special college or institutional awards and recognition, and inclusion of advising in a formal manner within the governance system of tenure and promotion review. Advising is not an "add-on"; it is an integral part of the total student experience and of the total faculty contribution to the university. It should be reflected as such in a university's reward and review systems.

To accomplish this, a director of advising must be an advocate for faculty who share the aim of improved learning through advising. The director must be able to collaborate with academic deans since they, not the director of advising, are critical to the tenure and promotion review process. And, the director must have the support and shared vision of the upper administration of the institution.

CONCLUSION

After years of observation, Light (2001) suggests that "good advising may be the single most underestimated characteristic of a successful college experience" (p. 81). For advising to reach its potential, a model of developmental advising needs to emerge. Faculty are well trained in their particular disciplines, but, in general, come to the advising aspect of their job with no more than good intentions and the desire to provide a sincere effort.

As suggested by the Quality poster mentioned earlier, good intentions and the desire to provide a sincere effort are a wonderful start. Administrators and faculty themselves must fashion quality by emphasizing development. Administrators and faculty leadership must also provide for the ongoing education of faculty about the institution, its value, its services, and resources so that advisors can communicate them to students. Only then will a quality advising program emerge.

Light provided great insight by showing that quality developmental advising is built upon the premise of shared responsibilities. The faculty member sets the tone for the faculty-student relationship. Guided by a faculty member, students, in turn, should explore their academic, career, and personal goals.

Advising and mentoring are more a process of inquiry than a process of selecting classes. Resources, ongoing training, and reward structures within the institution should reflect this shift. By doing so, faculty will recognize that the advising function matters. Quality academic advising does not happen by accident.

REFERENCES

Astin, A. W. (1997). *What matters in college? Four critical years revisited.* San Francisco, CA: Jossey-Bass.

Bennis, W. G., & Nanus, B. (1985). *Leaders: The strategies for taking charge.* New York, NY: Harper and Row.

Bowen, H. R. (1980). *Costs of higher education: How much do colleges and universities spend per student and how much should they spend?* San Francisco, CA: Jossey-Bass.

Corporate Impressions. (1998). New York, NY: Successories, Inc.

Crookston, B. B. (1972). A developmental view of academic advising as teaching. *Journal of College Student Personnel, 13,* 12–17.

Deming, W. E. (2000). *Out of the Crisis.* Cambridge, MA: MIT Press.

Fiedler, F. E. (1967). *A theory of leadership effectiveness.* New York, NY: McGraw-Hill.

Frost, S. H. (1991). *Academic advising for student success: A system of shared responsibility* (ASHE-ERIC Higher Education Report No. 3). Washington, DC: ERIC Clearinghouse on Higher Education, George Washington University.

Frost, S. H. (1993). Developmental advising: Practices and attitudes of faculty advisors. *NACADA Journal, 13* (2), 15–20.

Gordon, V. N., & Habley, W. R., & Associates. (2000). *Academic advising: A comprehensive handbook.* San Francisco, CA: Jossey-Bass.

Gray, W. H., III. (1997). *The case for all-black colleges.* The Washington Post Writers Group.

Light, R. J. (2001). *Making the most of college: Students speak their minds.* Cambridge, MA: Harvard University Press.

O'Banion, T. (1972). An academic advising model. *Junior College Journal, 42* (6), 62–69.

Snyder, T. D. (Ed.). (1993). *120 years of American education: A statistical portrait.* Washington, DC: United States Department of Education, Office of Educational Research and Improvement, Center for Educational Statistics.

U.S. Department of Education, National Center for Educational Statistics. (1995). *Digest of educational statistics.* Retrieved August 2002, from www.nces.ed.gov

8 RESOURCES TO IMPROVE FACULTY ADVISING ON CAMPUS

Betsy McCalla-Wriggins

Richard J. Light's (2001) book *Making the Most of College* emphasizes the significance of academic advising in a student's college experience. He stresses the importance of students' involvement in their academic experience and the role that faculty can play in encouraging students to become involved. Light sees the relationship developed through academic advising as a key factor in this important process: "Good advising may be the single most underestimated characteristic of a successful college experience" (p. 81).

Therefore, academic advising should be of utmost importance to the institution because of its potential to significantly contribute to students' success. In many cases, though, training of advisors is cursory at best. As with parenting, it is often incorrectly assumed that those charged with the responsibility to develop or enhance academic advising programs on campus already know what to do. Hence the frequent questions: Where do I begin? What resources are available to assist in this process?

This chapter will describe some of the significant national resources that focus on academic advising, career-life planning, and leadership, all of which are critical elements in creating a vision for a comprehensive, integrated, campus-wide academic advising system. It is important to note that while the focus of this chapter is on resources for academic leaders, the organizations and associations described also provide many excellent resources for those "doing the work," faculty and full-time advisors.

NATIONAL GUIDELINES FOR ACADEMIC ADVISING

National standards provide a framework and foundation through which to assess an existing system or establish a new one. Two specific standards are those developed by the Council for the Advancement of Standards in Higher Education (CAS) and the National Academic Advising Association (NACADA).

CAS Standards

The CAS was established to accomplish three goals: 1) to establish, adapt, and disseminate standards and guidelines for student services, student development programs, and preparation of professionals in the field; 2) to assist professionals and institutions in using standards for self-study and accreditation; and 3) to establish a regular system of evaluation of standards (Yerian, 1988). NACADA and CAS have worked cooperatively to develop standards for academic advising, and NACADA has a representative on the CAS council. CAS standards include 13 components, each with multiple assessment criteria.

Mission. Departmental advising programs can reflect the unique culture of that discipline but must support the overall institutional mission of academic advising.

Program. Faculty members are often accustomed to working independently, whether in the classroom environment or while engaged in research. However, when developing a departmental advising program, there need to be some common goals that each faculty member will strive for when working with students. All interactions and discussions with students need to be purposeful and focused on helping students to make informed major- and career-related decisions.

Leadership. This component speaks more to institutional support than departmental leadership. The president and academic vice president or provost must be very supportive of advising initiatives if such initiatives are to be successful. Having active, explicit, and financial support from these individuals sends a powerful message to all members of the educational community. Without this type of support, faculty advising interactions will be varied and dependent upon the individual within a department who takes on this function.

Organization and management. There are many ways that faculty-advising initiatives can be organized. Different colleges within the same university can choose different options and still deliver effective advising services. However, across all units there needs to be consistently administered policies and procedures. In addition, the specific responsibilities of advisors need to be clearly defined and widely published to both students and faculty advisors.

Human resources. This area is often of great concern to both faculty and students. As with any student service, there must be individuals with the time to do what is expected. While there is no "one size fits all" answer to this issue, those charged with developing and enhancing faculty-advising initiatives need to address this critically important area.

Funding and facilities. These two components of the standards are very connected to the human resources issue. If money is not provided for people, resources, materials, and space for students and faculty to engage in academic advising, advising will not take place. One important question for academic leaders to ask is "How much money in the department, college, or institution budget is specifically allocated to academic advising?" The answer will provide a great deal of information about how advising is viewed on campus.

Legal responsibilities; equal opportunity, access, and affirmative action; and ethics. As with all members of a higher education community, faculty advisors have legal and ethical responsibilities that they must fulfill. Often these are not covered in programs designed to educate new faculty because it is assumed that people know what is appropriate. However, these issues need to be included in faculty-advising training.

Campus and community relations and multicultural programs and services. Advising does not occur in a vacuum, and faculty advisors need to be aware of all the resources on campus available to assist students. Visits to other offices, attendance at and presentations by student services representatives are just two ways that the academic leader can facilitate connections across campus.

Evaluation. This last component is critical and frequently overlooked. Faculty advisors are often so busy "doing the work" that systematic evaluation never happens. However, the academic leader responsible for advising initiatives must insist that regular, systematic research and evaluation be a component of each department's advising program.

The CAS self-assessment guide is a comprehensive resource for leaders as they seek to establish or enhance the advising systems across campus or within a particular department or college (Yerian, 1988). This excellent tool provides a structured, step-by-step process to assess the status of the various components of advising. The rating scale for each criterion ranges from 1 (noncompliance) to 5 (compliance) to UK (unknown). As with any issue, individual perceptions vary, so this tool can be effective not only in assessing, but also in gathering data about perceptions of advising on campus. More information can be found at http://www.cas.edu.

NACADA Core Values

NACADA is an organization made up of more than 7,000 faculty, professional advisors, administrators, and others who have some responsibility for providing quality academic advising at colleges and universities. While institutions and individuals differ, NACADA has established a set of core values as a foundation for working with students. These values are based on the following beliefs about students: students are responsible for their own behavior; students can be successful as a result of their individual goals and efforts; students have a desire to learn; student learning needs vary according to individual skills, goals, and experiences; and students hold their own beliefs and opinions.

Regardless of the position an individual holds and whether advising is one of many responsibilities or the only responsibility, these core values remain consistent. According to NACADA, those who advise students are responsible to the students and individuals they serve; for involving others, when appropriate, in the advising process; to the college or community in which they work; to higher education generally; to the community (including the local community, state, and region in which the institution is located); and to their roles as advisors and to themselves personally (National Academic Advising Association, 2002b).

ACADEMIC ADVISING RESOURCES

To aid in implementation of the standards listed above, national organizations provide a wealth of information and contacts to those responsible for an advising system. This section will describe several of those and highlight specific resources for those leading faculty advising initiatives.

NACADA

NACADA grew out of the first National Conference on Academic Advising in 1977, and its membership has increased significantly over the past 25 years. Its mission is to champion the educational role of those providing academic advising to enhance student learning and development in a diverse world; *affirm* the role of academic advising in student success and persistence, thereby supporting institutional mission vitality; *anticipate* the academic advising needs of 21st-century students, advisors, and institutions; *advance* the body of knowledge on academic advising; and *foster* the talents and contributions of all members and promote the involvement of diverse populations (National Academic Advising Association, 2000).

To support the association mission, a wide variety of resources and activities have been and continue to be developed. These include publications, videos, conferences and institutes, networks, and awards and scholarships. Each of these is described in further detail, with highlights regarding their use by those responsible for the campus advising system. More information on any of the programs and services listed below can be found at http://www.nacada.ksu.edu.

Publications. NACADA publications include journals, monographs, and special resources. All may be ordered from NACADA's web site at http://www.nacada.ksu.edu.

NACADA Journal. The *NACADA Journal* is a semiannual refereed journal in which members publish results from both qualitative and quantitative studies related to academic advising. Two articles that focus on the role of faculty in advising are "Advising as Teaching" (Ryan, 1992) and "Developmental Advising: Practices and Attitudes of Faculty Advisors" (Frost, 1993).

Monographs. NACADA has published several monographs that provide an in-depth look at specific issues in academic advising.

Reaffirming the Role of Faculty in Academic Advising (Kramer, 1995) explores issues of training, accountability, evaluation, and recognition and reward as they relate to faculty. These are the most significant methods through which advising can be improved but are often the components not included in campus advising programs.

This monograph could be especially meaningful to those seeking to document, improve, and evaluate faculty advising.

Academic Advising as a Comprehensive Campus Process (Glennen & Vowell, 1995) is organized around three general areas: administrative support services, academic advising services, and student support services. This monograph describes how individuals throughout the institution influence and support the advising process, and it offers practical approaches that can be implemented in numerous institutional settings.

A number of studies have indicated how important the first four weeks on campus are for students' success. *First-Year Academic Advising: Patterns in the Present, Pathways to the Future* (Upcraft & Kramer, 1995) addresses the specific concerns of first-year students. *Transforming Academic Advising Through the Use of Technology* (Kramer & Childs, 1996) addresses how to apply technology to the advising process in a practical and effective way—based on institutional resources, leadership, and system thinking. Technology has been embraced by institutions of higher education to varying degrees. However, students entering college now have come to expect many processes, procedures, and information to be available 24/7 through the use of technology. *The "e" Factor in Delivering Advising and Student Services* (Kramer & Childs, 2000) builds on the previous monograph and explores the role of web technology in the advising interaction. Because of the number of technological options available, the high cost of these systems, and most institutions' limited resources, careful and deliberate decision making in this area is essential. These two publications would be of particular value to advising administrators considering ways to enhance advising through technology.

Advising Students with Disabilities (Ramos & Vallandingham, 1997) explores the challenges related to advising the growing numbers of students with disabilities now enrolling in institutions of higher education. Awareness of disability issues and rights is essential to academic advising. While this monograph could be of value to anyone advising students with disabilities, it would be an excellent resource for those charged with creating faculty-development programs.

Current Practices in Academic Advising, published in 1998, is the final report of the ACT fifth national survey of academic advising

(Habley & Morales). It summarizes current practices in advising from a random sample of more than 725 institutions across the nation. It is particularly useful for leaders wanting to get a sense of the current state of advising.

Special resources. One special resource is *Academic Advising: A Comprehensive Handbook* (Gordon, Habley, & Associates, 2000), published by NACADA and Jossey-Bass. It is the most extensive single publication that addresses the essential elements of the advising process—whether performed by faculty advisors or professional advisors. A must-have resource, this book can help institutions construct and administer quality academic advising programs, even those institutions whose budget limitations preclude the purchase of other resources. The 28 chapters are divided into five sections: foundations of academic advising; student diversity and academic advising; organization and delivery of advising services; training, evaluation, and recognition; and dealing with change in the future of academic advising.

Designing an Effective Advisor Training Program (Vowell, Wachtel, Grites, & Rozzelle, 1993) is available as a monograph or CD-ROM, and includes an overview of the issues of advisor development and the necessity of continuous in-service activities and rigorous evaluation of advising. In addition, there are samples of training models, topics, and agendas that are especially helpful to those charged with enhancing or creating a training program.

Videos. *The NACADA Faculty Advising Training Video* (National Academic Advising Association, 1995) is excellent resource for those charged with advisor development. It addresses the practical issues of advising students through a series of eight vignettes. Six of these show the developing relationship between a first-year student who is uncertain of her major and a new faculty advisor. The other two vignettes deal with situations unique to adult students. After each vignette, experts comment on the most effective methods for handling each situation. A comprehensive facilitator's manual accompanies the video and includes experiences, questions, and overhead transparency templates that can be used in a variety of ways.

Academic Advising: Campus Collaboratives to Foster Retention is a videotaped teleconference produced in 1999 by NACADA in collaboration with PBS Adult Learning Services. Panelists addressed the relationship between advising and retention and key findings of the National Advising Survey results; various models for delivery of advising; the best methods for training advisors; and dealing with cultural differences in the academic-advisement process. Many campuses used this teleconference as an opportunity to bring together different components of the community to begin the conversation on the importance of academic advising.

Conferences and institutes. NACADA sponsors many opportunities for advisors to meet face-to-face to discuss important issues. A complete listing of the specific events scheduled for the current year is available on the NACADA web site. This section outlines some of the highlights of these events.

National conferences. Each October, NACADA hosts the National Conference on Academic Advising. This conference allows advisors to meet, share, discuss, learn, debate, and recharge. As with many national conferences, keynote speakers present new challenges and research data. Thirty preconferences explore in-depth topics, such as producing a comprehensive faculty advising handbook, research on advising, the economic value of advising, enhancing advisor training, leadership styles, and designing and implementing a successful advising program (National Academic Advising Association, 2001). In addition, more than 260 concurrent roundtable sessions are presented by faculty and professional advisors and advising administrators on a wide variety of advising-related topics. Participants can gather a variety of options from which to design, develop, create, and enhance advising at their own institutions.

The NACADA/ACT Summer Institute on Academic Advising, an intensive five-day event, is another national effort designed to enhance the skills and knowledge of advisors. Each day participants attend a general session that addresses a broad concept in advising, engage in small-group discussions with others from similar institutions, and choose from a variety of workshops. In addition, each person develops an action plan to address some advising issue at his or her institution. Participants can receive feedback, suggestions, and implementation strategies, then present their plans in small groups for additional feedback and refinement (National Academic Advising Association & American College Testing, 2002).

Another national program of interest is the Advising Administrators' Institute. Led by individuals with multiple years of experience designing, creating, and managing advising programs, these forums provide excellent content information for those new to this responsibility or for those who want to enhance their skills. Participants examine case studies, discuss possible solutions, and relate those findings to their own institutions (National Academic Advising Association, 2001).

Regional conferences. Other opportunities to learn from experts in the field are provided through ten NACADA regional conferences, held in the spring. While the format and presentations are similar to the national conference, the conferences are usually two to two-and-a-half days in length.

NACADA regional meetings offer distinct advantages to those attending. A smaller number of participants is less overwhelming and provides opportunities for advisors to make presentations to their colleagues. Costs for transportation, registration, and lodging are usually lower than for the national conference, and the shorter length of the conference may be easier to coordinate with faculty schedules.

State conferences. In an effort to make more services available to NACADA members "where they are," individual states are offering "drive-in" workshops on academic-advising topics. Besides being more accessible, these sessions may also be focused on a more narrowly defined topic. As an example, "Merging One Mission: Faculty, Staff, and Students Working Together" and "Exploring Diversity in Advisement" were the themes of two recent state conferences. While the number of sessions is limited by the short duration of such conferences, these programs still provide faculty and professional advisors with the opportunity to share and learn.

By allowing advisors to attend these national, regional, and state activities, academic leaders demonstrate a strong commitment to advising and acknowledge the importance of enhancing those skills. They also provide a forum for institutions to share outstanding programs and receive recognition for jobs well done. Knowing that one's work will be reviewed by peers also emphasizes continual program assessment and evaluation.

Leaders can significantly strengthen the impact of these experiences by attending with their advising teams. Designating specific goals prior to the conference and requiring that participants present what they learned to their colleagues upon their return reinforce the knowledge gained and help coordinators focus on the information most useful for their particular situations. Leaders reinforce the value of advisement training by supporting such conferences even when financial resources may be limited. Generally, limited departmental resources are most often used for professional development activities within a faculty member's specific academic discipline. By providing consistent financial support for advising as well as discipline-related activities, however, academic leaders explicitly demonstrate their commitment to this important activity.

Networks. Networks provide participants with the opportunity to share and receive information around specific areas of interests. While the conference and drive-in workshops described earlier provide networking opportunities as well, the resources described here are not location specific.

Commissions and interest groups. These subgroups within NACADA are designed to address specific interests of the members. Some address issues related to specific student groups, such as adult learners, business majors, student athletes, undecided and exploratory students, and transfer students. Others focus on institution type, such as two-year institutions, small colleges and universities, and private comprehensive institutions. Commissions of more specific interest to advising leaders relate to advising administration, technology in advising, advisor development, and faculty advisors (National Academic Advising Association, 2002d).

In addition to meeting at the national conferences, members of these groups communicate through newsletters and electronic mailing lists (EMLs). For academic leaders who need immediate feedback on a specific topic, the EMLs of those commissions can be especially valuable. One question can generate multiple responses within a very short time frame. An EML that is particularly valuable to academic advising is the ACADV. An acronym of academic advising, this is NACADA's electronic network email system. Members of this network represent all areas of academic advising.

Member career services. This NACADA resource will be especially helpful to the academic leader who is seeking new staff. Postings of job openings here can generate a number of applicants, at the national conference, résumés of job seekers and interviewing space are available for active recruiting.

Consultants bureau. NACADA's Consultants Bureau services may be of particular interest to academic leaders who want an outside perspective on the state of advising at their institution. Recognized leaders in the field are available to provide assistance and feedback in the following areas: advising skills and techniques, advising special populations, career and academic advising, technology in advising, delivery system models, evaluation of advising, faculty development, orientation and retention, advisor training, and the legal implications of advising. Customized programs beyond the scope of these can also be developed. They can range from a one-day faculty development program to an ongoing, institution-wide advising-assessment system (National Academic Advising Association, 2002a).

National clearinghouse. The National Clearinghouse for Academic Advising disseminates pertinent resources and research that promote the advancement of academic advising. Originally developed and administered by University College at Ohio State University, the clearinghouse later was moved to the NACADA executive office and is currently being expanded. Through the clearinghouse, academic leaders can link to published materials as well as to web sites, handbooks, and advising tools developed by members.

Awards. Recognizing and rewarding top performance is an excellent way to encourage the continuation of outstanding work. The NACADA National Advising Awards Program provides academic leaders with an excellent opportunity to recognize individuals and programs.

Individual and program awards. Each year 15 to 20 individuals are recognized at the national conference in honor of their contributions to their students through academic advising. They receive free registration to that conference, a recognition plaque, and a one-year membership in NACADA.

In order to support and acknowledge the concept that advising is done by people in different roles, awards are given in three different categories: academic advising—primary role, faculty academic advising, and academic advising—administration. Any individual serving as a faculty advisor, full-time academic advisor, or advising administrator and employed by a regionally accredited postsecondary institution may be nominated. NACADA membership is not required.

Individuals distinguished in this way have provided evidence of excellence in advising or administration of advisement programs. They may have demonstrated strong interpersonal skills toward advisees, faculty, and staff or given exceptional service to students in terms of appointment availability, monitoring of student progress toward academic and career goals, or connecting the student to appropriate resources. They may be recognized for positive evaluations or student success rates. They may also be honored for implementation of intrusive advising. They may have demonstrated exceptional ability to engage in, promote, and support developmental advising or advisor-development programs. Or, they may have shown mastery of institutional regulations, policies, and procedures or administered a program that supports NACADA's core values or CAS standards (National Academic Advising Association, 2002c).

In addition to recognizing individuals, NACADA also sponsors an Outstanding Advising Program Award. A program that achieves this level of recognition addresses current problems and issues in academic advising and demonstrates systemic commitment to advising. It initiates new and creative approaches and documents student success (National Academic Advising Association, 2002e).

These national awards have been the catalyst for many universities and colleges to develop institution-specific award programs. Recognition can take many forms: a plaque; an article in the institution's newspaper; recognition at a significant public event such as convocation or graduation; support to attend state, regional, or national advising conferences; or release time to conduct research related to advising and the faculty member's specific discipline.

While recognizing individuals is important, academic leaders need to be inclusive and deliberate in developing recognition systems and programs. Given the contexts of academic freedom and tenure and promotion, the process of selecting one faculty member over another presents its own challenges in higher education. However, Syracuse University and the University of Wisconsin–

Whitewater have both successfully integrated advising into their promotion and tenure structures. Southwest Missouri State University has developed an "Excellence in Advising" award. More information on these award-winning programs is available through the NACADA Clearinghouse.

Scholarships and research grants. Research is a critical component of any profession, as is the support of scholarships for those entering the profession. Advising administrators can support these two efforts through the NACADA Research Awards and Scholarships program.

Individuals at the master's or doctoral levels who have recently completed important research that adds significantly to the body of knowledge on academic advising can be nominated for the NACADA Research Award. The award includes recognition at the national conference, a plaque, and a check for $500.

The scholarships, one for $1,000 and four for $500, are awarded to individuals who are pursuing graduate education at the master's or doctoral level. Recipients must be and have been NACADA members for two years, be currently enrolled in a graduate program, and have worked as an academic advisor for two years with a minimum of a half-time appointment (National Academic Advising Association, 2002c).

Other National Education Organizations

Although NACADA's mission and focus on academic advising make it the preeminent organization in the field, there are other organizations and institutions that offer resources or supplementary aids to those developing or coordinating academic advising initiatives.

American Association for Higher Education. The American Association for Higher Education (AAHE) promotes higher education's effectiveness in a complex, interconnected world. Founded in 1969, AAHE provides many resources for educators—from chancellors of state systems and presidents of institutions to department chairs and faculty.

Association resources are available in many forms: books, monographs, and papers; *Change* and the *AAHE Bulletin,* award-winning periodicals; and conferences. The National Forum on Faculty Roles and Rewards is an excellent conference that addresses the multiple roles of faculty, including the role of academic advising. A complete listing of the materials available through AAHE is available at http://www.aahe.org.

American College Personnel Association. The mission of the American College Personnel Association (ACPA) is to "support and foster college student learning through the generation and dissemination of knowledge, which informs policies, practices, and programs, for student affairs professionals and the higher education community " (American College Personnel Association, 2002).

While the stated purpose of this organization is directed to student-affairs professionals, administrators responsible for academic advising will find many ACPA resources to be of great value. In fact, academic advising is often seen as the central function that connects both the traditional academic and student service components of an institution.

For the academic leader who wants to support advising from "both sides of the aisle," a resource of particular value is the series titled *Higher Education Trends for the Next Century: A Research Agenda for Student Success* (Johnson & Cheatham, 1999). This collection of nine papers identifies issues that both academic and student affairs leaders need to address, including diversity, affordability, technology, the changing nature of work, and accountability.

In "Learning and Teaching in the 21st Century: Trends and Implication for Practice," Marcia Magolda and Patrick Terenzini (1999) state that "structurally and functionally, the present (academic affairs and student affairs) boundaries must be blurred to reflect the joint and synergistic efforts of students' in- and out-of-class experiences on learning" (¶ 1). They contend that both faculty advisors and student affairs professionals have important roles to play to help students make meaning of the whole of their college experiences.

An example of this collaboration is in place at Rowan University in Glassboro, New Jersey. The staff in the Career and Academic Planning Center and selected faculty of the College of Business have jointly developed a model to integrate academic and career decision-making activities into selected classes. Students receive the discipline-specific knowledge, academic and career information, and job-search-strategy skills needed to become successful upon graduation. This integrated approach actively engages students in exploring the connection between their academic field and meaningful employment.

In writing about collaboration among multiple departments in an institution of higher education, Schroeder (1999) discusses the strategies academic advisors and advising administrators should "use to identify undergraduate education opportunities that lend themselves to such cross-functional, collaborative responses" (Questions and Challenges section, ¶ 1). He suggests ways they might "enhance student success by forging alliances with colleagues in faculty development programs, academic advising, the learning center and academic enrichment programs—functional units that 'straddle' academic affairs and student affairs" (Questions and Challenges section, ¶ 1). Schroeder maintains that structures such as writing courses can help students explore "important student life issues such as diversity, binge-drinking, civility, and gender issues" (Questions and Challenges section, ¶ 1). He further states that partnerships among student affairs educators, "faculty, and academic administrators to create residential colleges that link courses and cocurricular experiences around general education themes [are effective methods for helping students] connect academic work and out-of-class experiences" (Questions and Challenges section, ¶ 1), enhancing student success.

Schroeder goes on to describe programs at various institutions that have been created as a result of collaborative efforts. Strategies for establishing these partnerships include a "'triggering' opportunity," "fundamental shifts of perspectives," developing "shared visions," alignment of resources, the "development of cross-functional teams committed to common purposes and educational outcomes," leaders who champion innovation and commit to initiatives, institution-wide thinking and acting, and taking "risks and cross[ing] the traditional boundaries separating their organizational functions to address common objectives" (Schroeder, 1999, Strategies for Establishing Collaborative Partnerships section, ¶ 1).

The person leading these advising initiatives may not have control over all the factors listed above. However, every individual has control over the lens through which he or she views life. The leader might gather a group of committed colleagues, faculty, student-affairs professionals, managers, and support staff together for a day off campus. This will encourage each person to dream and create collaborative projects that support and enhance student learning. Exciting, yet low-cost initiatives often come out of such an experience and can be the catalyst for a much larger, more encompassing program.

As with other professional associations, ACPA (http://www.acpa.nche.edu) provides many additional resources from state and national meetings to commissions and EMLs.

National Resource Center for the First-Year Experience and Students in Transition. The National Resource Center for the First-Year Experience and Students in Transition (FYE) has as its purpose the collection and dissemination of information about the first college year and other significant student transitions. This information is used to assist educators at the University of South Carolina and at institutions around the nation and world to enhance the learning, success, satisfaction, retention, and graduation of college students.

In addition to hosting national conferences, the center publishes a scholarly journal, a newsletter, and a monograph series. These resources could be especially helpful to the academic leader working with faculty who advise students in transition: those moving from high school to college, from community college to a four-year institution, and from a college or university into the world of work or graduate school. More information can be found at www.sc.edu/fye.

National Association of Student Personnel Administration. While the National Association of Student Personnel Administration (NASPA) is an association directed mainly toward student affairs administrators, many of the issues they address are also of interest to academic-affairs leaders. Specific topics in which they provide resources include diversity in higher education, health education and leadership, international exchange, minority undergraduate fellows, and principles of good practice in student affairs.

Like the other associations described in this chapter, NASPA holds national and regional conferences, publishes numerous publications, and identifies exemplary programs throughout the nation. More information can be found at http://www.naspa.org.

NASPA, in conjunction with the AAHE and ACPA, developed the publication *Powerful Partnerships: A Shared Responsibility for Learning.* It presents an excellent framework for how all components of the college community can work collaboratively to deepen student learning (American Association for Higher Education, American College Personnel Association, & National Association of Student Personnel Administration, 1999). Examples from specific institutions across the country describe ten principles about learning plus techniques to implement and strengthen learning. Student learning takes place all over campus, especially within the advising interaction. Students, faculty, and staff all share the responsibility for improving this dynamic learning environment.

Noel-Levitz. Noel-Levitz is a for-profit organization dedicated to supporting faculty, staff, and administrators as they seek to help students achieve success. This organization offers a multitude of services, two of which are specifically related to academic advising. A complete listing of all Noel-Levitz resources can be obtained at http://www.noellevitz.com.

Academic Advising for Student Success and Retention (Noel-Levitz, 2002) is a comprehensive advisor development program designed to increase student success and retention. Through this video-based program, faculty and professional advisors examine the principles and practices of student success. Studies show and experts agree that students persist at higher rates when strong advising is there to guide them. The program is commonly used in a variety of ways with groups of both new and experienced advisors. The components of the program include a four-volume video set, a step-by-step leader's guide, and an intensive, 258-page participant book/resource guide for use both during and after the training.

The annual National Conference on Student Retention sponsored by Noel-Levitz is another excellent resource. More than 100 sessions cover a wide range of programs, including academic advising, that institutions use to support and increase student retention and success.

CAREER- AND LIFE-PLANNING RESOURCES

Terry O'Banion (1972) maintains that developmental advising involves five stages: 1) exploration of life goals, 2) exploration of vocational goals, 3) choosing academic programs, 4) choosing academic courses, and 5) course scheduling. In addition, Astin, Parrott, Korn, and Sax (1997) report in the annual survey of college freshmen that, for a large majority, the major reason they go to college is to "get a better job" (p. 13). However, when asked to articulate what that means, students are often at a loss.

Given the expectations of students and the importance of exploring life and vocational options in developmental advising, the academic leader needs to be aware of resources in that area as well. This section will describe two national associations, a few selected publications, and three electronic resources that address these issues.

National Associations

Although the National Career Development Association and the National Association of Colleges and Employers do not target academic advising specifically, they do offer training and resources that complement or enhance it.

National Career Development Association. The National Career Development Association (NCDA), a division of the American Counseling Association, has as its mission "to promote the career development of all people over the life span" (National Career Development Association, 2001). To achieve this mission, NCDA provides the public and professionals involved with or interested in career development with services that include professional-development activities, publications, research, public information, professional standards, advocacy, and recognition for achievement and service.

NCDA hosts an annual national conference, and most states also have organizations and meetings. *The Career Development Quarterly* is the journal of the association. Selected publications for NCDA include *A Counselor's Guide to Career Assessment Instruments* (Kapes & Whitfield, 2001) and *The Internet: A Tool for Career Planning* (Harris-Bowlsbey, Dikel, & Sampson, 1998). Additional information is available at http://www.ncda.org.

National Association of Colleges and Employers. The National Association of Colleges and Employers (NACE) is a non-profit association established in 1956 to build bridges between the graduates of America's institutes of higher education and employers in the world of work. The organization provides information on national and regional employment and salaries as well as on what employers expect in a new hire. A four-magazine series,

Planning Job Choices, is a guide to career planning, the job search, and work-related education for the college graduate. Since academic planning requires career information, advisors need to be aware of current employment projections and trends. Advisors who are aware of students' employment expectations can also help them to see the connections between the skills developed in curricular and cocurricular experiences and those needed for professional employment.

The salary survey published by NACE presents very specific information about starting salaries offered by employers in more than 70 disciplines. JobWeb (http://www.jobweb.org), NACE's Internet web site, provides links to hundreds of professional and job-related resources. With so many students coming to college with "a good job" as a goal, the more career- and occupation-related resources advisors have available, the more they can help students achieve that goal. The NACE homepage is located at http://www.naceweb.org.

Publications

While there are many publications that address career decision making, those described in this section are recommended for the academic leader who wants to obtain an overview of this area.

Career Information, Career Counseling, and Career Development (Isaacson & Brown, 2000) is intended to "help those who are now engaged, or who expect to be engaged, in facilitating the career development process" (p. 17). Two chapters may be of particular interest to the individual developing an advising initiative. "Theories of Career Choices and Development" gives the reader an overview of the many theories of career choice and will help faculty advisors be more comfortable in this area. "Career Development in Four-Year Colleges" discusses specific career development programs in these settings. It provides an overview of the activities advisors may use with students in exploring career options as well as some details on program evaluation.

What Color Is Your Parachute? (Bolles, 2002) is an annual guide that has been on the bestseller list for years. It offers many activities to help individuals identify their interests, values, and skills. These assessment activities provide both the student and the faculty member with a great deal of information with which to assess specific career options, industry settings, and employment opportunities.

The chapter entitled "Integrating Academic Advising and Career Life Planning" (McCalla-Wriggins, 2000) in *Academic Advising: A Comprehensive Handbook* presents numerous ways these two functions can work collaboratively. There are multiple ways to integrate these functions, but academic leaders may find the description of the totally integrated model of particular interest. In this model, undecided students receive academic advising from individuals who also provide career- and job-search counseling. Academic- and career-planning issues are woven into conversations with students from the very beginning of their campus experience. While this model may be the most challenging to implement because of already existing administrative structures, it demonstrates explicitly how academic advising and career and life planning are interconnected and part of the same process.

Electronic Resources

There are multiple software and Internet resources that the academic leader may want to consider in providing academic- and career-decision-making resources for students and their advisors. Three are particularly comprehensive and currently used on many campuses across the country. All offer similar information, differing mainly in their interfaces and means of navigation.

Discover, a software program dealing with career planning, is separated into four halls. Hall 1 of Discover includes a self-assessment of interests, values, and abilities that produces a list of suggested occupations and information about a wide variety of careers. Hall 2 provides detailed information about thousands of occupations. Hall 3 lets students explore undergraduate and graduate programs at specific institutions, searching by keyword, major, or geographic location. Hall 4 guides the student through the job-search process. Discover may be purchased from ACT (http://www.act.org/discover).

Sigi Plus, from Educational Testing Service (ETS) (http://www.ets.org/sigi), is another software package available for purchase by institutions. Like Discover, it includes a tool for self-assessment of values, interests, and skills plus detailed information on education and training for hundreds of occupations. Students may search colleges and graduate schools to find their perfect match.

Web-based MyRoad (http://www.myroad.com), hosted by the College Board, includes components for self-assessment, exploration of majors and careers, details of specific occupations, and a search function to choose colleges by type, major, location, size, and intercollegiate sports offered. Individual annual subscriptions are available at a nominal cost, but institutions may purchase contracts that allow their students to use all services free of charge.

LEADERSHIP RESOURCES

When an individual is selected to be an academic leader, there are high expectations that the person is competent not only in the content areas but also in the art and science of leadership. Many administrators have wonderful ideas about ways to improve the advising on campus but have not been successful because their leadership skills were not developed. Listed here are three organizations that can help an academic administrator enhance those leadership skills.

Center for Creative Leadership

Through customized programs, the Center for Creative Leadership's education sector group brings leadership-development resources to educators to assist them with the tough job of reforming and restructuring schools. Educational leaders reflect on their strengths and weaknesses by seeing themselves as others in their school community see them. Specially designed assessment activities sharpen insights about the impact of leaders' behaviors. Leaders also participate in realistic, intensive, "action learning" simulations that bring alive their typical responses within the context of the complex, high-pressure world of educational leadership. Activities include individual assessments; surveys on organizational climate, interests, skills, and team development; and a leadership index and team leader profile. Complete information is available at http://www.ccl.org.

Covey Leadership Center

While this organization has published a number of trade books, it has more intensive resources specifically directed to leadership. "The 4 Roles of Leadership" and the "Principle-Centered Leadership Week" are experiences designed to help participants "significantly improve their strategic thinking, long-term and position influence on others" (Covey Leadership Center, 2002).

"The 4 Roles of Leadership" two-day workshop helps participants create personal action plans or "blueprints"; shows them how to align "systems, processes, and structure" with objectives; facilitates personal empowerment; and helps participants develop an "essential balance between character and competence" (Covey Leadership Center, 2002).

Based on Steven Covey's books *The 7 habits of Highly Effective People, Principle-Centered Leadership,* and *First Things First,* "Principle-Centered Leadership Week" is a five-day retreat where participants learn to "build a high performance, high-trust culture; identify desired results and unify [their] teams to achieve those results; and renew [their] leadership role and gain a better understanding of its impact on [the] organization" (Covey Leadership Center, 2002). More information can be found at http://www.franklincovey.com.

JAMES MACGREGOR BURNS ACADEMY OF LEADERSHIP

This organization, housed at the University of Maryland, states the following as its mission: "[It] fosters principled leadership through scholarships, education, and training, with special attention to advising the leadership of groups historically underrepresented in public life" (James MacGregor Burns Academy of Leadership, 2002). Information on the seminars, courses, studies, and publications available through this center may be found online at http://www.academy.umd.edu.

An excellent resource for those charged with transforming a faculty advising system is the academy's publication *Leadership Reconsidered: Engaging Higher Education in Social Change* (Astin & Astin, 2000). Published in conjunction with the Kellogg Foundation (http://www.wkkf.org), the book gives very specific suggestions on how students, faculty, student affairs professionals, and college presidents can incorporate ten individual and group qualities of transformative leadership into their daily interactions. Demonstrating leadership behaviors is critical: "Our students are probably going to be influenced at least as much by what we academics do as by what we say in our classroom lectures and advising sessions" (Astin & Astin, 2000, p. 4).

COMMON ELEMENTS IN SUCCESSFUL FACULTY-BASED ADVISING PROGRAMS

As described in this chapter, there are numerous resources available to support the development of faculty-based advising programs. When embarking on the journey, it is important to identify the common elements in successful programs. First, exemplary programs benefit from a commitment to the advising initiative from the very top level of the institution and receive guidance and leadership from administrators. Faculty are actively involved in the planning and implementation of advising initiatives, including a well-articulated philosophy of academic advising.

Also, in successful programs the advising function is visible campus-wide, in all departments, and there is a designated coordinator or director of advising. Faculty and student affairs staff work together in a team approach and both participate in advisor development and training activities. Communication networks are clearly established, and the information that advisors need as they work with students is readily accessible. Faculty's regular involvement in students' academic careers begins early.

Regular and systematic evaluation of the academic-advising function and of those who advise is another hallmark of successful programs. Last, but certainly not least, is that faculty receive recognition and reward for academic advising.

Gaining information about successful programs at other institutions is helpful. Many details are available through NACADA's National Clearinghouse for Academic Advising, but actually visiting campuses with successful programs can be enlightening. However, since each institution has its own culture, the faculty-advising initiatives that will be most effective are those that reflect the mission and unique characteristics of that college or university.

CONCLUSION

As is evident throughout this chapter, academic leaders who are charged with the responsibility to create or enhance an effective academic advising system often face many challenges. However, they have many resources available to assist them in meeting these challenges.

Through collaboration and utilization of both internal and external resources, the academic leader can create an advising environment that supports a vision for higher education like that suggested by Dr. Monica Manning (1999), keynote speaker at the National Conference of the Association for General and Liberal Studies:

> Higher education, and liberal education in particular, could be about providing learners of any age with the opportunity to reflect on the purpose and meaning they create with their lives and the contribution to the world they can make with their gifts. That, to me, is the highest calling of the academy. (¶ 8)

Faculty advisors are in a unique position to assist students as they explore these potentially life-changing issues. When asked to reflect on factors that contributed to their success, the majority of successful students cited similar elements. According to Light (2001), "At key points in their college years, an academic advisor asked questions, or posed a challenge, that forced them to think about the relationship of their academic work to their personal lives" (p. 88).

REFERENCES

American Association for Higher Education, American College Personnel Association, & National Association of Student Personnel Administration. (1999). *Powerful partnerships: A shared responsibility for learning.* Retrieved December 2001, from http://www.acpa.nche.edu/pubs/powpart.html

American College Personnel Association. (2002). *Mission statement.* Retrieved January 2002, from http://www.acpa.nche.edu

Astin, A. W., Parrott, S. A., Korn, W. S., & Sax, L. J. (1997). *The American freshman: Thirty-year trends.* Los Angeles, CA: University of California, Higher Education Institute.

Astin, H., & Astin, A. (Eds.). (2000). *Leadership reconsidered: Engaging higher education in social change.* Battle Creek, MI: W. K. Kellogg Foundation.

Bolles, R. (2002). *What color is your parachute?* Berkeley, CA: Ten Speed Press.

Covey Leadership Center. (2002). *4 roles of leadership.* Retrieved February 2002, from https://register.franklincovey.com/register/moreinfo_4roles.cgi?program_id=8andsource=WEB0121

Frost, S. H. (1993). Developmental advising: Practices and attitudes of faculty advisors. *NACADA Journal, 13* (2), 15–20.

Glennen, R. E., & Vowell, F. N. (Eds.). (1995). *Academic advising as a comprehensive campus process.* Manhattan, KS: National Academic Advising Association.

Gordon, V. N., & Habley, W. R., & Associates. (2000). *Academic advising: A comprehensive handbook.* San Francisco, CA: Jossey-Bass.

Habley, W. R., & Morales, R. H. (1998). *Current practices in academic advising: Final report on ACT's fifth national survey of academic advising* (Monograph Series No. 6). Manhattan, KS: National Academic Advising Association.

Harris-Bowlsbey, J. A., Dikel, M. R., & Sampson, J. P. (1998). *The Internet: A tool for career planning.* Tulsa, OK: National Career Development Association.

Isaacson, L. E., & Brown, D. (2000). *Career information, career counseling, and career development.* Needham Heights, MA: Allyn and Bacon.

James MacGregor Burns Academy of Leadership. (2002). *Mission statement.* Retrieved January 2002, from http://www.academy.umd.edu

Johnson, C. S., & Cheatham, H. E. (Eds.). (1999). *Higher education trends for the next century: A research agenda for student success.* Washington, DC: American College Personnel Association.

Kapes, J. T., & Whitfield, E. A. (2001). *A counselor's guide to career assessment instruments* (4th ed.). Tulsa, OK: National Career Development Association.

Kramer, G. L. (Ed.). (1995). *Reaffirming the role of faculty in academic advising* (Monograph Series No. 1). Manhattan, KS: National Academic Advising Association.

Kramer, G. L., & Childs, M. W. (Eds.). (1996). *Transforming academic advising through the use of technology.* Manhattan, KS: National Academic Advising Association.

Kramer, G. L., & Childs, M. W. (2000). *The "e" factor in delivering advising and student services.* Manhattan, KS: National Academic Advising Association.

Light, R. J. (2001). *Making the most of college: Students speak their minds.* Cambridge, MA: Harvard University Press.

Magolda, M. B., & Terenzini, P. T. (1999). Learning and teaching in the 21st century: Trends and implications for practice. In C. S. Johnson & H. E. Cheatham (Eds.), *Higher education trends for the next century: A research agenda for student success.* Washington, DC: American College Personnel Association. Retrieved February 2002, from http://www.acpa.nche.edu/seniorscholars/trends/trends4.htm

Manning, M. M. (1999). *Liberal education for our life's work.* Keynote address at the National Conference of the Association for General and Liberal Studies, Richmond, VA.

McCalla-Wriggins, B. (2000). Integrating academic advising and career life planning. In V. N. Gordon, W. R. Habley, & Associates (Eds.), *Academic advising: A comprehensive handbook* (pp. 162–176). San Francisco, CA: Jossey-Bass.

National Academic Advising Association. (1995). *NACADA faculty advising training video* [Video]. Manhattan, KS: Author.

National Academic Advising Association. (1999). *Academic advising: Campus collaboratives to foster retention* [Video]. Manhattan, KS: Author.

National Academic Advising Association. (2000). *Mission statement and strategic plan 2000–2005.* Retrieved February 2001, from http://www.nacada.ksu.edu/Associnfo/stratpln.htm

National Academic Advising Association. (2001). *Academic advising: Discover the many voices* (National Conference Program). Manhattan, KS: Author.

National Academic Advising Association. (2002a). *Consultant's bureau.* Retrieved February 2002, from http://www.nacada.ksu.edu/Profres/consult.htm

National Academic Advising Association. (2002b). *NACADA statement of core values of academic advising.* Retrieved February 2002, from http://www.nacada.ksu.edu/Profres/ corevalu.htm

National Academic Advising Association. (2002c). *National advising awards program.* Retrieved February 2002, from http://www.nacada.ksu.edu/Awards/advcall.html

National Academic Advising Association. (2002d). *Organizational structure.* Retrieved February 2002, from http://www.nacada.ksu.edu/Associnfo/structur.html#committeechairs

National Academic Advising Association. (2002e). *Outstanding advising program award.* Retrieved February 2002, from http://www.nacada.ksu.edu/Awards/procall.html

National Academic Advising Association & American College Testing. (2002). *Summer institute on academic advising.* Retrieved February 2002, from http://www.nacada.ksu.edu/SummerInst/brochure02.htm

National Career Development Association. (2001). *NCDA mission statement.* Retrieved January 2002, from http://ncda.org/about/mission.html

Noel-Levitz. (2002). *Academic advising for student success and retention.* Retrieved December 2001, from http://www.noellevitz.com/ret_advising.asp

O'Banion, T. (1972). An academic advising model. *Junior College Journal, 42* (6), 62–69.

Ramos, M., & Vallandingham, D. (Eds.). (1997). *Advising students with disabilities.* Manhattan, KS: National Academic Advising Association.

Ryan, K. C. (1992). Advising as teaching. *NACADA Journal, 12* (1), 4–8.

Schroeder, C. S. (1999). Collaboration and partnership. In C. S. Johnson & H. E. Cheatham (Eds.), *Higher education trends for the next century: A research agenda for student success.* Washington, DC: American College Personnel Association. Retrieved January 2002, from http://www.acpa.nche.edu/seniorsscholars/trends/trends7.htm

Upcraft, M. L., & Kramer, G. L. (Eds.). (1995). *First-year academic advising: Patterns in the present, pathways to the future.* Columbia, SC: University of South Carolina, National Resource Center for the Freshman Year Experience and Students in Transition.

Vowell, F. N., Wachtel, E., Grites, T. J., & Rozzelle, R. W. (Eds.). (1993). *Designing an effective advisor training program.* Manhattan, KS: National Academic Advising Association.

Yerian, J. M. (1988). *Putting the standards to work.* College Park, MD: Council for the Advancement of Standards for Student Services/Development Programs.

9 OUTSTANDING FACULTY ADVISING PROGRAMS: STRATEGIES THAT WORK

Franklin P. Wilbur

In *Making the Most of College,* Richard Light (2001) distills years of interviews, observations, and research on factors closely related to a student's success in college and concludes that "good advising may be the single most underestimated characteristic of a successful college experience" (p. 81). In his quest to understand why the college years for some students are a time of development, growth, discovery, and success, while for others they are a period of frustration, struggle to meet requirements and deadlines, and generally a rather flat, uninspiring extension of high school, Light affirms that faculty can and do play powerful roles in students' success, their overall feeling of satisfaction with their experiences, and their retention to completion of degree.

Often the best advising models are based on a system of collaboration between faculty and staff. While students benefit from the availability, commitment to advising, and global institutional knowledge of professional staff, faculty advisors offer students more in-depth knowledge about particular majors and share their enthusiasm of scholarship within their disciplines. Academic advising, when done right, offers students and faculty an additional opportunity to connect in meaningful ways.

With increasing frequency, advising is viewed as an important aspect of teaching in which faculty, as well as professional staff and student peer advisors, help students to explore their environment, make informed choices in planning their courses of study, take responsibility for much of their own learning, and set the stage to become effective lifelong learners. Developing an effective advising system does not happen accidentally, particularly with faculty, who have many competing demands on their limited time and energies. Those campuses on which advising is viewed by students as a strength have usually taken many deliberate actions to build commitment among the campus community to work together to better orchestrate and support all aspects of student learning. This chapter considers successful advising practices from campuses throughout the country that have received national recognition for the effectiveness of their advising systems. The intent is that readers will envision a plan for strengthening, maintaining, and assessing various aspects of advising on their campuses, "jump start" innovation by learning from and networking with colleagues, and begin to prioritize the areas most in need of attention.

A CAMPUS STATEMENT ON ACADEMIC ADVISING

In order for a campus to begin improving its advising system to better meet the needs of students, there must be agreement as to what academic advising is and how it should happen. Developing a campus statement regarding academic advising can not only clarify the activity itself as integral to student learning, it can also make clear the roles and responsibilities of both individuals and the institution as a whole to help ensure that the advising process will contribute to overall student success.

The following statement, crafted at Hamilton College in Hamilton, New York, a selective four-year liberal arts institution, captures their definition of advising and the necessary conditions for its successful execution:

> Academic Advising at Hamilton College is one of the many ways in which students engage with faculty on an individual basis. Advisors and advisees work together to craft a unique, individual academic plan based upon each student's strengths, weaknesses, and goals. Hamilton College views the advising relationship as an on-going conversation that transcends mere course selection and attempts to assist students as they explore the breadth of the liberal arts curriculum, experience college life, focus on a major concentration, and prepare for life after Hamilton.
>
> Students are responsible for making their own decisions based upon their best judgments informed by the best

> information and advice available to them; arranging advising appointments; preparing for advising meetings; seeking out contacts and information related to planning their academic program; and understanding degree and program requirements.
>
> Faculty are responsible for proactively engaging advisees in the academic planning process; monitoring the academic progress of their advisees; making appropriate referrals to other campus offices; and communicating clearly to their advisees the regular time during which they are available for consultation.
>
> The College is responsible for providing appropriate recognition for the role that faculty play in the academic advising system; assuring that there are clear policies, procedures, and resources to support the advising process; assisting faculty to develop effective advising skills; and conducting ongoing assessment of the advising program. (Hamilton College, n.d.)

The Hamilton statement also includes a section that explains to students the nature of a liberal-arts education, strategies to get the most out of their years on campus, and specific learning goals that should be achieved during the undergraduate years. For Hamilton and other institutions that have spent time developing a statement on advising as a community, the efforts have been rewarded in not only clarifying for students, parents, alumni, faculty, and staff what quality advising is and its intended outcomes, but also what support elements have to be in place for advising to work.

Advising statements define a philosophy and suggest goals, organization, and conditions for successful advising. Such statements can be useful in orienting new students to the campus, in helping them to understand institutional resources and ways their learning is supported, and in learning their own roles and responsibilities in the process. Advising statements also help to prioritize resource allocation, build information systems, focus assessment and support activities, and remind campus leaders of their special obligations to support and reward those seeking to serve effectively in advising roles.

Other advising statements to review are those from Monroe Community College in Rochester, New York; Penn State University; University of Wisconsin; Fox Valley Technical College; and Syracuse University, all of whose URLs may be found in the Additional Resources section of this chapter.

EFFECTIVE CAMPUS LEADERSHIP AND ADVISING

Often what stimulates attention to the status of academic advising is negative feedback from current students or alumni regarding advising experiences, unacceptable retention rates, or problems with special populations. The assignment to "fix" academic advising can come to an academic vice chancellor, dean, faculty chair, or other member of the campus community, and the challenges can be daunting. Campuses that build effective advising programs receive support from leaders such as presidents and provosts, who set the tone and say, without equivocation, that advising is viewed as highly important in fostering student success and that it is considered a key role for faculty. Further, leaders both say and show that advising will be supported and will be considered a factor in the faculty reward process. Without leadership at the institutional and operational levels, efforts to strengthen advising will likely come to little more than statements of intent.

In the mid-1990s, the vice chancellor at Syracuse University (SU) began an initiative to improve academic advising by stating that advising was an important aspect of teaching and that it would receive more attention and resources in the future to meet the needs of students. Further, he appointed a single individual, an associate vice president within academic affairs, to take responsibility for organizing the campus and devising an operational plan to systematically and comprehensively improve advising. This process was achieved through involving key administrative and faculty campus leadership and basing recommendations upon a thorough needs analysis and understanding of national best practices. At SU, this mandate, support at the top, and a clear action plan led to a national academic-advising award within three years of the start of the project.

At the University of Central Arkansas, the work of several appointed campus committees and advice from outside professional consultants resulted in a commitment from the leadership to establish the position of coordinator of academic advising and create an academic advising center, consisting of faculty and staff specially trained and prepared for work in the center. Every college within the university identified a faculty member to be assigned to the advising center as a major part of their official teaching load. A new, centrally located building was constructed to house the center. The strong commitment of high-level leadership and special efforts to create a broad sense of faculty ownership for advising significantly contributed to the overall improvement of academic advising on this campus.

At the University of Arizona, support for advising came from the vice president for undergraduate education following proposal submissions from three separate committees: Associated Students at University of Arizona, the Deans' Committee on Faculty Advising, and the University Professional Advising Council. The breadth of the university communities involved ensured that all interests were being represented, and resulted in the establishment of the Academic Advising Task Force for the University of Arizona. The charge of the task force was to provide a set of recommendations that could be supported by the university community, as well as plans for the implementation and assessment of those recommendations.

REWARDS AND RECOGNITION

Wherever academic advising works well, you will find practices in place that recognize advisors and reward them for their efforts and their effectiveness. While Chapter 5 goes into greater detail regarding this topic, following is a sampling of what some institutions around the country do and say that make advising something that "counts" in the campus-reward system.

At the beginning of a multiyear initiative to improve all aspects of academic advising, Gershon Vincow, at the time the vice chancellor for academic affairs at SU, issued a statement that sent a clear message to deans, chairs, and faculty that advising was going to be a strong "signature" of a Syracuse education and that faculty would be appropriately recognized and rewarded for success in this area. The following is an excerpt from his 1993 address to the campus community:

> As we continue to seek ways of improving advising and mentoring of students, it is essential that we give this aspect of teaching and learning appropriate recognition in the faculty reward system. [Each school and college committee] is encouraged to give similar treatment to advising and mentoring in their deliberation concerning faculty promotion. Each tenure case considered in the future will explicitly evaluate the contributions of the faculty member to lower-division undergraduate advising, undergraduate major advising, and graduate advising (including thesis and dissertation supervision) and include a statement concerning this evaluation which is forwarded to the Vice Chancellor for Academic Affairs for review. (Vincow, 1993)

This announcement that advising was considered an important aspect of the teaching and learning process and would count in the tenure and promotion process caught the attention of the entire campus community and paved the way for the creation of a comprehensive plan to improve advising. No serious change at Syracuse would have been possible without this critical leadership declaration.

Another effective way to stress the importance of advising is to develop a formal program of campus advising awards. These have special significance when they are the result of nominations from students and are supported with assessment data. Penn State University and Indiana University–Purdue University Indianapolis (IUPUI) are but two of many campuses that have initiated advising awards at the departmental, school, and institutional levels. At Penn State, for example, the "Excellence in Advising Award" is listed in the same award category as the institution's undergraduate teaching awards. This procedure is in keeping with Penn's statement on the role of a faculty advisor, which states, "Faculty members at Penn State perform the function of advising students as an important component of their professional responsibilities, namely teaching" (Pennsylvania State University, 2002b). The University of Wisconsin–Whitewater Master Advisors Program also includes its "Excellence in Advising Award" with awards for service, teaching, and research and recognizes winners together at its college retreat. At Monroe Community College, Outstanding Faculty Advisor, Outstanding Adjunct Faculty Advisor, and Outstanding Retired Faculty Advisor annual awards are one of the highlight celebration events of the academic year. Fox Valley Technical College evaluations reveal that appreciation luncheons and awards for advisors are very highly rated by faculty advisors. These and other such practices show appreciation for advising and its important role in fostering student success.

UNDERSTANDING NEEDS: GATHERING INFORMATION FOR IMPROVEMENT

Every major campus improvement initiative should begin with an effort to truly understand the problems, strengths, and relevant issues related to academic advising from multiple perspectives. When SU, for example, began to devise a campus plan to strengthen advising, they sought answers to questions such as:

- What aspects of advising do students, staff, and faculty feel are currently working well?
- Where does the advising system fail to meet student needs?
- Do students and advisors have the information they need, when they need it, to have meaningful conversations about program options, to build schedules, and to make decisions or referrals?
- Does the campus electronic communication network as it currently stands facilitate or impede communications related to student advising and monitoring academic progress?

It is also important to understand how faculty regard their advising roles. SU asked faculty to respond to the following questions:

- What exactly is my role as an academic advisor? What is expected of me?
- How do I keep in contact with the students assigned to me?
- What information do I need to know, particularly outside of my department?

- Do my students, my peers, and those in administrative positions consider advising important?
- Does advising really "count" in the campus reward system?
- Is my advising effective? How can I know? How can I improve?

Through the use of such questions in focus groups, campus surveys, and individual conversations, campus leaders can get a good sense as to where the greatest needs are and can decide how to prioritize initiatives. It is also possible to learn a great deal by examining routinely administered campus surveys, including postgraduate surveys, to see what students have to say about the quality of the advising they expected and received at different points in their academic careers.

The University of Arizona is another example of a campus that did an in-depth, university-wide assessment of advising using a variety of tools to best understand what worked and to identify the weaknesses prior to preparing recommendations to strengthen their system of advising. Details of their process can be found online at http://w3.arizona.edu/~uge/aatf/. Fox Valley Technical College in Wisconsin, a two-year institution, annually administers an internally devised Faculty Advising Survey and the ACT Survey of Academic Advising every other year to continually ascertain what their advising needs are and if they are being met.

Examples and sources of instruments that can be used to assess advising at any type of institution can be found through the web sites of the National Academic Advising Association (NACADA) at http://www.nacada.ksu.edu/Profres/Assessment%20of and the American College Testing (ACT) organization at http:// www.act.org/products.html.

ADVISOR TRAINING AND SUPPORT

Those engaged in advising students will, almost without exception, agree that it is a complex and often demanding process that few, if any, faculty feel equipped to handle without adequate training, information, and support. An institutional commitment to preparing faculty for this aspect of their professional lives is an important element of any quality advising program. While the delivery systems, format, time of year, required versus optional events, use of technology, and other factors may differ dramatically between and even within institutions, as noted in Figure 9.1, particular topics are frequently common among the strongest programs.

FIGURE 9.1

COMMON ADVISING PROGRAM TOPICS

- communications skills
- academic rules and regulations
- intra-institutional transfer
- the role of learning communities
- assisting students with special needs
- listening skills
- helping a student in crisis
- multiple advisor communications
- student development issues
- minors and dual majors
- internships and study abroad
- academic support services
- time management and study skills
- knowing when and how to referrals
- using campus electronic resources
- helping students in transition
- record keeping
- information on careers

Institutions across the nation currently use a variety of training tools, techniques, and approaches to address important topics and to help faculty feel capable and comfortable in an advising role. Advisor training should not be viewed as a one-time activity, but rather as an ongoing commitment to continue to raise the skill levels and provide updated institutional information to all those involved in student advising roles. For example, Penn State's Center for Excellence in Academic Advising supports advisors and maintains a web site with resources, tools and techniques, frequently asked questions (FAQs), news, and more (http://www.psu.edu/dus/cfe/). In addition, there is the Penn State Monograph for Faculty Advisors, which won a 2001 NACADA publication award.

The University of Central Arkansas offers professional development workshops throughout the year, weekly staff meetings, and an online newsletter for advisors (http://www.uca.edu/divisions/academic/undergradstudies/advising/newsletter.htm).

The University of Wisconsin–Whitewater Master Advisors Program has, as a key component, a Master Advisors Group, comprised of faculty identified by department chairs as genuinely interested in advising and related issues. Master advisors receive additional advising training to prepare them to be advising resources, to develop advising initiatives, and to assist in the delivery of advising workshops.

More detailed information regarding faculty-advisor training programs can be found in Chapter 4.

LINKING ADVISING AND FIRST-YEAR PROGRAMS

Many campuses now make it a priority to establish meaningful, comfortable advising relationships with faculty early in a student's career. In particular, campuses are finding it effective to integrate academic advising into a wide variety of first-year programs, including summer preview opportunities, freshman forums and seminars, opening week activities, learning communities, and other initiatives intended to effectively integrate students into campus life and help foster their success. The following examples are intended to illustrate successful mechanisms for building authentic, comfortable, meaningful relationships between students and their advisors from the very earliest stages of a student's integration into a campus community.

At SU, the first student contact with an advisor begins with a telephone conversation during the spring or summer prior to the student's arrival on campus. A relationship is started, questions are addressed, and plans are made to meet during the first few days of the semester. Once students arrive on campus, freshmen participate in forums and seminars that have been designed to provide a highly personalized introduction to the university and the immediate community, to begin to help them understand campus resources, and to help them make an effective transition from high school to full-time college study. In SU's College of Arts and Sciences, experienced volunteer faculty who have been especially trained for this role lead all Freshman Forums. Each forum is limited to 15 students to keep the experience highly personal and allow for maximum interaction and bonding within the group. Important in the dynamics of the forum model is the commitment of each of the faculty leaders to serve as the academic advisor to the students in the groups. Due to the contact from the earliest stages of the students' campus experiences, the advisee-advisor relationship is usually comfortable and strong, extending well beyond simply planning class schedules for the next semester. Social events, including dinner at the professor's home, field trips into the community, links to campus learning communities, involvement with residence-life staff, and a freshman lecture series are additional components of this highly successful program. This approach to building advising relationships is a powerful and proven way to immediately affect in positive ways the dynamics of the advising process. More information is available at http://thecollege.syr.edu/undergraduate/Freshforum/default.html.

Other examples include IUPUI's efforts, which extend their formal orientation programs into first-year seminars. The instructional teams responsible for the courses are comprised of a faculty member, librarian, academic advisor, and student mentor. And while each team tailors the syllabus to its specific discipline or school, there are basic curriculum components common to every section: culture and context of the university; critical thinking; technology skills; library training; communication skills—both verbal and nonverbal; campus resources; advising and IUPUI Principles of Undergraduate Education. A detailed overview of IUPUI first-year seminars can be found at http://www.universitycollege.iupui.edu/LC/.

Bridgewater State College's Haughey First Year Advising Program is a model that offers a series of advising sessions taught collaboratively by faculty and staff. Students progress through the sessions, beginning with large-group orientations and ending with individual sessions with their faculty advisor. Each session has a defined goal and set of objectives.

The University of Alabama at Birmingham's faculty and professional advisors join forces in University 101, a three-credit course designed to teach critical-thinking skills. University 101 incorporates advising assignments to ensure that freshmen, particularly those at risk, develop the necessary academic skills and strategies for successfully transitioning from high school to the university. The advising component requires students to meet individually with advisors to have conversations about their short- and long-term education goals. Student assignments tied to advising include developing individual plans for achieving their goals and a follow-up assignment later in the course, where they evaluate their plans. That the advising assignment is worth 12% of the final grade stresses its importance.

Monroe Community College's Liberal Arts Faculty Mentor Program offers students the opportunity to develop a long-term mentoring relationship with a faculty member in one of the courses in which they have enrolled. This program offers students the advantage of choosing an advisor they already know from class.

CAMPUS INFORMATION SYSTEMS THAT SUPPORT THE ADVISING PROCESS

The availability of timely, accurate information on student progress, academic programs and requirements, and campus support services is essential to the advising process, and many campuses have begun to take advantage of technology to improve communication. A number of institutions with award-winning advising programs have paid particular attention to building and maintaining robust campus student information systems and work to train advisors to effectively use electronic resources in support of student success.

Purdue University Calumet (PUC), for example, recently implemented Curriculum Advising, Program Planning (CAPP), which has been phased in over several years. In the initial phase of CAPP, an automated degree-audit tool replaced the manual paper process; next, an automated audit function was added to advisors' desktops; finally, the CAPP audit report was implemented for use during advising appointments. Changes and enhancements continue with input from a CAPP crew committee, an advisory committee, campus deans, department heads, and academic advisors. Some of the most valuable sessions in the creation and evolution of the CAPP system, which is still a work in progress, have been brainstorming sessions where participants are invited to informally share ideas and give input.

Penn State assists its schools and colleges in developing advising web sites while maintaining campus-wide standards via "Guidelines for Advising Web Sites," (http://www.psu.edu/dus/uac/webmain.htm), which states, "Sites should be designed to give information to students enrolled in the University, prospective students and their families, and members of the University advising community" (Penn, 2001a). It goes on to list exemplary web sites and the standard online links to other areas, such as registrar, bursar, financial aid, and so on that should be included on all Penn advising web sites.

Ball State University also recently developed the Automated Course Transfer System (ACTS), which stores all identified course equivalencies and produces a "Course Equivalency Report" that identifies the transfer courses accepted and not accepted at Ball State, and a "Reference Degree Audit" that applies the transfer credit to an intended major and highlights the courses students could take at their current institutions prior to transferring. Michael McCauley, director of academic systems, states that Ball State has seen a dramatic increase in transfer student enrollments since the implementation of ACTS (personal communication, January 9, 2002). IBM and its Best Practices Partner Group recognized ACTS.

Having accurate, timely information at one's fingertips is extremely useful for all those engaged with the process of advising. Electronic resources are invaluable for making referrals and keeping in more frequent contact with students, other faculty, and staff advisors.

USING CAMPUS MEDIA AND ORGANIZING PUBLIC EVENTS

Every campus needs to consider how to best communicate academic advising information. Advising web sites enhance communication in a variety of ways, and major fairs, workshops, and videos are other common vehicles for information dissemination to inform, teach, and excite students about various learning opportunities and support services. The examples cited below are a brief sampling of best uses of the web, as well as a variety of other public events and media options currently used to enhance advising on campuses.

The University of Central Arkansas Academic Advising Center web site (http://www.uca.edu/divisions/academic/undergrad studies/advising/advise1.htm) is direct-linked from the UCA home page and offers a wealth of information for both advisors and students. Among the advising activities at UCA are an annual campus-wide majors fair and "Don't Cancel That Class," a program where advisors offer to make a presentation to a class if the professor has to be absent from a session.

Penn State offers the DUS Navigator, an NACADA award-winning online yearlong advising program for freshman. Located at http://www.psu.edu/dus/navigate/, this program is designed to help students become better planners and decision makers and to prepare them for more productive interactions with their academic advisers. IUPUI, in addition to having online information (http://uc.iupui.edu/AA/), hosts "Major Decision Workshops" several times during the fall semester to assist students preparing to declare a major. Monroe Community College's "Academic Advising Atlas" provides information for students and online help, as well as videos, for helping students to choose a major.

Such practices serve to encourage students to consider for themselves their interests in a broad range of academic and cocurricular offerings, create a sense of excitement about new learning opportunities, and help students take more responsibility for exploring the campus environment on their own. As a result of such personal initiative, students often find their conversations with their advisors to be more focused and purposeful.

ASSESSING EFFECTIVENESS OF ADVISING

Every strong advising program identified by NACADA or other national organizations has integrated an effective system to monitor quality. An effective assessment plan needs to gather data at every stage in the process to ensure continuous improvement, to provide feedback to individual advisors and the units in which they work, and to provide evidence that will be used, along with other aspects of teaching, to make a case for tenure, promotion, and salary increments. While there are many instruments designed and available nationally, each campus has to determine what system of data collection will provide them with the most accurate and timely feedback on the advising process. Sometimes something as simple as a short feedback form that can be completed by students at the end of an advising session proves quite helpful to advisors. Other times, more comprehensive survey instruments and focus groups are needed to capture broader student experiences with advisors and related campus resources over time. In addition to monitoring advising for current students, some of the best programs assess students' expectations prior to arriving on campus, as well as regularly contacting alumni regarding their reflections on the advising process and how it helped or failed to help them achieve their educational goals.

At Penn State, for example, each academic unit must assess its advising process as it relates to the goals stated in the senate policy for advising. The University Advising Council's guidelines for advising assessment, which include developing strategies, describing the current state of advising, and evaluating the advising program, can be found online at http://www.psu.edu/dus/uac/asindex.htm.

Fox Valley Technical College uses the ACT Student Opinion Survey—Two-Year College Form to solicit valuable information from students. Recently, the Research and Evaluation department added faculty advising questions to their program evaluation surveys. The University of Central Arkansas has clearly articulated goals for the Advising Center, and the center tracks advising activities and conducts surveys regularly to assess student satisfaction with advising services.

Additional resources and suggestions can be found in Chapter 5, which includes best practices in assessment of faculty advising.

TAKING STOCK: A CAMPUS ADVISING CHECKLIST

In consideration of NACADA recommendations and a study of exemplary advising programs nationally, a checklist has been included to assist campuses in taking inventory of what components of an advising system are currently in place and to help identify where there are voids or inadequacies. While by no means comprehensive, this list is a starting point to gather information, stimulate conversation and debates, and to eventually lead to prioritizing areas most in need of attention. The process of "taking stock" works best with broad participation of the campus community, both to share perceptions and experiences and to help to build ownership and participation in improvement initiatives. The checklist is located in Appendix 9.1.

CONCLUSION

In this chapter principles and practices associated with the best practices in faculty academic advising, as identified by national organizations such as NACADA, have been identified and examples have been provided. Keep in mind that what may be a "best practice" for one campus may simply not be appropriate somewhere else, depending on campus culture, mission and vision, labor contracts, and special needs of students. Successful innovation and improvement in advising begins with a thorough understanding of present practices. Examples from other campuses may help faculty, staff, and administrators begin to see a range of options for addressing particular needs. In studying the processes used to improve and maintain strong advising systems, one thing is very clear: each college or university involved their communities in assessing need and in devising and owning new initiatives. Even though it is wise not to "reinvent the wheel," practices from other campuses should be adjusted and customized to create a best fit. The "not invented here" syndrome has doomed many campus improvement projects from the start. The quality of academic-advising services and support provided to faculty and staff say a lot about the institution's values and priorities. Successful advising programs are designed, implemented, and maintained with caring and well-chosen leadership, each school determining the right combination of people with the skill, influence, credibility, and commitment to do the job.

When done right, a comprehensive system of advising can be a tremendous source of satisfaction for all parties, including staff, faculty, parents, and the students it is designed to serve. Not only can exemplary advising contribute to student satisfaction and academic success, it can result in alumni feeling warmly connected to their alma mater. Ask alumni what they valued most about their time at their college or university and their response will seldom involve buildings or facilities. Rather, remarks will center on teachers, staff, and fellow students who, through their teaching, encouragement, and support, demonstrated they cared and were committed to students' success.

REFERENCES

Hamilton College. (n.d.). *Hamilton College statement on advising.* Internal document.

Light, R. J. (2001). *Making the most of college: Students speak their minds.* Cambridge, MA: Harvard University Press.

Pennsylvania State University. (2002a). *Guidelines for advising web sites.* Retrieved March 2002, from http://www.psu.edu/dus/uac/webmain.htm

Pennsylvania State University. (2002b.) *Role of the adviser.* Retrieved March 2002, from http://www.psu.edu/dus /cfe/myrole

Vincow, G. (1993, January). *Annual address to the faculty.* Unpublished speech, Syracuse University.

ADDITIONAL RESOURCES

Beck, R. J. (2002). *Undergraduate academic advising.* Center for Academic Excellence, Tufts University. Retrieved March 2002, from http://ase.tufts.edu/cae/ occasional_papers/advising.htm

Buck, J. B., Moore, J. W., Schwartz, M., & Supon, S. B. (2000). *The Penn State adviser* (2nd ed.). University Park, PA: Pennsylvania State University, Office of Undergraduate Education.

Fox Valley Technical College. (2001). *Academic/faculty advising guidelines.* Appleton, WI: Author.

URLS

Monroe Community College's advising mission and philosophy statements: http://www.monroecc.edu/

Pennsylvania State University's advising policy: http://www.psu.edu/advising/

Pennsylvania State University's role of the adviser: http://www.psu.edu/dus/cfe/myrole

Syracuse University's statement on academic advising: http://sumweb.syr.edu/registrar/AdvisingMinors.html

University of Wisconsin–Whitewater Master Advisors Program goals of academic advising: http://www.uww.edu/lettsc/advising/ADVRES.htm

APPENDIX 9.1

BUILDING AN EFFECTIVE CAMPUS ACADEMIC ADVISING SYSTEM: AN ADMINISTRATIVE LEADER'S CHECKLIST

	Yes	No	To Some Degree	Don't Know
1. Does your institution have an official statement defining its position on academic advising, explaining what advising is and the various roles and responsibilities of students, faculty, and staff?				
2. Are formal practices in place to recognize and reward those who excel in advising?				
3. Is advising recognized on your campus as an important aspect of teaching or service, and are expectations regarding advising competence articulated in tenure and promotion guidelines?				
4a. Is the effectiveness of academic advising assessed regularly, both at the individual-faculty and staff level, as well as at the department, school or college, and institution levels?				
4b. Is data collected from all sources (for example, campus surveys, alumni surveys, focus groups, and discussions) used as part of the continuous improvement process for advising?				

APPENDIX 9.1, CONTINUED

	Yes	No	To Some Degree	Don't Know
4c. Is advising-assessment information reported as part of the institution's self-study plan for accreditation?				
5a. Does your campus information system facilitate the availability of timely, accurate information regarding students academic progress, support services, and academic options for advising purposes?				
5b. Is it possible, using your campus student information system, for advisees and advisors to conduct degree audits and to experiment with "what if" scenarios when exploring such options as changing majors, enrolling in a study-abroad program, adding a minor or additional major, and so on? Is an adequate technical infrastructure in place for such information flow?				
6a. Is there training in place, offered on a regular basis, for all faculty, staff, and students (peer advisors), who are assigned to advising roles?				
6b. If training is in place, is the adequacy of such support regularly assessed?				

APPENDIX 9.1, CONTINUED

	Yes	No	To Some Degree	Don't Know
7. Do you feel that your campus has effective communications and coordination between and among advisors from academic and student affairs?				
8. Are advisors aware of campus student-support services and knowledgeable and comfortable with making referrals?				
9a. Do you have adequate campus leadership in place to continually monitor and work to improve the quality of academic advising?				
9b. Has a clear administrative mandate or charge been given to the individual or team charged with improving advising?				
9c. Are your goals for advising realistic, specific, and measurable?				
10a. Do recognized leaders in academic advising from your campus have access, through organizational memberships, to national advising resources?				
10b. Is their involvement with regional and national meetings supported?				

APPENDIX 9.1, CONTINUED

	Yes	No	To Some Degree	Don't Know
11. Do you regularly provide coverage through campus media (for example, newspapers, magazines, television, campus recruitment videos, radio) regarding academic opportunities, support services, and the role of advisors in helping students to explore options?				
12. Does your campus ever sponsor "academic opportunities" fairs or other events that enhance student awareness of various programs and provide forums for sharing?				
13. Is academic advising well integrated into special programs for first-year students, such as learning communities, freshman forums and seminars, and summer preview events?				
14. Do you feel confident enough about the quality of academic advising services on your campus that you could highlight them in your admissions materials?				
15. Should you consider establishing or enhancing a professional advising center(s) to supplement faculty and staff advising?				

10

EVOLUTION AND EXAMINATION: PHILOSOPHICAL AND CULTURAL FOUNDATIONS FOR FACULTY ADVISING

Susan H. Frost and Karen E. Brown-Wheeler

With the university currently evolving into an open, flexible system—a system increasingly supported by enabling structures—faculty advising demands examination now more than ever. Academic advising, a vital and organic component of teaching at any university, perpetually changes in tandem with the evolution of academic disciplines, philosophies, and cultures of teaching. This chapter explores the cultural and philosophical foundations of advising by considering the evolution of the city, the evolution of the university, and the evolution of advising as three parallel and mutually reinforcing achievements.

Even though this chapter refers solely to evolutionary trends within "the university," the theories and proposals elucidated here go well beyond traditional university walls. Using the term "university" broadly is our own attempt to capture the essence of the marketplace of ideas that we as teachers and educators embody. However, by locating the university as a philosophical and cultural set of values rather than as a specific place, we address our ideas to advising in four-year liberal arts colleges, community colleges, state colleges, and state universities.

The evolution of the modern research university has contributed from the beginning to our contemporary understanding of advising as a vital and organic component of teaching. Frederick Rudolph and Laurence R. Veysey, two historians specializing in university development, traced the history of the university in their 1960s scholarship. Since then, other leading scholars—historian

Thomas Bender, sociologist Saskia Sassen, theologian Rebecca Chopp, and higher education scholar Susan Frost (a coauthor of this chapter)—have all embraced an idea of "evolution" to explore the developing city's relationship to the university, to urban planning, and to disciplinary development. The scholarship of these thinkers together significantly influences this chapter's discussion of evolution and examination as they elucidate the complexities of academic advising.

In *The American College and University,* Frederick Rudolph (1962) asks, "How and why and with what consequences have the American colleges and universities developed as they have?" (p. viii). Rudolph describes university development in America as progressing from aristocratic, colonial colleges to state and land-grant universities to the democratic institutions we have today—institutions committed to the growth of knowledge and expansion of educational opportunity. Equally interested in the rise of the research university, Laurence R. Veysey (1965) argues in *The Emergence of the American University* that conflict drove the university's emergence—a conflict regarding "the basic purpose of the new university and . . . the kind and degree of control to be exerted by the institution's leadership" (p. viii). Perhaps as a result of his interest in conflict, Veysey also explores the relationship between American society and the university—a surprising connection, Veysey tells us, because "ever since the late nineteenth-century the better university campuses have maintained the character of oases, sharply set off from the surrounding society in many of their fundamental qualities" (p. x).

Just as Veysey traces the connection between society and the university, Bender, Chopp, and Frost (1988) reflect on significant connections between the city and the university. Bender is interested particularly in the *parallel* histories of the city and the university, suggesting that educational institutions, like cities, depend upon structures to advance their own particular identity in the world. Drawing on Bender's interest in the relationship between the university and the city, Chopp (2001) imagines the evolution of the university as that of a city—a passage from village to metropolis to global city. For Chopp, few formal systems characterize the village, while formal bureaucracies characterize the metropolis. Through Sassen (1991), she suggests that fluid structures characterize the global cities of today, allowing the city's culture to produce its own singular identity, rather than depending upon imposed structures to produce a fixed and rigid—and often ill-fitting—identity. The same progression can be located in universities (Chopp, 2001).

Chopp suggests that, in its initial evolutionary phase, the university organized itself as a *village,* a civic organization run more by general consensus than by strict design. Later, the university evolved into a more bureaucratic, *metropolis* model, one that is compartmentalized in space, function, and identity. In its more recent form, the university has appeared to organize itself much like a *global city.* Newly emergent, the global city requires open, flexible systems that have replaced the closed and rigid systems of the metropolis. This characteristic of the global city helps new ideas develop out of a culture that is supported, but not defined, by its structures.

Academic advising can similarly be divided into three phases of evolution, depending upon the philosophical and cultural milieu of the university. These phases include advising as an undefined and unexamined activity; advising as a defined, but unexamined activity; and advising as a defined and examined activity (Frost, 2000). Advising functioned primarily as an unexamined and informal activity before such formal curricula as majors and electives were introduced. However, as formalized curricula dominated at institutions of higher learning, advising became a more defined and necessary activity. Yet, it remained largely unexamined. Finally, as advisor training and evaluations became more prominent, advising at most institutions of higher learning evolved into a fully defined and examined activity.

Currently, bureaucracies govern and support most universities, resulting in rigid organizational structures reminiscent of the 20th-century metropolis. Despite all of its evolutionary sophistication, however, this highly structured system may not be the most suitable form for supporting and enhancing academic advising. Perhaps another evolution is necessary—one that emulates the global city by providing an environment more conducive to faculty advising. With these advantages in mind, this chapter asks, can we in higher education replace the current defining bureaucracies of advising with more flexibility in order to foster positive development?

In considering this question, this chapter connects the role of advising with the role of teaching. Bender has argued that academic disciplines and schools of thought perpetually evolve, as do philosophies and cultures of teaching and advising. Theorizing advising as a developing concept—as a vital and organic component of the culture of teaching—this chapter proceeds to explore the development of advising, examining whether current support for academic advising is appropriate for the evolved, and evolving, university in general. Might the current systems actually hinder faculty advising by casting advising as an obligation, rather than highlighting it as a form of teaching? What are some more conducive, organic ways to support faculty in this work?

EVOLUTION OF ADVISING: FROM VILLAGE TO GLOBAL CITY

Undefined and Unexamined: Advising in the Village

Initially, the university functioned as a village. Universities began as organic, civic organizations based on general-consensus values and cultural images, where educated citizens held civic debates in public venues. Likewise, the values and techniques of the Sophists, apparently the first paid teachers, were crucial to the development of Western higher-education philosophy. In fact, their early teaching methods anticipate the model of the university as a village. In his landmark work "The Idea of a University," John Henry Newman (1993) enthusiastically describes the way the early Athenians paced among their students, fielding their questions on topics ranging from physics to astronomy. As Frost (2000) has noted elsewhere, these "gathering[s] seemed as much social as serious, for until that time teaching adults had not been acknowledged as an intellectual activity or granted standing of its own" (p. 4). Socrates, among the first of the Sophists' students, founded his pedagogy upon the debating technique we know as Socratic dialogue; further, some scholars identify the Academy of Athens, founded by Socrates's student Plato in 387 B.C. as the first university in Europe. At this early stage of university development, institutions of higher learning were not organized according to a given system, but rather in response to concerns communicated freely and openly. Leaders met needs as they emerged, and needs, not a predetermined system of government, set the agenda for action.

In this village stage of the university, any advising that took place was undefined and unexamined; there were neither general education requirements to decipher, curricula to follow, nor formal graduation dates pushing students through to the end of the university system. Career guidance was unnecessary as the teachers and students believed theirs was the best and only way to pursue the life of the mind. Although Newman (1993) assures us that "Mind came first, and was the foundation of the academical polity," he also acknowledges that the professors themselves were often "statesmen or high functionaries," and so "it soon brought along with it and gathered round itself, the gifts of fortune and the prizes of life" (p. 58). We can therefore deduce that the students were inspired and encouraged by the successful example of their professors to embrace the political and academic life they embodied. As it was not essential to the earliest universities, what advising took place was informal and unexamined.

Medieval universities commonly functioned as guild systems, similar to today's graduate schools. These universities sought primarily to produce doctors, lawyers, ministers, or scholars. Therefore, the aim of faculty at this time was not to help students map their own individual courses through higher education, but rather to help students follow the paths already paved for them—the same paths followed by the faculty who instructed the students. The activity of advising thus resembled modeling behavior. As such, it was informal and largely unexamined. Class sizes were small, student populations were homogeneous (to import a few terms from today's university); therefore, certain types of advising central to today's complex universities simply were not needed.

Crucially, advising in the university during the village stage occurred in settings that were no different than teaching settings. The inherent connection between teaching and advising has grown less clear as institutions of higher learning have become increasingly varied and complex. Even today, advising and teaching are connected, but that connection needs strengthening in today's larger and more diverse universities.

Toward Examination: Advising in the Metropolis

In the late 19th and early 20th centuries, the introduction of formal curricula—in particular, the introduction of electives into those curricula—emerged with the increasing size and diversity of student populations. This combination resulted in a stronger resemblance between the university and the metropolis, as the place and shape of faculty advising in the university necessarily changed to accommodate this development. In other words, as the university became highly differentiated and compartmentalized, so too did advising. In response to elective choices in the curriculum, faculty advisors needed formally to help students navigate their own individual paths through the curriculum—a process significantly different than the faculty advisor's own journey through higher education. These changes in curriculum, reflecting changes in educational philosophy, ushered in the era of the university as metropolis and led to a greater compartmentalization of advising.

Advising and academic disciplines simultaneously became increasingly compartmentalized. As American universities established academic departments around 1900, faculty evolved professionally and graduate schools evolved formally. Simultaneously, the industrial revolution created the wealth contributing to professional research, and, ultimately, to the dominance of research universities. After World War II, universities began expecting faculty to publish their research results, and the inception of the National Science Foundation (NSF) in 1950 recognized the preeminence of research in today's university. Such recognition contributed not only to the university's evolution into a metropolis model, but also to a shift in advising duties away from faculty.

While research and teaching ideally support and enhance one another, many institutions now privilege research over teaching in tenure and promotion decisions. Granted, research provides outstanding opportunities for advising. As Richard Light (2001) and the Boyer Commission (1998) have illustrated, for example, working with faculty on research projects is one of the components essential to student success. However, research activities are often separated from both teaching and advising. Moreover, with the inherent connection between advising and teaching, faculty who feel pressured to devote most of their time to research might well be tempted to give advising short shrift. The demands of research universities on faculty time could serve as an example of a system that supports faculty but often limits or confines faculty work in other ways.

The imposition of time pressures on valuable citizens is not exclusive to universities. According to Sassen's model of the metropolis, for example, leaders of the metropolis must manage large numbers of busy, mobile, and productive citizens. Soon, advising in the university as metropolis began to resemble a management project to save time for faculty, resulting in such concrete and quantitative goals for students as course requirements and graduation deadlines. Ultimately, these quantifiable demands took precedence over less formalized and more qualitative advising goals such as enhancing self-knowledge and achieving self-realization. University leaders invented complex systems to manage high volumes of student-advisees.

This increased complexity in universities required that advising become a defined activity. Yet in the first half of the 20th century, advising remained a largely unexamined activity. As the century progressed, universities continued to implement such sophisticated innovations as advisor training and evaluations. Further, the National Academic Advising Association (NACADA) emerged not only to legitimate advising as a profession, but also to increase the level of attention devoted to advising.

By the end of the 20th century, new bureaucracies—namely, advising offices separate from academic departments—were firmly in place. The university was beginning to resemble the metropolis in structure. For, as advising gained recognition as a profession—often as separate from a faculty career—many universities established separate advising departments or offices not staffed by faculty. Within these office walls, advising became increasingly compartmentalized—even bureaucratized—underscoring just how far the university had evolved into a metropolis in its own right. On the one hand, these shifts helped to establish advising as an activity worth examining, as proven by an entire discipline devoted solely to research and publication in the field of advising. On the other hand, however, such changes also confined advising as a field within the university.

While structural changes within the academy profoundly influenced the university's development from village to metropolis, this development also resulted from significant demographic shifts. The GI Bill, passed after World War II, allowed unprecedented numbers of students to attend college. And over the course of the rest of the century, student populations became increasingly more diverse in gender, race, ethnicity, and economic class. Formal systems were needed to manage a tremendous volume of students, each facing increasingly broad choices; however, as formalized structures emerged to help support advising, advising became an increasingly defined, complex, and ultimately limited activity.

The size and diversity of today's student population demands certain kinds of advising. For example, first-generation college students may benefit more from different types of guidance than those students whose parents and grandparents attended college. Further, many current university students undergo a kind of "culture shock" that must also be addressed with effective advising. Such advising opportunities are neither positive nor negative in and of themselves, but they require a different set of advising skills than those used simply to help students select courses. Some faculty might be intimidated by the demand for this kind of "cultural guidance" and willingly turn over the responsibility to trained, nonfaculty counselors. While this exchange potentially results in positive consequences if the student gets necessary professional intervention, it may also have negative consequences. For example, when student issues are assigned to nonfaculty counselors, students do not experience the opportunity to develop meaningful relationships with faculty members—a crucial component of student success.

A second modern development affecting the evolution of universities is the increasing presence of technology on university campuses. Technology has assisted the growth of the university and contributed to the success of the university as metropolis. It has also opened up new avenues of learning inside and outside the classroom, and undeniably contributes meaningfully to student and faculty success. For example, email and online discussion groups allow students and faculty to connect more regularly than in the past. But while technology streamlines certain bureaucratic processes and enhances faculty-student interaction, it can also—paradoxically—limit student-faculty interaction by allowing students to register for classes online. This development may well be time-efficient, but it also eliminates the need for the student to see an advisor, resulting in a missed opportunity for both student and faculty.

Nevertheless, some institutions use technology to permit faculty to have more meaningful advisory contact with students. For example, Richland Community College in Texas has placed its orientation materials on CD-ROM. This allows students to view (and to review) these materials at their convenience, while the faculty and advisors who once led the orientation sessions now use that time to meet with students one-on-one in an advising center.

The university as metropolis in its mature form, heralded by the founding of the NSF, is the form most prevalent today, a form in which advising is not necessarily associated with faculty and teaching. While the shift to the university as metropolis required new systems of advising, these new systems evolved as increasingly goal-oriented, further removing students and faculty from the shared experience of inquiry and exploration, and from the shared experience of teaching and learning.

Advising in the university as metropolis underwent many notable developments—structural, demographic, and technological. In this setting, advising necessarily became increasingly formalized. The increased examination accompanying such formalization, including advisor training and evaluation, was often meaningful and productive and resulted in many positive advising strategies. Technology had both positive and negative effects on advising. Further, recognizing advising as a distinct profession and introducing nonfaculty advisors to higher-education institutions provided students with opportunities for more and different kinds of advising. And yet, these developments may ultimately minimize the impact of faculty advising by depriving students of the crucial faculty relationships that foster success. Formal structures gave advising a firm foundation and secured for it a place of prominence within the university; however, such complex structures, once intended to facilitate the examination and definition of advising, have become restrictive. Currently, the bureaucratic measures appear to be waning in productivity and usefulness.

Given this surprising and unexpected failure of highly evolved structures, can current bureaucratic systems ever function again as helpful and enabling systems for faculty advising? Or, conversely, have they become too limiting and confining, hindering faculty in their teaching and advising mission? This next section explores possible new support structures for advising based on open systems, one of the cornerstones of the global city.

Redefining and Reexamining: Advising in the Global City

If advising is in some ways separate from faculty life and confined by bureaucratic aspects of the university, then where will it find its place among university activities in the next stage of the university's evolution? Chopp and Frost argue that today a more open model for the university is developing—a model greatly dependent upon networks and strategy, blurred boundaries, strategic projects, and constructed identities. Sassen calls this form the "global city"; the corresponding stage in academia would be the global university.

Global cities such as Los Angeles, Tokyo, and New York emerge through a combination of ideas, identities, economics, material structures, and new patterns of immigration; and most universities seem to be shifting in ways that compare to Sassen's urban descriptions. Student and faculty populations are now more diverse than ever, as are combinations of disciplines in significant interdisciplinary projects (Light, 2001). This willingness of both students and faculty to cross existing boundaries has extended beyond the campus as well. Universities, once considered nearly self-contained—as illustrated by the truth in the caricatural "ivory tower"—now seek partners endlessly: with one another, with neighborhoods, with science parks and biotech incubators, with international cities, as well as with nonprofit and community-based organizations. This new focus on partnerships might create opportunities for academic advising to come from within—and to reach beyond—the confines of the university.

Two relevant aspects that Sassen identifies in the global city may help to explain the university in its emerging form: structure and culture, and identity.

- **Structure and Culture.** In the metropolis, structures are fixed, and cultures and traditions are retained or lost based on their fit with the structure. In other words, culture represents the essence of the city. However, in the global city, culture and traditions are fixed, while structures change to accommodate them. Culture *produces* the essence of the city.
- **Identity.** If culture *represents* the essence of the metropolis, then culture *represents* its identity. If culture *produces* the essence of the global city, then culture *produces* its

identity. In the global city, identity, particularly, the way people understand the city, reflects change and evolution more easily and expediently.

If, as Frost argues, these points are crucial for understanding how culture and identity function in the university, it seems important to acknowledge the culture of the university as first and foremost a culture of pursuing and transmitting knowledge—as a culture of teaching. Rather than culture merely *representing* identity—as is the case with bureaucratically imposed identities—the global city and perhaps the newly emerging university reverses this relationship, allowing culture instead to *produce* its own identity. Recognizing the university as a culture of teaching would in turn allow advising, as an essential component of teaching, to manifest itself as a part of faculty culture and identity.

Ideally, a university culture of teaching would readily embrace a university culture of advising as it has evolved through the decades. As we have noted previously, research is frequently and erroneously considered antagonistic to such teaching activities as advising, which leads faculty to regard their research identity as detrimental to their identity as advisors. However, nothing could be further from the truth. In fact, faculty research culture could be completely in harmony with faculty's identity as advisors. And it is junction that shall characterize the next evolutionary phase of advising in the global university, a phase worth elucidating with specific strategies.

ADVISING IN THE UNIVERSITY AS A GLOBAL CITY

Developmental Advising and Advising Alliances

Open systems are crucial to the global city or university, but it may be unclear how to foster such systems. First and foremost, advising must be regarded as a developing system. If regarded as a fixed entity, advising will fail to thrive within open systems. In "Advising Alliances: Sharing Responsibility for Student Success," Frost (1994) addresses the creation of open systems for advising within universities and emphasizes the importance of planning skills in developing advising strategies and in advising itself. She then proposes several questions for planners to guide the planning process and to foster the open systems she labels "advising alliances." Such questions speak to the particular identities of the faculty and students. These questions include:

- Who are our students? What specific traits and circumstances define their needs?
- Who are our advisors? What strengths do the most valuable advisors bring to our students?
- What structures will best serve our students and advisors?
- Within these structures, how can we meet student and institutional needs and link all available resources?

Thoughtfully answering these questions will ensure that advising systems grow out of the culture of the university rather than the structural impositions that prescribe them. Furthermore, all levels of the university—students, faculty, and advising staff—should be involved in the planning process, thereby emphasizing the blurred and permeable boundaries of the global system. This will naturally create planning teams. As teams take responsibility for the components they plan, alliances will form, and another valuable pattern for advisors and students will emerge. Ideally, advisors and students adopt the patterns of the teams and also form advising alliances (Frost, 1994).

Essential to any notion of advising alliances is the concept of developmental advising. Developmental advising understands advising as a system of shared responsibility in which the primary goal is to help the student take responsibility for his or her decisions and actions. Many faculty trained in a more prescriptive and intrusive type of advising may be intimidated by advising outside their academic specialty or discipline, but this fear is contrary to the developmental approach. After all, in developmental terms, developmental advising actually requires an "upside-down" approach to advising—developmental advising should start with the general and work its way into the particulars, rather than the other way around. Students and faculty should work on the big questions—What do I want my life to look like? What are my goals?—and then fit the particulars (course requirements, credit hours, and so on) into the larger picture. Unfortunately, most advisors feel pressured to provide the particulars before exploring a student's life plan. Of course, providing faculty with general advising training (including an overview of course requirements and other particulars), underscoring how advising is an integral part of what faculty do, is both important and worthwhile. Yet Light (2001) has found that the two main areas where students need especial guidance from their advisor are making connections and enhancing time-management and study skills. This finding emphasizes that students require interest and support, not just discipline-specific expertise.

Shifting the focus away from discipline-specific expertise, Frost (1994) suggests that "developmental advisors rarely make decisions for students [p. 56]. . . . Developmental advising emphasizes process, not product" (p. 55). Students in Light's study spoke most highly of advisors who asked them to articulate why they wanted to go to medical school or what they meant when they said they wanted to acquire a good liberal arts education or why they chose to attend a particular university. This evidence suggests that helping students to articulate and achieve their goals is an essential part of advising, and not simply discipline-specific. In fact, helping students (and faculty) to articulate and achieve their goals is a crucial element of Sassen's global city, where culture determines systems. As the Boyer Commission (1998) notes, an idea that cannot be fully articulated is an idea that is not fully formed and, therefore, cannot be realized. Articulating the importance of advising via a mission statement, for example, can help universities implement advising as a global activity on their own campuses.

The Importance of Community

The global university emphasizes connections—a crucial element of advising according to Light (2001). For Light, helping students understand the connections between their outside interests and their academic work is of particular importance. A good way to do this, he proposes, is by encouraging students to undertake projects that incorporate their outside interests with their academic interests; a primary factor in the success of these projects is the willingness of an academic advisor to recommend appropriate faculty members to guide or supervise the students in their work. In this way, increased faculty community and knowledge of other faculty's work can enhance advising.

Intellectual community is equally important to student and faculty success. Increased connections between faculty aid both students and faculty in their work. This potential was evident at the first meeting of the executive committee of a newly formed commission at a large research university. Twelve highly respected, well-known, and dedicated faculty members gathered around the table and were surprised to find that, even at such a high level of the university, not everyone knew each other. Even if they had recognized each other by name, the faculty members did not fully understand what members in other departments or schools actually did. However, by the end of their work, these faculty enthusiastically exchanged contact information, realizing with excitement how their research interests overlapped and intersected. Discovering these common bonds not only served to cement a very real sense of community on that particular committee, but also laid the groundwork for potential collaboration in the future.

While strengthening academic connections enhances faculty community, some nonacademic-based community-building events and incentives may benefit the role of advising as well. And while welcoming activities abound to help incorporate new students to a university, far fewer programs exist for new faculty. Andre Auw (1991) describes the positive results of taking a fractionalized department on a retreat where they were not allowed to discuss academic or job activities for the first day. Instead, the faculty members found common ground in areas outside the workplace, sharing interests beyond their academic pursuits. It was only after these other connections had been established that department members could work through their difficulties in the workplace. Afterward, the department set up a series of potluck suppers for the faculty to meet informally and maintain the connections formed on the retreat.

Finally, while advising offers outstanding opportunities for faculty and students to form community bonds as they explore life goals together, the university itself must help unite a community of advisors. Although the relationship between student and faculty should remain the primary advising relationship, students continually seek advice from others on campus—the financial aid office, the career center, individuals in their student-life activities, their peers. For this reason, the university should work to recognize the importance of advising—to make advising a global concern—as it begins to view itself as a perpetually evolving community of advisors.

The Role of Interdisciplinarity

This evolving community of advisors depends upon interdisciplinarity as one trait of the developing global university. Students are increasingly demanding interdisciplinary courses while interdisciplinary work has become more frequent among faculty members. This means that advising too will be shaped by a heightened awareness of interdisciplinarity, rethinking the very activity of advising as itself highly interdisciplinary.

On one level, this means removing bureaucratic barriers to interdisciplinary advising, reinforcing the view of advising as a global concern and a priority. In many current bureaucratic systems, where funding is often channeled through departments, programs that are "outside" departments frequently find themselves orphaned or accused of draining resources from existing departments. Similarly, advising students from "outside" one's department, even if the student and faculty member desire the interaction, might be discouraged as stepping outside one's bounds. In a global system, on the other hand, advising can—and should—happen everywhere and by everyone on campus, without the hindrance of institutional boundaries.

On another level, increased interdisciplinarity might help to diminish current boundaries separating advising, teaching, and research. This is where Sassen's idea of encouraging open systems is especially important, as boundaries in the global city are blurred, flexible, and permeable. Further, the open, global systems characterized by reduced boundaries reflect an institution's culture, and they do so by allowing structures to develop from the ground up. One example of such development is fostering student and faculty initiatives rather than privileging administratively implemented programs. If advising is recognized as a part of the global culture of the university, then it, too, can be fostered and supported as such.

Interdisciplinarity and Extracurricular Activities

Extracurricular activities are an often-overlooked feature of university culture and community—a feature that provides significant opportunities for advising. For example, Light (2001) notes that one way to identify at-risk students is to gauge their involvement in extracurricular activities, noting little social involvement as an indicator of academic hardship. While extracurricular activities give advisors a way to discern the level of their advisees' involvement and adaptation, they also provide faculty with important opportunities to become involved in the university community as faculty advisors for clubs or activities. Such activities give faculty a chance to work with students outside the classroom, and while their academic disciplines and the extracurricular activities may be related, they need not be academically similar. For example, at Rutgers University in the early 1990s, the advisor of the cycling club was a well-respected astrophysicist, and this activity allowed him to interact with students who never took his classes or studied physics.

While we recognize the tremendous demands already placed on faculty members' time, the benefits to faculty for participation in activities "outside" their academic interests might include joy, a "release" from academic pressures, the opportunity to work with a diverse group of people toward a common goal or cause, and opportunities for self-knowledge (Light, 2001). These benefits might also increase faculty retention, another central issue at many universities. After all, if involvement is essential to student satisfaction, could the same hold true for faculty satisfaction?

External Rewards for Advising

In any system, good advising needs to be recognized. Given all the demands on their time, it is understandable that faculty, and untenured faculty in particular, might be tempted to give advising less attention than some of their more quantitative pursuits (such as publishing and teaching). In addition to being recognized, faculty should be rewarded for good advising. As the Boyer Commission (1998) notes, "Faculty course loads must also allow for research mentoring as part of normal operations rather than as poorly compensated overloads" (p. 32). For a university still operating as a metropolis, advising needs to be recognized by individual departments as an important faculty pursuit, but for a school to evolve into a global university, advising must be understood as a top university priority and recognized as such.

In many important ways, advising is one-on-one teaching. One way to make advising more "quantifiable" is to recognize advising as an inherent part of teaching and to document it accordingly. While faculty commonly receive student and peer evaluations of their performance in the classroom, it is not as common for faculty to document and examine the effort of one-on-one teaching (such as mentoring a graduate student or supervising an independent study or thesis). Peter Seldin (1997) maintains that a teaching portfolio is a good place to include documentation of mentoring students, thus underscoring the inherent connection between teaching and advising. Teaching portfolios not only serve as useful documents to present to external evaluators regarding tenure and promotion decisions, but portfolios can also be a tremendous aid for self-reflection and growth for the faculty who create and maintain them, helping to identify teaching and advising strengths and weaknesses and to document the evolution of faculty-teaching philosophies.

In keeping with the focus on teaching and documentation, the Boyer Commission (1998) offers another strategy for "quantifying" teaching and, therefore, advising. As the report admits,

> Evaluating good teaching will always be difficult, but effective integration of research and teaching should be observable. Deans and departments must be pressed to give significant rewards for evidence of integrated teaching and research. . . . When publication is evaluated, attention should be paid to the pedagogical quality of the work as well as to its contribution to scholarship. (p. 33)

Therefore, evidence of integrated advising and research—such as mentoring student research assistants—should be rewarded as well. The Boyer Commission also notes the impact of class size on advising. Large lecture classes will probably never be completely eliminated, and professors cannot realistically be expected to get to know students well enough to mentor them in such settings. Therefore, small-class opportunities should be provided. In the words of the commission, "the teaching schedule of each faculty member needs to provide for small group situations for baccalaureate students and a context that places them in joint exploration" (p. 32).

When talking about external motivations for behavior, time and money are always part of the conversation, and they should not be left out of discussions of advising. While monetary rewards of any kind are generally welcome, the Boyer Commission emphasizes that "rewards for . . . outstanding mentorship need to be in the form of permanent salary increases rather than one-time awards" (p. 34). Faculty at Emory have mentioned that release time would help them enhance their teaching and advising performance, while the Boyer Commission similarly recommends that "committee work at all levels of university life . . . be greatly reduced to allow more time and effort for productive student-related efforts" (p. 34). While this may sound like wishful thinking, more open structures of a global university could facilitate this change.

Finally, we encourage universities to think in new and innovative ways when it comes to rewarding faculty. Financial rewards are always gladly received—and some schools do give their faculty members additional pay for the hours they spend advising or working in the advising center—but they are often not the *only* rewards faculty would welcome. For example, the winner of a teaching prize at one university is awarded with a coveted prime parking space. At parking-starved universities, this is a truly meaningful distinction.

Structural and Institutional Support for Advising

A strong university counseling program is vital to a strong university advising program. Faculty members are often rightfully wary of discussing personal, emotional, and mental health problems with students who should indeed be discussing such issues with trained counselors. But if trained counselors are unavailable, students often seek help wherever they can find it. This puts unnecessary and perhaps even dangerous pressure on faculty and deprives students of the opportunity for appropriate assistance when needed. While a counseling program is undoubtedly an expensive and resource-intensive investment, it is greatly beneficial to the university at large. Universities with medical schools may be able to form partnerships with counseling programs, offering invaluable opportunities for medical, professional, graduate, and undergraduate students—satisfying one population's need for experience with another's for assistance.

A successful advising program in any university also considers very carefully the question of accessibility. For example, at one particular university, academic advisors are located in one building, the career center in another, and the tutoring program in a third building—each approximately a 15-minute walk from the other and—as a result—the source of numerous complaints from students. Such distances make resources less accessible and cause students to lose motivation. However, if physical proximity of advising resources is impossible, electronic proximity poses a solution. Links from one web page to another, or a central web page, would help students with awareness of and access to a variety of advising resources.

Finally, while students repeatedly emphasize the importance of a long-term relationship with a faculty member, faculty advisors certainly do not have to go it alone. Advising can—and should—take place at every level of the university, particularly with peer advisors. While training resident advisors, dorm advisors, and other types of peer advisors may take an initial investment of time, the rewards are incalculable. Peer advisors understand the student's situation better than anyone else, and their availability (particularly if they live in the student's residential area) can be a tremendous asset.

Faculty Culture and Identity

Bearing in mind Sassen's consideration of culture and identity in the global city, it is important to remember that the identity of advisors profoundly influences the identity of the university. Students attest that the faculty who advise them, both formally and informally, indelibly shape their sense of the institution during the students' academic careers. Faculty are the university, and advising is one crucial way to ensure that their identity—the true culture of the university—is advanced.

CONCLUSION

Advising is an essential component of the university's teaching mission. As a developing system, it is helpful to examine the evolution of advising in three stages: 1) as an undefined and unexamined activity, 2) as a defined yet unexamined activity, and 3) as a defined and examined activity. Considering the evolution of advising in conjunction with the evolution of the university helps us to reach a deeper understanding of advising and its place within the university.

Each stage of the university as city has something positive to offer with respect to advising, and so the emerging global university must integrate the best components of each model—in sum, it must redefine and reexamine advising to fit its emerging form and needs. The university as village allowed for advising as an organic activity—small class sizes and plentiful student interaction meant that advising was almost constant and nearly indistinguishable from teaching. Key aspects of the university as metropolis—formal curricula, support structures for advising, advising training and evaluation, and educational technology—were indispensable to the positive growth of advising and to student success. Finally, the university as global city incorporates the positive aspects of past incarnations with the flexibility of open systems. This creates potential for a return to advising as an organic activity that is closely aligned with the mission of teaching and an outgrowth of faculty culture.

Philosophies of advising are inextricably tied to philosophies of teaching and higher education, to theories of what a university should be, and to what university education should provide. The predominance of research universities today has sometimes unfairly, and rather incongruously, resulted in minimizing the importance of teaching—the primary mission and identity of faculty. In order to move beyond this impasse, research universities—and indeed, all colleges and universities—must exist as educational institutions for shared inquiry and exploration, not simply for the transmission of knowledge.

Academic advising is an innovative form of teaching that helps students become involved in their own choices. Providing students with a sense of commitment to their future plans and responsibility for their decisions is the cornerstone of the academic advisor's work. "Planning skills are becoming essential life skills" (Frost, 1994, p. 56), and advising is an ideal format in which to teach these skills. The move toward learning-centered colleges among community colleges underscores this need—Florida's Valencia Community College is one example, where its all-purpose handbook is called a LifeMap and helps students plan not only their coursework but their broader goals as well. Other institutions ask students to create e-portfolios: extensive resumes linked to an online repository of student materials. Such portfolios, that are ideally created with the guidance and input of an advisor, give students a greater sense of their achievements, helping them to see the big picture. Perhaps the emergence of the global university has within it echoes of a return to the village model and to the Sophists—valuing, once again, inquiry over mastery.

At its very core, the university is a community of teachers and learners with unfixed and permeable identities. Faculty can and do learn from their students. Students can teach other students, and faculty can teach other faculty. Of course, the traditional teaching relationship between faculty and students will continue; however, students and faculty must also recognize that they are partners in learning, and that advising emphasizes and underscores this partnership. As the Boyer Commission (1998) noted, "Undergraduates who enter [research] universities should understand the unique quality of the institutions and the concomitant opportunities to enter a world of discovery in which they are active participants, not passive receivers" (p. 11). Such partnership can emerge only through successful faculty advising. And it is through these successes that advising has the power to advance the global university as a community of learners—a community embarking together on a journey of discovery.

REFERENCES

Auw, A. (1991). *Gentle roads to survival.* Boulder Creek, CA: Aslan Publishing.

Bender, T. (Ed.). (1988). *The university and the city: From medieval origins to the present.* New York, NY: Oxford University Press.

Boyer Commission on Educating Undergraduates in the Research University. (1998). *Reinventing undergraduate education: A blueprint for America's research universities.* Stony Brook, New York: State University of New York at Stony Brook for the Carnegie Foundation for the Advancement of Teaching.

Chopp, R. (2001, November 17). *Beyond the founding fratricidal conflict: Scholarship of religion and a renewed public academy.* Presidential address to the American Academy of Religion, Denver, CO.

Frost, S. H. (1994). Advising alliances: Sharing responsibility for student success. *NACADA Journal, 14* (2), 54–58.

Frost, S. H. (2000). Historical and philosophical foundations for academic advising. In V. Gordon & W. Habley (Eds.), *Academic advising: A comprehensive handbook.* San Francisco, CA: Jossey-Bass.

Light, R. J. (2001). *Making the most of college: Students speak their minds.* Cambridge, MA: Harvard University Press.

Newman, J. H. (1993). The idea of a university. In C. Eliot (Ed.), *Essays, English and American.* Danbury, CT: Grolier.

Rudolph, F. (1962). *The American college and university: A history.* New York, NY: Knopf.

Sassen, S. (1991). *The global city: New York, London, Tokyo.* Princeton, NJ: Princeton University Press.

Seldin, P. (1997). *The teaching portfolio: A practical guide to improved performance and promotion/tenure decisions* (2nd ed.). Bolton, MA: Anker.

Veysey, L. R. (1965). *The emergence of the American university.* Chicago, IL: University of Chicago Press.

11 PRACTICAL LEGAL CONCEPTS FOR FACULTY ADVISING

Wesley R. Habley

Few subjects raise more concerns for a faculty advisor than the legal ramifications of the academic advising role. While this is important, the legal concepts and principles presented in this chapter will show these concerns are largely unfounded.

In approaching the issue of practical legal concepts for faculty advisors, several things become immediately apparent. First, it is critical for faculty members to recognize that the role of a faculty advisor is not a casual and informal relationship in the eyes of the courts. Those who serve as faculty advisors act on behalf of the institution in providing students with information and guidance. Second, since most faculty members are not lawyers, it seems counterproductive to rely on the use of legal briefs and case citations as a means of illustrating practical legal concepts. It is not a matter of understanding case law as much as it is of understanding the implications of case law as they can be applied to advising situations. Finally, there is no substitute for competent legal advice. In that spirit, the author provides the caveat that this chapter is written by a person who is not a lawyer and is intended for faculty members who are not lawyers.

This chapter is organized into three major sections:

1) A review of three general legal concepts.
2) An overview of ten basic principles of contract law integrated with practical suggestions for application to academic advising. Although no cases are cited in this section, many of the principles discussed are

grounded in judicial decisions related to contract law.
3) The management of student records and student privacy rights.

GENERAL LEGAL CONCEPTS

The first general legal concept requires the recognition that few judicial outcomes are universally applicable to every institutional setting. Judicial outcomes are predicated on several critical factors:

1) The legal jurisdiction of the courts (state or federal)
2) If federal, the level at which the case was decided (federal district, court of appeals, or Supreme Court)
3) The institutional type (public or private)
4) The basis for the decision (procedural or substantive)
5) Scope of decision (applies only to that specific case or to similar cases in the same jurisdiction)

A second general legal concept is the notion of judicial nonintervention. Simply stated, the concept of judicial nonintervention means that the courts are generally reluctant to intervene in certain areas, including academic matters. Under most circumstances courts will not replace decisions made by experts with their own opinions and judgments. This concept was clearly articulated by Justice Lewis F. Powell in *University of Michigan Regents v. Ewing.* Powell wrote, "Judicial review of academic decisions, including those with respect to the admission or dismissal of students, is rarely appropriate, particularly where orderly administrative procedures are followed" (Regents of the University of Michigan, 1985, p. 16).

The third general concept is that court cases related to academic advising are most likely to be based in contract law. While the concept of judicial nonintervention expands the authority of colleges to make and implement academic policy, it is not a grant of immunity from litigation. Colleges and the individuals they employ may become a party to litigation if they fail to comply with state and federal statutes. Many colleges and universities also become parties in tort litigation involving either negligence or defamation (libel or slander). Although statutory and tort litigation are fairly common in higher education, cases involving faculty advising are not. As a result, this chapter focuses primarily on issues of contract law, the area that produces the preponderance of the cases related to academic advising.

The final general concept is that the agreement between a college and a student is not a single, written, formal contractual document containing terms of agreement between the student and the college. And although the college clearly identifies some of the conditions students are expected to meet, other expectations are not as clearly delineated. Because there is no written formal contract and because at least some policies, procedures, and expectations are not clearly explicated in university publications, many elements of the agreement between the student and the college constitute an implied contract. Faculty advisors would do well to reflect on the semantic difference between the terms *infer* (to derive a conclusion) and *imply* (to hint, suggest, or intimate). It is important to note that the absence of explicit language either in the written policies and procedures of the college or in the advisor's application of those policies can lead to multiple interpretations of those policies. That is, an implication made by a faculty advisor may be interpreted differently based on the inference taken by the student.

BASIC PRINCIPLES OF CONTRACT LAW

The following are ten practical legal principles, rooted in contract law, for faculty advisors to keep in mind as they work with undergraduate students. Included with a description of each of the principles is a discussion of the implications for faculty advisors.

Publications and Other Written Materials Constitute a Part of the College Contract With Students

From the point of initial contact as a prospective student through enrollment and on to graduation, students receive a wealth of printed material from the institution. In addition to the more common publications such as recruitment brochures, college catalogs, student handbooks, course registration information, and program planning worksheets, students receive both formal and informal written communications and correspondence from a variety of institutional representatives. Information included in these publications and materials may be construed as part of the student contract with the college. While one can never be certain that a student will read, much less understand, these materials, clarity and consistency in these communications is essential.

Implications. The implications for faculty advisors are clear. First, all publications and other materials should be reviewed for clarity and consistency. Are the policies and procedures clearly written, or are they ambiguous and prone to multiple interpretations? In addition, college policies and procedures often appear in more than one publication. It is important that the wording be consistent from one publication to another.

Second, publications should be reviewed to determine the degree to which they reflect advising practice. If materials do not coincide with practice, then either the practice or the materials need to be modified. At face value, this appears to be a relatively simple practice. Yet the wealth of publications and materials emanating from multiple sources on campus suggests that this task may be more complex than it seems.

A third implication for faculty advisors is the necessity to participate in training activities that include a periodic department-wide review of requirements for majors and minors to ensure that the information provided by faculty advisors is current, clear, and consistent. Through such training, faculty advisors are more likely to provide students with unambiguous expectations for performance.

The Contract Is Usually the One in Effect at the Time of First Enrollment

Although this principle appears to be straightforward, many institutions now stipulate that enrollment must be uninterrupted for a student to meet the requirements in force when he or she first enrolled. As more students are extending the time it takes to complete a degree, this principle becomes increasingly important. Some students drop out of college for a semester or more for very legitimate reasons. Others attend college only when they are unencumbered by financial, family, or career concerns. Still others return after a long hiatus from higher education.

Implications. It is important for faculty advisors to understand the college policy on catalog applicability. In addition, faculty advisors should check to make sure that the student's enrollment has been continuous. Only then can advisors determine the major, minor, and general education requirements that apply to each advisee.

Under Certain Circumstances, Institutions Can Make Reasonable Alterations in Programs, Policies, and Procedures

As mentioned earlier, the courts' general position of judicial nonintervention recognizes the expertise of faculty in academic decisions. However, there are some circumstances in which the courts may not rely on the precedent of judicial nonintervention. The first consideration involves the definition of a reasonable time period from approval of a program or policy change to its implementation. When modifications are made in programs or policies, it is essential that reasonable notification be given to students. While the courts have provided no absolute definition of the term *reasonable,* it appears that the test of reasonable notification is defined by the scope of the modification. Thus, with a minor change in a cognate course required for the major, it is logical to assume that a short notification period and an informal communication strategy are in order and would probably seem reasonable. On the other hand, a change in the core courses that are required in the major or an overhaul of the general education program would necessitate a considerable time period from approval to implementation. Such a major curricular change suggests the need for a systematic and formal communication strategy to ensure students are fully aware of the change.

A second consideration on changes in program, policy, or procedure is that the changes are reasonable if they are not applied retroactively to students. For example, it is not reasonable to impose a new set of core requirements on individuals who have already completed all, or almost all, of the existing core requirements within a major.

A final consideration on changes in programs, policies, and procedures is that it is not reasonable for institutions to make changes that substantially alter the nature and character of the program without providing current students with the opportunity to complete the original program. Such a situation is likely to exist in cases of financial exigency where faltering programs are discontinued. This situation could also take place in an academic department that wishes to significantly modify or delete a program concentration with a major.

Implications. The advising implications of this principle involve both timing and medium of communication. After spending months (even years) driving curricular changes through the governance process, it is indeed tempting for faculty to move for immediate implementation of the changes. Yet the timing of each curricular change must account for its impact on students who are near program completion, on students who are currently in the program, and in some circumstances, on students who intend to enroll in the program. It is clear that faculty advisors play a key role in assessing the impact of curricular changes on advisees. In addition, faculty advisors should assist in designing a communication strategy that informs students of the impending changes. While minimal changes can be shared informally with students, as change increases in scope and complexity, more formal and official communications are necessary.

Descriptions of Services Provided and Their Anticipated Outcomes Should Be Accurate

Although colleges are long past the stage where wisdom, truth, character, enlightenment, understanding, justice, liberty, honesty, and courage are extolled among the outcomes of a collegiate experience, institutions need to be aware that the services described and the outcomes promised must be delivered. On the surface, this does not appear to be a major problem, but in reality such statements have a large impact on the implied contract. As an illustration, consider the answers to the following questions at your institution:

- What do you say to students who successfully complete remedial or developmental courses in basic skill areas?
- How does your institution (or department) represent its record in job placement?
- How does your institution (or department) represent its record in graduate and professional school placement?
- How does the institution position itself in relation to internships, cooperative programs, student teaching assignments, or study abroad opportunities?
- How does your institution (or department) represent academic advising?

Implications. First, advisors should avoid the tendency to suggest that general benefits always accrue to individual students. In addition, this principle requires faculty advisors to be knowledgeable about a wide variety of on-campus services. This knowledge base should include the types of services available to students, the means for participating in these services, and the intended outcomes of the services. Finally, faculty advisors should avoid making broad claims about student outcomes.

Due Process Is Not Usually Required in Academic Decisions

This principle is an extension of the concept of judicial nonintervention. While students have certain due process rights in matters of student conduct, similar guarantees do not exist in academic matters unless the institution has developed such a procedure. If the courts determine that the campus has established an academic due process policy that was not followed, the campus may be required to exhaust its internal remedies before the case is heard.

Implications. Although due process is not usually required in cases related to academic advising, it is critical that faculty advisors understand the mechanisms in place for students to challenge academic decisions. On many campuses, student challenges to academic decisions move through the administrative hierarchy, from faculty advisor to the department chairperson to the college dean's office to the chief academic affairs officer to the president or chancellor and, in some cases, to the board of trustees. Because this is often the case, faculty advisors must not only understand the appeal process, but also communicate the locus of decision-making authority to advisees who challenge academic decisions. On other campuses, challenges to academic decisions may be handled through hearing panels or other established mechanisms. In addition to understanding these procedures, faculty advisors should become aware of their own discretionary authority. On some campuses faculty advisors exercise broad discretionary authority in the application of policies and procedures, while on other campuses faculty advisors have clearly defined limitations on their discretionary authority. A faculty advisor who exceeds these limitations inadvertently contributes to the implied contract.

Practice Establishes Precedent

Precedents are established by practice. As a result, it is not necessary for a policy to be published for it to become part of the implied contract. Such *de facto* policies are based on academic custom and usage. *De facto* policies differ from *de jure* policies, which are established (usually in writing), widely practiced, or both. On the surface, this principle appears to have limited impact on faculty advising. Nevertheless, legal issues may arise either when faculty advisors apply the practice differentially among advisees or when faculty advisors (usually within the same department) have different interpretations of the same vague or unwritten policy. This principle is similar to the first principle that suggests that advising practice should coincide with published materials. It is, however, much easier to ascertain advisor compliance with published policies and procedures than it is to determine if there is reasonable consistency among faculty advisors in the interpretation of vague or unwritten policies.

Implications. The implications of this principle again underscore the need to clarify the discretionary power exercised by the faculty advisor. In addition, there is also a more far-reaching implication. This principle suggests that faculty advisors within an academic department should meet on a regular basis to review the interpretation of unwritten practices that establish advising precedents. Possible questions for discussion include:

- Are course substitutions consistent?
- Are course waivers consistent?
- Are specific courses in the major required or recommended?
- Are courses within the general education requirement required or recommended?
- How does the department apply independent study credit?
- How does the department determine transferability of specific coursework from other colleges?

These questions represent only a fraction of the *de facto* advising practices subject to individual interpretation.

The Role of Faculty Advisor Has Legal Status in the Eyes of the Court

A faculty advisor is an agent of the institution. This means that the role of faculty advisor is not a casual and informal one. While many colleges publicly state that meeting academic requirements and adhering to various policies and procedures is a student responsibility, from a legal standpoint, it is not possible for advisors (or institutions) to disclaim the responsibility for advice given to students. And it is not possible to disclaim responsibility for the consequences, intended or otherwise, of the advice given. This principle holds true not only for faculty members who have been delegated the authority to provide advising services but also for faculty members who are not formally assigned as advisors. By virtue of their roles as institutional agents, the advice faculty members provide may become a part of the implied contract.

Implications. Once again, it is critical that faculty members recognize that the advice they give puts them in the position of representing the university. A college that relies on a boldly printed catalog disclaimer on "student responsibility" and assumes that the disclaimer absolves faculty (and the institution) of the consequences of inappropriate or inaccurate advising should rethink its position. While it is important to publish disclaimers reminding students of their responsibilities, such disclaimers would probably serve only to mediate the institution's position in court. It is far less likely, however, that the institution's case will be sustained if the sole defense is a published disclaimer.

Advisors' Verbal Statements Can Become Part of the Implied Contract With Students

This principle is particularly true in the absence or vagueness of published procedures or guidelines. Verbal statements would be less of an advising issue if the institution designed and adhered to a set of clearly articulated and consistently applied program requirements, policies, and procedures. Unfortunately, some printed policies are ambiguous, others may be conflicting, and still others are nonexistent. As a result, an advisor's well-intended verbal attempts to clarify these policies may become a part of the implied contract.

Implications. To avoid misunderstanding with advisees, faculty advisors should pay careful attention to the implications of word choice. For example, opening a simple declarative sentence with the words, "Other students have . . ." may be subject to multiple interpretations by an advisee. Does the statement mean any student has . . . ? Does the statement mean the advisee should . . . ? Does the statement mean the advisee must . . . ? Does the statement mean all students will . . . ? Without additional information, a simple declarative statement by a faculty advisor may take on multiple meanings. Any of these meanings could be interpreted as part of an oral implied contract.

The Advisor Is Usually Not Involved in Court Proceedings

In many instances a breach of contract claim does not wind up in litigation until several others in the administrative hierarchy have participated in an appeal process. As a result of an unsatisfactory outcome at the campus level, an aggrieved student is likely to name the board of trustees, the president, the chief academic officer, the college dean, or the department head in breach of contract litigation. If the faculty advisor is named in the litigation, it is important to note that the remedy in a contract law dispute requires the institution to fulfill the implied contract with the student. The remedy involved may require the awarding of disputed credit, the granting of the degree sought, or underwriting the cost of additional coursework to complete degree requirements. Unlike litigation brought under tort or statutory law, the remedy in a contract law case does not involve punitive monetary damages.

Implications. Faculty advisors often ask if they should purchase liability insurance under the assumption that they could be held liable for information shared in the academic advising relationship. Under most circumstances the answer to that question is no. In contract law, the responsibility of the institution and its representatives is to fulfill the contract or to make the contract good. It is possible, however, that faculty advisors could be held liable under statutory law or under tort law if they knowingly acted in an arbitrary or capricious manner that resulted in student harm.

Faculty Advisors Have Minor Tort Liability

The conditions under which tort litigation could take place are fairly specific. The first condition is that either the advisor was not delegated authority or that the advice given was knowingly contrary to institutional policy. The condition of delegated authority has already been discussed in several previous principles. If the advice given was contrary to institutional policy, one of two scenarios is possible. Either the advice was given without knowledge that it was contrary to institutional policy or the advice was given with full knowledge that it was contrary to institutional policy. Each of these situations could create legal problems for the advisor and for the institution. Advice given that unknowingly conflicts with institutional policy could wind up, in time, in a breach of contract suit. Should the student win the suit, the institution would need to take steps to fulfill the contract. If clearly conflicting advice was knowingly given by the faculty member to create a difficult situation for the student, then it is possible that the advisor could be held negligent under tort law and could be liable for punitive damages. Finally, if the advice was given as an expression of the faculty member's dissatisfaction with the particular policy in question, it is possible that the faculty member could be liable for some portion of the breach of contract settlement with the aggrieved student.

The second condition is that the advice given by the faculty advisor resulted in an action taken by the student. Without action on the advice, there is no recourse for the student.

The third condition is that the action taken by the student resulted in the deprivation of some liberty or property. While the first two conditions are plausible, the third circumstance is most likely to occur only when the institution fails to take internal corrective action (for example, granting a waiver or substitution) that results in the failure of the student to complete degree requirements in a timely fashion. A student who fails to graduate on time may be deprived of liberty or property (for example, additional tuition, forgone income, or room and board to complete the necessary courses).

While these three conditions could place a faculty advisor in an unenviable legal position, it is this author's assertion that it is highly improbable an advising situation would reach this level of legal complexity.

MANAGEMENT OF STUDENT RECORDS

While issues related to contract law have a major impact on the practices of faculty advisors, it is also important for advisors to understand statutory regulations and polices and procedures related to the maintenance, dissemination, and privacy of student records. Since 1974, colleges and universities have been subject to the Family Educational Rights and Privacy Act (FERPA) regulations, also known as the Buckley Amendments. FERPA was designed to protect the privacy of student educational records; to establish the rights of students to inspect and review their educational records; to provide guidelines for the correction of inaccurate or misleading data (except grades); and to permit students to control disclosure of their education records, with certain exceptions. Under the Buckley Amendments, colleges may disclose "directory" information. Directory information means information contained in an education record of a student which would not generally be considered harmful or an invasion of privacy if disclosed. It includes, but is not limited to, name, address, telephone number, date and place of birth, major field of study, participation in officially recognized activities and sports, weight and height of members of athletic teams, dates of attendance, degrees and awards received, and the most recent previous educational agency or institution attended. The Buckley Amendments define education records as those directly related to the student and maintained by an educational agency or institution.

The control of directory information may be more stringent because current and former students (18 or more years old) may withhold permission to disclose this information under the FERPA, as amended. On many campuses students may exercise this option by notifying the registrar's office in writing of their intentions. Such notification remains in effect until specifically revoked by the student.

Although FERPA establishes minimum federal standards for the treatment of the student educational record, many states and several colleges and universities have extended the FERPA policies to further restrict access to student records.

The myriad of regulations regarding the management of educational records can create a great deal of confusion for a faculty advisor. To reduce this confusion, several suggestions follow.

First, it is incumbent upon faculty advisors to understand the records policy on their own campus. Almost without exception, the campus registrar administers the student records policy because the registrar is the individual charged with the maintenance and distribution of academic records. The registrar is in a position to share and interpret the student records policy with faculty advisors. In addition, he or she should be consulted on record keeping issues within departments.

Second, it is most prudent for faculty advisors to refer requests for student information directly to the office of the registrar. Faculty may receive such requests from external agencies or from parents. Although these requests appear to be fairly straightforward, faculty members who are unaccustomed to responding to such requests could inadvertently relinquish restricted information about a particular student.

Third, advising files are considered to be educational records maintained by the institution. As a result, FERPA requires that advising files and the records contained therein be made available to advisees for examination upon request. Electronic versions of student advising files are also included under the FERPA definition of educational records. Because the student may review the advising files at any time, those files should include only information that is pertinent to the advising relationship.

In addition, it is recommended that advising files include faculty notes on advising interactions with each student. Such notes should include the topics discussed, the actions taken, and recommendations made. Because these notes are included in the advising file, they are subject to review by students. As a result, the notes should include only objective and factual information. Subjective advisor comments and notes that include advisor opinions on student characteristics or behavior should be avoided. If conference notes reviewed by students include the subjective opinions of the faculty advisor, they may create stress in the advising relationship. Even more critical, subjective opinions may support student allegations in the event that legal action is taken at a later date. Because of this concern, many advisors take the time to review advising notes with the student at the conclusion of the advising appointment.

It is important to note that FERPA does allow for advisors to maintain private notes that are not subject to review by advisees. Such notes must be kept in the sole possession of the faculty advisor and may not be shared with any other person except a temporary substitute for the faculty advisor. Even if such notes may be useful in providing background information in unusually problematic advising situations, faculty advisors do not have privileged communication status in the courts. Although private notes may include greater detail than notes maintained in the advising file, these notes, like those in the official advising file, should also be objective and factual.

CONCLUSION

In an attempt to demystify legal issues that relate to the role of faculty advisor, this chapter provided a basic overview of general legal concepts, a review of principles and implications of contract law, and a discussion of records management and student privacy. It is by no means exhaustive and should not be construed as providing legal advice. While the chapter includes a number of suggestions for faculty advisors, several broadly based implications are apparent. First, there are legal ramifications associated with the role of faculty advisor. Those ramifications are not complex. They focus on clarity and consistency, both in written materials and in communications between advisor and advisee. None of these ramifications should, in any way, stifle the development of quality relationships between advisors and advisees. It is important for faculty advisors to clarify with each advisee the responsibilities and authority of the faculty advisor. Finally, those responsible for faculty advising should include legal issues as an important component of advisor training. Such training must be campus specific because there are few legal principles that apply to every campus. Training should include a review of the campus policy on records administration and student privacy conducted by the registrar as well as an overview of contract law provided by college legal counsel. By understanding the implications of various principles of law, faculty advisors should be in a position to provide quality service to advisees with confidence and commitment.

REFERENCES

Regents of the University of Michigan v. Ewing, 474 U.S. 214 (1985).

ADDITIONAL LEGAL RESOURCES

Becker, B. A. (2000). Legal issues in academic advising. In V. N. Gordon & W. R. Habley (Eds.), *Academic advising: A comprehensive handbook* (pp. 58–70). San Francisco, CA: Jossey-Bass.

The Family Educational Rights and Privacy Act (FERPA), 20 U.S.C. Section 1232g (1974).

Gehring, D. D., & Letzring, T. D. (Eds.). *The College Student and the Courts* (quarterly newsletter published by College Administration Publications).

Kaplan, W. A., & Lee, B. (1995). *The law of higher education* (3rd ed.). San Francisco, CA: Jossey-Bass.

12 FACULTY ADVISING AND TECHNOLOGY

Eric R. White and Michael J. Leonard

Like nearly every other human endeavor, academic advising has been the beneficiary of the technological advances made primarily in the last 25 years. Technology has especially been applied to the more routine functions of academic advising, resulting in an altered definition of academic advising—one that encompasses a more sophisticated and student-centered approach and that frees faculty advisors to pursue the more meaningful aspects of the endeavor. The introduction of technology in academic advising has thus served its historical purpose: liberating the user and allowing more time for those aspects of advising that depend upon interpersonal exchange and the expertise that faculty advisors possess.

THE INFUSION OF TECHNOLOGY INTO ADVISING

The immediate pretechnological era for advising usually included the use of printed check sheets for majors, forms and cards that required signatures of both student and advisor, and arena registrations where students gathered either all at once or staggered over a period of time to collect the necessary forms that then constituted an academic schedule.

At those institutions that have embraced technology, these relics of the pretechnological era have virtually disappeared. They have been replaced with electronic degree audits, email exchanges, web-based advising interactions, and touch-tone telephone and Internet registration protocols. For routine advising tasks, what was once done on paper is now done electronically, and what was once done via a face-to-face meeting is now handled through email exchanges and virtual advising interactions on the Internet.

As with all changes, the availability of such technology did not necessarily mean universal acceptance. Skepticism, still very much alive in higher education, has been a stumbling block for academic advising administrators. Related campus offices usually accept technological advances first. It is often these changes by offices peripheral to the advising endeavor that have prodded advising administrators to rethink how those who engage in advising will manage their day-to-day work.

Advisors who found the one-on-one contact with their advisees the most satisfactory part of their work often saw technological changes, especially the personal computer, as the downfall of the personal advising interview. This perceived alienation needed to be addressed by advising administrators by introducing faculty advisors to the new technologies and assisting them to achieve a level of comfort with the technology.

In most instances students have been ready to accept new technologies without question. Especially with first-year students, this is simply a case of not knowing what the previous mechanisms were for handling a specific advising interaction. And within a period of about five years, students' memory of a previous advising tool is lost.

While some advisors lament the intrusion of technology into their work, new technologies are here to stay. Some advisors remember the flaws or limitations of the original products, but over time these flaws have been eliminated and enhancements added. Faculty advisors who have not kept abreast of the rapidly changing technology may base their distrust on previous releases and therefore be unwilling users of the technology.

The business of convincing them that, in some cases, new ways of doing things is better remains the challenge for advising administrators. Administrators must demonstrate to faculty advisors that new technologies need not be burdensome, that many chores previously done by hand can now be accomplished electronically, and that much more information is available than ever before.

Likewise, faculty advisors need to know that the new technologies are empowering students to access materials and to interact with their own advising databases in new ways. For example, at many universities students can access their own degree audits or create "what if" scenarios by plugging their completed courses into a template for any major at their college or university. In the past these functions were available only to the advisor.

Faculty advisors need to develop a level of comfort with available technologies so they can function with optimal effectiveness. This means knowing how to navigate the advising web sites of the institution, how to determine the availability of courses, and how to use an electronic catalog when no paper copy exists.

THE WEB

The World Wide Web provides access to an abundance of information that can assist faculty in their work as advisors, teachers, and researchers. Browsing the web, bookmarking important web sites for later access, and using the navigational tools in a web browser have become basic skills for faculty to carry out their various professional roles. These tools have now become as fundamental to a faculty member's work as was knowing how to use a card catalog a mere ten years ago.

Locating Key Academic Web Sites

In their role as advisors, faculty members often express concern that they do not know where to obtain information about their institution's academic programs, policies, rules, and procedures. An increasing number of key academic resources (college catalogs, advising handbooks, policy manuals, and rulebooks) have been placed on the web, and in some cases have completely superseded the paper versions. Even when paper versions continue to exist, they often quickly become out of date, inaccurate, and incomplete compared to their dynamic web counterparts. It is critical that faculty know where to find these academic documents on the web and how to use them.

Many school web sites have links to advising resources on their home page or on department and school sites. At some institutions, there is an institution-wide academic advising web site that will help students and faculty navigate the myriad of web pages that comprise the institution's body of academic information. Department web sites and printed handbooks may include lists of web sites that contain key academic resources.

Searching the Web

One of the most significant (and often the most frustrating) challenges in using the web effectively is locating specific information dispersed across the millions of web sites that currently exist. This is usually accomplished using search engines—web pages that take input (keywords, phrases, and other text) from the user, search through a massive number of web pages, and return a list of pages that contain the requested keywords.

Many institutions include a search engine on their home page so that users can limit their search to institution-specific web pages. For such search engines, colleges often use commercial search companies such as Inktomi and Google. For a college site, these search engines will look through only those web pages belonging to that institution. When used as stand-alone commercial sites, the same search engines will typically look through a significant portion of all web pages on the Internet.

Knowing how to use a search engine effectively can save much time and frustration. Unfortunately, there is not a single standard for conducting searches used by all search engines. Most search engines provide a help page that explains some of the characteristics and features of that particular search engine and offers suggestions on how to receive the most accurate results.

Probably the most basic and important factor to know about a search engine is what form of logic it uses to search for the words and phrases entered by the users. For example, if a search engine uses "or" logic, it will find and retrieve all web sites that contain any one of the words entered. If it uses "and" logic, it will retrieve only those web sites that contain all of the words in the search. The type of logic that is used and how to control it is usually explained on the search engine's help page.

EMAIL

Email is a virtually ubiquitous mechanism for communication on college and university campuses. In some cases, email has become the accepted medium of written communication, replacing paper.

In fact, email has proven itself to be an effective means of communication between advisors and their advisees.

Despite the sometimes halting first steps to incorporate email into the communication repertoire of advisees and advisors, it is clear that it is time to capitalize on this technology in advising. Email not only removes the cumbersome task associated with paper communication, it also eliminates the frustration of telephone tag that often hampers communication.

One concern advisors sometimes have about email is that students will not read or respond to messages (students have this prerogative with paper communication as well), but as less time is invested in email communication, the frustration associated with a lack of response can be lessened. If faculty advisors inform their advisees that email will be used to communicate and that responses to email inquiries are expected, such problems can be eliminated.

POTENTIAL SHORTCOMINGS OF EMAIL

As with all forms of communication, there are potential problem areas with email. Advising coordinators should make a discussion of email advising limitations a part of the professional development of faculty advisors. The most critical topics of discussion include the following.

Loss of nonverbal cues. Students may mean one thing in an email message, but without seeing a frown, a shrug of the shoulder, or a tear, an advisor might miss the most critical aspect of the interaction.

Inappropriate information. The partial anonymity of email could encourage some students to share more than should be handled in an email message. It is recommended that email correspondence be limited to the more routine or mundane aspects of advising.

A corollary to this concern is that students might share confidential information. Because email technology does not always ensure confidentiality, all conversations of a confidential and private nature should take place in private, face-to-face communications.

Identity. One can't always be sure who is sending an email, so advisors have to be careful that they are responding to their advisee and not to someone else using the advisee's email address. Commercial email addresses can compound this problem because of students' propensity to use nicknames that often obscure the their identity.

Volume. One of the most recurrent student complaints about advising is the lack of availability to see an advisor. The judicious use of email can cut down on this problem. In fact, given the ease of email communication, faculty advisors might find themselves flooded with such communications. It is far easier for a student with a question to go to a computer and send off an inquiry than to make an appointment to see an advisor.

Complex questions. Students sometimes ask complex or multiple questions in one email inquiry. In some cases, asking the student to make an appointment might be more appropriate than trying to respond by email. In the case of complex questions, the advisor might not interpret the question correctly or the student might have left critical information out of the inquiry. In addition, without face-to-face interaction, the advisor might miss some nonverbal cue or the opportunity to quickly follow up with a question of clarification or a nod of understanding.

Effective Email Communication

Woolston and Lipschultz (1997) provide a useful summary for faculty advisors of what works and what does not when engaged in an email dialogue. Faculty advisors should consider this list when contemplating correspondence via email with their advisees.

What works. Email is effective for quick communications such as short questions and responses, following up on advising meetings, announcements, surveys, back patting, and sharing good news. It can also be effective for longer communications, such as cathartic messages from anguished students or messages in which the advisor or student thinks out loud. Email is also useful for other aspects of advising, such as retention, distance correspondence, and establishing a relationship.

What does not work. Some communications are better done in person. Long questions and long answers, for instance, aren't appropriate for email, nor are short answers to long questions. Long and involved suggestions are also probably better done face-to-face. Disapprobation doesn't work well in email communications. And too many messages can become a problem for advisors. Advisors should avoid promising a short (one- to two-day) response time.

Advisors should also be careful when sending messages to multiple recipients that the information is appropriate and applicable for all.

LISTSERVS

Most faculty members are familiar with the concept of a listserv, a type of software that facilitates email communication among groups of individuals. Faculty may be members of listserv discussion groups related to their interests and concerns in a particular academic domain. Faculty may also moderate listservs for their classes, allowing (or requiring) students to participate in email discussions related to the class. Listservs can also be used to broadcast information from a single source (such as a department office) to a large group of individuals (such as the faculty in a department or all of the students in a college or major). When listservs are used as a one-way broadcast medium, individuals within the group cannot send messages to the rest of the list directly, as they can in most professional and course-related listservs.

Listservs as Advising Tools

A listserv consisting of a faculty member's assigned advisees can make communication with those advisees much easier. With an advising listserv, faculty advisors can send a single email message simultaneously to all of their advisees, perhaps informing the students when they will be away from the university for an extended period, when their office hours have changed, or when it is time to discuss course selections for an upcoming semester.

But faculty advisors can use listservs as much more than mass-communication tools. Listservs of advisees can be used to promote discussion among advisees, much as a listserv of students enrolled in a particular class can facilitate discussion among them. Moderated by the faculty advisor, a discussion list of advisees could address such topics as the purposes and meaning of general education in the undergraduate curriculum, concerns about choice of major, the variety of educational opportunities available at the institution, learning about and preparing for specific careers, and similar issues. The thread of the discussion could be archived for other students to read later, particularly those who are later added to the faculty member's advising roster. Discussion topics could be changed on a regular basis or after they have ceased to generate new ideas, questions, or points of debate.

At most institutions, listservs comprising the students enrolled in an instructor's courses or the advisees assigned to a faculty member can be set up through the institution's information technology (IT) office or by IT support staff in the faculty member's department. To use the listserv simply as a way of disseminating information to advisees, the faculty member needs to know only the email address of that list. To use the listserv as a discussion medium requires more knowledge of how to manage a list.

STUDENT INFORMATION SYSTEMS

Student information systems (SIS) are integrated suites of software programs that typically include components for human resource management, business transactions, course management, and access to student records through the web or other electronic means. SIS programs may be developed locally by an institution solely for its own use or purchased from outside vendors and then modified for a specific institution's use. Some widely used commercial SIS programs include SCT Banner, Datatel, and PeopleSoft.

From the perspective of academic advising, some of the most useful features of an SIS are degree audit programs, advisor access to student records, faculty access to course enrollment information, appointment scheduling, and, for students, online course registration and access to their own academic records. Often these SIS features are available on the web 24 hours a day, every day.

Degree-Audit Systems

One of the most popular components of SIS software is a degree audit program, which allows the advisor and student to easily check his or her progress toward graduation. Typically, a degree audit program takes a student's electronic academic record (courses taken, grades earned, and so on) and matches it with the requirements for a particular major, showing which graduation requirements have been fulfilled and which are yet to be completed. Some audit systems will permit "what if" requests to be submitted by a student or advisor for any major offered by the institution or even for majors at other schools. The audit itself may be presented as a printout, an administrative screen view, a web page, an email message, or some combination of these.

The results presented by most degree audit systems will include such student-specific information as the student's major, class standing, grade average, assigned advisor, minor(s) declared, exceptions and substitutions approved, and requirements waived. More sophisticated degree audit programs may also provide color-coded web views and the opportunity to request different types of audits (for example, audits showing only the requirements that have not been completed, requirements that have been completed, courses required for entering the major, or core requirements). Web view audits may also include live links to course descriptions, the college catalog, and departmental lists of approved supporting courses.

The obvious advantage of an automated degree audit system is the speed and ease with which a student's academic progress can be checked by the student or the student's advisor. The not-so-obvious disadvantage is that the costs involved in establishing and maintaining such a system can be significant to the institution. One million dollars or more is not an uncommon price for the purchase of a commercial SIS; the ongoing monetary outlay for upkeep may be just as significant. The staff time involved in establishing and maintaining such a system, including the continuous updating of degree requirements and making degree substitutions and exceptions for individual students, can also be significant.

Faculty Access to Advisees' Records

Most SIS types provide online access to individual student records for a variety of users (faculty, administrators, professional advisors, support staff, students, and sometimes even parents). Advising administrators should ensure that access is made available to faculty advisors to assist them in their day-to-day activities with advisees.

The kinds of institutional data that are available to advisors through an SIS vary with the system and with the institution, but typically advisors should be able to view their advisees' transcripts, grade reports, and course schedules. Other student-specific information that may be available includes admissions data, semester and cumulative grade averages, credits earned, placement test results, mailing addresses, telephone numbers, email addresses, and possibly ID photographs.

Through the SIS, advisors can help students calculate semester and cumulative grade averages based on anticipated grades, assist students with online course registration, and look up transfer course equivalency. Some systems prevent advisees from registering for courses until they have met with an advisor and the advisor issues a code that will activate registration.

Institutional Data

A plenitude of institutional data is available to assist faculty members in their work with their advisees. Whether a faculty member wishes to create a comprehensive advising roster with specific data about each advisee or to conduct research on advising, there are ways to access the necessary data other than relying on predetermined output from SIS. For faculty advisors who wish to do research using student data, most institutions can provide access to student records stored in the institution's student records databases. Data warehouses, snapshots of student records extracted from the "live" student records database, allow researchers to access student data directly using common database or spreadsheet software rather than depending on programmers to write arcane ad hoc programs in order to access the live databases directly. Data warehouses may be updated on a regular schedule, perhaps only once a week or once a month, so the data are not as accurate as those found in the live database. This may not be a significant issue, however, for purposes of downloading an advising roster or conducting research.

Note Taking and Record Keeping

For ethical, professional, practical, and legal reasons, it is important that advisors keep notes of all advising contacts with their students. These notes may be informal, handwritten on paper, and stored in the faculty member's office or a departmental file room, or they may be more formalized and recorded electronically in centralized institutional databases.

Some SIS provide the opportunity to record advising notes electronically. Electronic notes may be free-format text, abbreviated codes that summarize the content of the advising contacts, or both. One of the specific advantages of recording advising contacts electronically is that the notes can be shared with other faculty members, advisors, or staff who might have contact with a specific student. And faculty advisors can quickly review previous contacts with individual students or read about contacts students have had with other academic advisors who use the system. This ability to share records is particularly helpful when the student changes advisors since it eliminates the need to transfer paper advising notes.

STUDENT-SPECIFIC WEB APPLICATIONS

Faculty members need to know what web applications their advisees are using to support their own educational planning. Do they register on the web? If so, how does that work for them? Do they need a code from an advisor to activate their registration? What other procedures, such as schedule adjustments, extensions for course completions, declaring or changing majors, and withdrawing from the institution, can students process via the web? Do they need an advisor's or an administrator's permission to do it? Can they take placement tests or course examinations on the web? Are there electronic forms on the web that students can use, for instance, to apply for admission, request financial aid, or to register for study abroad? Knowing what processes students use to effect academic actions at an institution can assist faculty in their advising.

Interactive Advising Systems

The trend in today's web services for students and academic advisors is toward integrated systems that provide multiple services and more sophisticated levels of interaction. These web systems include most or all of the following features.

An emphasis on the student perspective. The student perspective refers to using terminology that students use (such as "records" or "registration" instead of "registrar") and examining ways students use the web to obtain institution-specific information or process academic transactions.

Decision-making tools. Sophisticated web systems use artificial intelligence to provide students who have questions or are preparing to make important academic transactions with informed decision-making assistance.

Customization. Advanced systems permit users, whether students, faculty, or staff members, to customize the look and feel of the web site, in effect allowing each user to create a "my advising site" with unique specifications and preferences.

Proactive communications. Employing "push" technologies, these web systems determine who the student is (by requiring the student to log in to the system using a unique ID and password) and then use that knowledge to "push" individualized information to that student without the student asking for it. The individualized information is displayed in an on-screen message area as soon as the student logs in to the advising system. For example, an institution's records office may want to push a message to a student to remind him or her to file the appropriate paper (or electronic) form to graduate at the end of the current semester. The bursar's office may want to push a message indicating that the student needs to pay an outstanding tuition bill by a certain date. An advising office may want to push a message to the student indicating that the student needs to declare a major before the end of the current semester. In all cases, the pushed messages are sent only to a select group of students based on specific characteristics.

Increasing complexity of interaction. When the web was new, there was very little interaction between a user and a web page. Web pages displayed static textual information, and web users simply read what was on the page. As web sites advanced in complexity, they began to provide increasing levels of interaction with the user. Now, students can typically participate in varying levels of interaction, from *viewing* personal records (grades, schedules, transcripts, and financial aid information) to *updating* personal records (home/local addresses, telephone numbers, and passwords) to *manipulating* data (calculating grade averages based on predicted grades or modifying class schedules based on personal preferences about course meeting times, instructors, credits, and general education category) to *making decisions* with the help of the advising system (to drop courses, take a leave of absence, or withdraw from the institution).

Advisors are not neglected in this equation. Advanced web-based advising systems can also provide academic advisors with support services that include many of the same characteristics as the student-specific components.

eLion

The Pennsylvania State University's "eLion" is a specific example of an interactive advising system. Created by a team of faculty, professional advisors, IT staff, and representatives from the university's records office, eLion provides web-based services to faculty, advisors, and students. The original intent of the system was to supplement student-advisor relationships and engage students in interactive inquiry for informed educational planning. The system is available almost 20 hours a day, seven days a week, making it much more accessible than any one advisor would be. The information and advice that it provides on a variety of academic topics is consistent, accurate, and complete

Through eLion, faculty members can download class lists in a variety of formats, view a list of students who are enrolled in their classes but who do not meet the prerequisites for those classes, and submit and review end-of-semester grades for students in their classes.

Faculty and professional advisors can view online advising rosters; send email directly to all assigned advisees at once or to specific advisees selected from their rosters; view their advisees' academic records, including placement test results, course schedules, semester grades, and complete academic transcripts; assist students in calculating grade averages; and request degree audits for any student, for any major.

Currently enrolled students can register for courses, check their financial aid, explore majors, find out about their assigned advisor, pay their bills, request degree audits, declare a major, calculate grades averages, determine grades necessary to raise averages to a desired level, apply for work study jobs, and receive individualized, expert advice about dropping a course late or withdrawing from the university.

Providing interactive advising to students is not intended to replace contacts with advisors; rather, it is intended to raise the level of discourse between students and advisors by replacing some of the routine information giving activities with more substantial activities such as mentoring, discussing the meaning of one's education, and long-term educational planning.

The most interactive component of the student section of eLion is the "late course drop" application. At Penn State, students are permitted to late drop courses from the 11th day through the 12th week of a 15-week semester. In order for students to make a well-informed decision about late dropping a course, they need to know the late drop policies as well as the outcomes of, restrictions for, and alternatives to late dropping courses. Prior to the introduction of the eLion late course drop application, students were required to obtain written permission from an academic advisor before they could late drop a course. Waiting until the last minute, however, students often simply obtained the necessary signature without receiving much, if any, advice about late dropping a course.

The challenge that the eLion development team faced was designing an interactive program that would use artificial intelligence to provide advice to students about late dropping a course. The program would consider the student's past academic record, his or her responses to questions posed by the interactive application, and the expert consensus of academic advisors at Penn State related to late dropping courses. This program was also designed to simulate a one-on-one advising contact between a student and an advisor (albeit a virtual advisor).

After logging in to eLion and selecting the late drop application, students are greeted by the virtual advisor, who asks, "Which one of your courses are you thinking about late dropping?" Students are then presented with their current schedule and can indicate the course. Students are then informed of the deadline for late dropping the selected course (part-semester courses have different late drop deadlines than full-semester courses) and are shown how many total late drop credits they are permitted to use (this varies with a student's status), how many have already been used, and how many remain.

On the subsequent web page, students are asked to indicate which major they would like to use in being advised about dropping a particular course (the consequences of dropping a particular course vary from major to major). The impact of late dropping an introductory biology course on a premed major will be quite different than the impact of dropping that same course on a English major. Students may choose to be advised using their current major or any other Penn State major.

Next, students are asked why they are thinking about late dropping the course. Students are presented with a list of eight common reasons derived from surveys of the advising community at Penn State.

After students indicate a reason for wanting to late drop a course, advice is given on how to deal with that particular issue. For example, if students indicate that they have fallen too far behind in the class, the virtual advisor suggests ways of rearranging their schedule to have more time to spend on class work, speaking to the instructor about the availability of tutoring or individual assistance, or (when the course is required by the major) considering late dropping a different course to free up more time to spend on the required course.

On the next screen, students are asked to indicate what grade they expect to earn in the course and whether they have verified the grade with the instructor. Often students who are planning to late drop a course will change their mind after talking to the instructor and discovering that there are ways to salvage the class and earn an acceptable grade.

On the next screen, the students are given possible implications of dropping the specific course with the expected grade, such as the need to repeat the course if it is required in the student's major, the possible impact on financial aid, and the effect on the student's chances of qualifying for a particular major. Students may then select another major for which to receive advice or a different reason for late dropping the course; either would result in a different advising scenario.

Finally, a summary of the advice and the outcomes of late dropping the specific course are displayed, and students are asked whether or not they wish to late drop the course at that time. If students indicate that they definitely do want to late drop the course, then the late drop is processed, the change is verified in an updated schedule, and a message that the course has been dropped is sent by email to the students and to the assigned advisor.

This scenario is just one of many that could occur, depending on students' academic record, the course in question, and the answers to questions posed in the application. Other specific factors that affect the advice include student-specific factors (such as registration status; implications of becoming a part-time student;

status as a student-athlete, university scholar, or participant in a study abroad program) and course-specific factors (number of credits; whether the course is required in the specified major; whether the requested drop is taking place before, during, or after the late drop period for that course). In cases where the scenario is too complex to be explicated through eLion, students are referred to an academic advisor to discuss the situation in more detail before deciding whether or not to late drop a course.

A similar eLion application is available to students who are contemplating withdrawing from the university before the current semester ends. A series of questions helps determine students' reasons for considering a withdrawal, the pros and cons of taking such a serious action, alternatives to withdrawing, and the specific outcomes that will or might result if the withdrawal is processed.

Other types of interactive advising provided by eLion include an application that calculates the student's semester and cumulative grade averages based on predicted grades and another application that calculates the grades a student would need to earn in order to raise the cumulative grade average to a specified level within a specified amount of future credits. In addition to displaying the numerical outcomes of these calculations, eLion also provides advice about the predicted grades or target averages, such as warning the student if predicted grades would result in deficiency points or alerting the student that it is mathematically impossible to earn the grades needed to reach a desired cumulative average.

Both of these applications are also available in the advisor's section of eLion so that advisors can use them during individual advising contacts and discuss the results with the students in person. eLion also permits the advisor to send the results of some of these applications (such as grade average calculations, target grade calculations, degree audits) directly to the student's email account.

Some universities have already implemented interactive academic advising web services such as eLion, and others are working toward that goal. Students are coming to expect this level of engagement, and they will expect advisors to provide even better academic advising as they relate to advisors with more complex and challenging issues.

FUTURE APPLICATIONS

As new technologies emerge, the ways that academic advising is delivered to students, electronically and in person, will undoubtedly change. There are, however, some current advances in technology that appear to be on the brink of having a significant impact on advising.

Handheld Computers

Handheld computers, sometimes referred to as personal digital assistants (PDAs) or just "handhelds," have become much more common since 2000. Small enough to be held comfortably, these diminutive computers can store and display appointment calendars, to-do lists, address books, documents (including full-length books), spreadsheets, email, and handwritten notes. Now even high school students are beginning to carry handhelds in favor of daily planners and notebooks. When these students arrive on college campuses, they will expect to find institution-based services that will accommodate their use of handheld devices. Some colleges and a few academic departments already provide special versions of their web pages that can be downloaded into handheld devices for future reference. These specially developed web pages may contain official institution news, recent updates, contact information, academic calendars, and even parking information.

It is not difficult to conceive of handheld versions of advising handbooks, college catalogs, course schedules, transcripts, degree audits, and other types of academic information being made available to students and advisors alike. Faculty advisors could also make their web pages, office hours, biographies, and advising philosophies available for their advisees to download to their handhelds.

That handhelds are not just a fad is evident in several recent developments. The University of South Dakota, for example, issued handheld computers to all incoming freshmen in fall 2001 to enhance the educational experience of students at the university and to equip them for future learning. At the University of Virginia, students enrolled in several different courses used handheld devices to read and electronically annotate their assigned texts. As prices decrease and functionality increases, handhelds will become more prevalent in many areas of society, especially in higher education, business, and medicine.

Video Conferencing

Traditional video conferencing, which provides live, two-way audio and video transmission, usually requires specially equipped studios for all of the conference participants. The advantage is that some of the participants can be located in a studio on campus while other participants can be anywhere else in the world, as long as an appropriate studio is also located there. Some colleges have used video conferencing to provide orientation programs to groups of students who live a large distance from the institution but only a short distance from each other and from a studio that can receive the orientation program and provide the necessary two-way communications.

Another, more flexible type of video conferencing is made possible through inexpensive web cameras (web cams) that connect to personal computers. Using software provided with the web cams and existing modem or Ethernet connections, two people can carry on a conversation from the privacy of their own offices and homes but with the added advantage of being able to see each other. At this point the video transmission is typically not high quality, but it is sufficient to allow the participants to read each other's facial expressions, and to some extent, body language—important factors in providing and receiving academic advice. Some institutions, particularly those with a significant enrollment of distance education students, have already begun to use web cams as a method of providing academic advising to their students. Web cams might also be useful in providing advising to students who are studying abroad, on leaves of absence, taking summer courses away from the institution, or who have not yet matriculated at the college. Faculty might use these inexpensive communication devices to advise students at a distance.

Webcasts

Webcasting is a relatively new technology that permits data such as PowerPoint presentations to be broadcast live, along with simultaneous audio from one or more presenters, via the web. Participants in a Webcast need only to log in to a specific web site from which the presentation is being broadcast. Webcasts may also provide a "chat" feature that permits participants to type questions to the presenters or comments to other participants. In some

Webcasts, participants may also be able to provide their questions and comments via live audio. Webcasts are currently used primarily for professional development purposes, such as the ongoing training of physicians, business professionals, and even academic advisors. But the potential exists for Webcasts to be used in advising situations as well. Since the participants in a Webcast can be located anywhere as long as they have a connection to the Internet, it is not necessary for them to go to a special studio or purchase special equipment. In addition, Webcasts can be archived, including the participants' typed comments and questions, for later viewing by those who could not participate in the live Webcast as well as by those who want to review what they saw and heard during the original Webcast.

Webcasts could be used to provide new student orientation programs as well as advising sessions dealing with exploration of majors, career decision making, and other topics of interest to a particular group of students. Because these presentations can be archived, they would need to be "produced" only once, but could be used many times by many students at different times and locations. Individual faculty members could produce live Webcasts to introduce themselves to and answer questions for new advisees and then make the archived Webcasts available to students in later semesters. Panels of faculty advisors could produce Webcasts to communicate information about the similarities and differences in related majors or to discuss the variety of career opportunities available to students in their departments.

PROFESSIONAL DEVELOPMENT AND TRAINING

Technology, especially the web, has placed a great deal of information about academic advising and the advising profession in front of faculty advisors. Of particular note are the following sites.

The National Academic Advising Association

The web site for the National Academic Advising Association (NACADA) is more than a compendium of the various services of the association. It also includes pages that can be used for the professional development of advisors. Advising administrators should use the site in their professional development efforts. The frequently asked questions section addresses a full range of issues important to faculty advisors, such as cultural issues in advising, privacy concerns, working with undecided students, and advising assessment.

The NACADA web site also includes the association's Statement of Core Values and the Academic Advising Standards and Guidelines developed by the Council for the Advancement of Standards in Higher Education (endorsed by NACADA), which provide an ethical, value driven, and quality assurance basis for academic advising. These documents provide the acceptable standards for establishing and maintaining an academic advising program.

Faculty advisors might also find the section on past winners of Outstanding Advising Programs of interest, especially when contemplating changes to their own advising program.

The NACADA Commission on Technology in Advising maintains its own web site. This site provides access to a great deal of information through links to other sites. In the section Academic Advising Resources on the Internet, faculty advisors can find links to information on such topics as academic advising guides and manuals; advising special populations; business, law, and health professions; graduate school information, mailing lists, and discussion groups; and test preparation and testing services.

One of the projects of the commission is the Advising Technology Education Center. This site includes information, for example, on design considerations for a successful advising web site. Such information would provide insights into what constitutes a useful advising site not only to advising administrators but also to faculty advisors.

NACADA also maintains a National Clearinghouse for Academic Advising. Via this site, advisors and advising administrators can request information and sample documents as well as citations on all aspects of advising. Such information can be especially useful when developing professional development programs.

The Mentor

The Mentor: An Academic Advising Journal, published by the Division of Undergraduate Studies at Pennsylvania State University, is an online publication devoted to academic advising. This site is available free of charge and can be used for a variety of purposes. Advising administrators can use the various posted articles or forum topic discussions for professional development activities. Administrators can also encourage faculty advisors to submit articles for publication.

Local Information

Even at a local level there is much advising information available to faculty. As part of professional development activities, faculty advisors need to be made aware of such resources, how to navigate them, and perhaps how to develop their own. The Internet provides the opportunity for online catalogs and advising handbooks, documents that once were out of date soon after they were published, but now can be maintained more easily for accuracy. Faculty can be encouraged to provide their input into the nature of such sites. Faculty can also be encouraged to develop their own sites, perhaps including a statement of their advising philosophy and the expectations they have of advisees.

Listservs

There are also a number of listservs available to advisors. ACADV, an acronym of academic advising, is NACADA's electronic network email system. This network provides a forum for discussions and announcements for professional advisors and for faculty academic advisors. Topics of discussion have included attrition and retention issues, FERPA (Family Educational Rights and Privacy Act) and the confidentiality of student records, legal issues in advising, general education, advising special populations, and theories of advising.

TECADV-L (Technology in Advising Listserv), sponsored by NACADA's Technology in Advising Commission, is a related professional listserv for those interested in technology in academic advising. On this listserv, topics have included cyber orientation, electronic advising records, technology in the classroom, advising software, exemplary advising web sites, web-based course evaluations, email advising, and related issues. Information about these and other listservs sponsored by NACADA can be found at the end of this chapter.

ONLINE ASSESSMENT OF ADVISING

The assessment of advising is a critical aspect of the advising endeavor. With the advent of the Internet and the web, advising assessments can now move out of the paper-and-pencil realm into online applications. Assessment needs to be an ongoing process, driven by the mission, goals, and objectives of the advising unit.

As might be expected, the most contentious aspect of advising assessment is when there is a determination that the effectiveness of individual advisors needs to be measured. Before taking such an approach, an advising administrator should determine what expectations exist for a faculty advisor in terms of behaviors. If this cannot be determined up front, then such an assessment is probably doomed to fail. Likewise, the development of such instruments should be a collaborative effort. Assessment really should be a professional development activity.

Given current technologies, it is relatively simple to communicate with a population of advisees regarding their attitudes toward their advisors, the nature of their advising interactions, and what they have learned as a result of the relationship with the advisor.

While there does not yet seem to be sufficient data as to advisees' likelihood of responding to an email survey versus a paper one, anecdotal evidence suggests that the immediacy and ease of the online form can lead to a larger return rate. This, of course, assumes that the online form is well constructed and easy to read and respond to and that the request comes from someone the respondents feel can make changes suggested by the data.

When an identifier is asked of the advisee (often a student number) with the assurance than no individual respondent will be associated publicly with a particular response item, advising administrators are in a position to associate individual responses with available descriptive data elements in the college or university databases. For example, did females respond differently to various items than males, or did students with lower semester standing or lower cumulative grade point averages have different responses? Using the identifier to find demographic information about the respondent in the database means that students do not have to be asked for the same descriptive and demographic data over and over again as they complete various surveys and questionnaires. This can help in response rates when students realize they are not being asked for data that they have already provided to the institution.

Allowing administrators to correlate responses to various elements in the database can help assessors pinpoint issues of concern. Are they with high achieving students, students in a particular department, students from a particular secondary school, or students assigned to a particular advisor? Being able to separate data with regard to significant respondent characteristics is a critical aspect in assessment.

While technology has not yet produced a perfect assessment instrument, it can certainly enhance the administration of data collection, data aggregation, and the interpretation phase of the operation. Having more useful data available quicker allows for appropriate changes to be made more quickly. Doing assessment online has made this process less tedious and less subject to error in the collection of student characteristics and has enhanced the potential for more sophisticated assessment instruments.

MAKING THE TECHNOLOGY ADVISING NEXUS WORK

The *sine qua non* of effectively connecting technology to academic advising is institutional support. Without financial backing from the administration, faculty will likely not have the hardware, software, or technical support they need to be optimally effective academic advisors. Without the appropriate institutional Zeitgeist that encourages and expects the use of technology by faculty in support of their professional responsibilities, faculty will be less inclined to use technology in their advising interactions and it is unlikely that the human infrastructure necessary to support technological services will be readily available and used by faculty.

Given the requisite institutional support, there are minimum standards in terms of access and knowledge that need to be met for the technology advising nexus to work.

What Must a Faculty Advisor Have?

The following are suggested minimum standards that administrators of faculty advising programs should strive to meet in support of quality academic advising.

- All faculty advisors should have a personal computer in their own offices with user-friendly software, including, at a minimum, email, a web browser, and word processing.
- All faculty advisors should have high-speed Internet access on their personal computers and, at a minimum, modem access to the Internet on laptop computers.
- When appropriate, all faculty advisors should have access to their institution's SIS, including online access to degree audits, grade reports, transcripts, course schedules, and other types of student-specific academic information.
- All faculty advisors should have access to a variety of training resources to assist them in learning how to use or to improve their use of various types of hardware and software.
- All faculty advisors should have ready access to IT support staff who can assist them in training and problem resolution.

What Must a Faculty Advisor Know?

The following are suggested minimum standards of technological knowledge that faculty advisors should strive to meet in support of their advising responsibilities.

- All faculty advisors should know how to use a personal computer.
- All faculty advisors should know how to access student-specific institutional data (degree audits, transcripts, and so on).
- All faculty advisors should know how to correspond with their advisees via email and how to manage a personal email system.
- All faculty advisors should know how to browse the web (including how to locate key academic resources), how to bookmark important resources, how to manage these bookmarks, and how to search the web efficiently.
- All faculty advisors should know, at a minimum, how to join and participate in professional listservs, and when appropriate, how to create and manage advisee listservs.

- All faculty advisors should know what technology resources are routinely being used by their advisees in support of educational planning.

CONCLUSION

This chapter has examined a variety of ways technology can be used to enhance (not replace) one-on-one advising relationships between faculty and students. It is clear, however, that technology is not being used to its optimum extent in advising interactions at many institutions of higher education, even when technology might be the best source of information, the best method of communication and interaction, or the best way to ameliorate an academic problem.

For any technology to be beneficial to the faculty-student advising relationship, it must be 1) available, 2) understood, and 3) applied. If any of these conditions is missing, then the technology will be ineffective. High-powered PCs, high-speed networks, interactive student information systems, and the newest upgrades of hardware and software in the service of academic advising are useless (albeit expensive) tools unless employed effectively and efficiently. Those who are responsible for the administration of faculty advising programs must ensure that faculty have access to appropriate technologies, know how to use them, and employ them in support of the advisor-student relationship.

REFERENCE

Woolston, D., & Lipschultz, W. (1997). *E-mail advising: Art, science, or waste of time?* Concurrent paper session at the 21st National Conference on Academic Advising, Kansas City, MO. Available: www.personal.psu.edu/faculty/w/p/wpl100 /EMAILSAM. HTM

SUGGESTED RESOURCES

Gordon, V. N., Habley, W. R., & Associates. (2000). *Academic advising: A comprehensive handbook.* San Francisco, CA: Jossey-Bass.

Kramer, G. L., & Childs, M. W. (2000). *The "e" factor in delivering advising and student services.* Manhattan, KS: National Academic Advising Association.

Lipschultz, W. P. (1999, January). What can and should we do with e-mail? An outline for a systematic approach. *The Mentor: An Academic Advising Journal, 1* (1). Retrieved February 15, 2002, from http://www.psu.edu/dus/mentor The Mentor: An Academic Advising Journal: www.psu.edu/dus/mentor/ National Academic Advising Association (NACADA): www.nacada.ksu.edu

NACADA Technology in Advising Commission: www.psu.edu/dus/ncta/Palm @ USD: www.usd.edu/palm/

Penn State's eLion: eLion.psu.edu

Trends in Electronic Student Services (a WCET Webcast): www.wiche.edu/telecom/projects/laap/Information.htm#Webcasts

University of Virginia Students Test e-Books: www.virginia.edu/topnews/releases2001/ebook-may-23-2001.html

BIBLIOGRAPHY

Aims Community College. (2002a). Aims Community College academic advising institutional philosophy statement. In *Academic advising summer institute 2002 session guide* (pp. 139–146). Manhattan, KS: National Academic Advising Association.

Aims Community College. (2002b). Edu 206a: Introduction to the process and techniques of academic advising. In *Academic advising summer institute 2002 session guide* (pp. 139–146). Manhattan, KS: National Academic Advising Association.

Alexitch, L. (1997). Students' educational orientation and preferences for advising from university professors. *Journal of College Student Development,* 38, 333–343.

Altschuler, G. C. (2001, November 11). Take this advice, or don't. *New York Times,* [Educational Life Section] p. 4A.

American Association for Higher Education, American College Personnel Association, & National Association of Student Personnel Administration. (1999). *Powerful partnerships: A shared responsibility for learning.* Retrieved December 2001, from http://www.acpa.nche.edu/pubs/powpart.html

American College Personnel Association. (2002). *Mission statement.* Retrieved January 2002, from http://www.acpa.nche.edu

American College Testing. (1994). *Normative report of the survey of academic advising.* Iowa City, IA: Author.

Arnstein, D. (1978). Improving instruction: Reform the institution, not the faculty. *Liberal Education, 64,* 266–277.

Astin, A. W. (1985). *Achieving educational excellence.* San Francisco, CA: Jossey-Bass.

Astin, A. W. (1997). *What matters in college? Four critical years revisited.* San Francisco, CA: Jossey-Bass.

Astin, A. W. (1998). *The American freshmen: National norms for fall 1997.* Los Angeles, CA: University of California at Los Angeles, Higher Education Research Institute.

Astin, A. W., Parrott, S. A., Korn, W. S., & Sax, L. J. (1997). *The American freshman: Thirty-year trends.* Los Angeles, CA: University of California, Higher Education Institute.

Astin, H. (1985). Providing incentives for teaching underprepared students. *Educational Record, 66*, 26–29.

Astin, H., & Astin, A. (Eds.). (2000). *Leadership reconsidered: Engaging higher education in social change.* Battle Creek, MI: W. K. Kellogg Foundation.

Atkinson, R., & Tuzin, D. (1992). Equilibrium in the research university. *Change, 24,* 21–31.

Auw, A. (1991). *Gentle roads to survival.* Boulder Creek, CA: Aslan Publishing.

Banta, T. W., & Associates. (2002). *Building a scholarship of assessment.* San Francisco, CA: Jossey-Bass.

Bardovi-Harlig, K., & Hartford, B. (1993). The language of comembership. *Research on Language and Social Interaction, 26* (2), 227–257.

Beattie, J. (1995). Assessment in higher education. *Higher Education Management, 7,* 281–296.

Beck, R. J. (2002). *Undergraduate academic advising.* Center for Academic Excellence, Tufts University. Retrieved March 2002, from http://ase.tufts.edu/cae/occasional_papers/advising. htm

Becker, B. A. (2000). Legal issues in academic advising. In V. N. Gordon & W. R. Habley (Eds.), *Academic advising: A comprehensive handbook* (pp. 58–70). San Francisco, CA: Jossey-Bass.

Beede, M., & Burnett, D. (1999). *Planning for student services: Best practices for the 21st century.* Ann Arbor, MI: Society for College and University Planning.

Bender, T. (Ed.). (1988). *The university and the city: From medieval origins to the present.* New York, NY: Oxford University Press.

Bennis, W. G., & Nanus, B. (1985). *Leaders: The strategies for taking charge.* New York, NY: Harper and Row.

Berberet, J. (1999). The professoriate and institutional citizenship. *Liberal Education, 85,* 32–39.

Berdahl, R. (1995). Educating the whole person. *New Directions for Teaching and Learning, 62,* 5–11.

Bergquist, W., & Phillips, S. (1977). *A handbook for faculty development* (Vol. 2). Washington, DC: Council for the Advancement of Small Colleges.

Biggs, D., Brodie, J., & Barnhartt, W. (1975). The dynamics of undergraduate academic advising. *Research in Higher Education, 3,* 345–357.

Blix, A., Cruise, R., Mitchell, B., & Blix, G. (1994). Occupational stress among university teachers. *Educational Research, 36,* 157–169.

Bolles, R. (2002). *What color is your parachute?* Berkeley, CA: Ten Speed Press.

Bond, L. (1996). Norm- and criterion-referenced testing. *Practical Assessment, Research and Evaluation, 5.* Retrieved August 2002, from ericae.net/pare/getvn.asp?v=5&n=2

Bowen, H. R. (1980). *Costs of higher education: How much do colleges and universities spend per student and how much should they spend?* San Francisco, CA: Jossey-Bass.

Boyer Commission on Educating Undergraduates in the Research University. (1998). *Reinventing undergraduate education: A blueprint for America's research universities.* Stony Brook, New York: State University of New York at Stony Brook for the Carnegie Foundation for the Advancement of Teaching.

Boyer, E. (1990). *Scholarship reconsidered: Priorities of the professoriate.* Princeton, NJ: The Carnegie Foundation for the Advancement of Teaching.

Buck, J. B., Moore, J. W., Schwartz, M., & Supon, S. B. (2000). *The Penn State adviser* (2nd ed.). University Park, PA: Pennsylvania State University, Office of Undergraduate Education.

Burgan, M., Weisbuch, R., & Lowry, S. (1999). A profession in difficult times: The future of faculty. *Liberal Education, 85,* 6–15.

Carnegie Commission. (1980). Carnegie council's final report. *The Chronicle of Higher Education,* pp. 9–12.

Chickering, A. W. (1994). Empowering lifelong self-development. *AAHE Bulletin, 47* (4), 3–5.

Chickering, A. W., & Gamson, Z. F. (1987). Seven principles for good practice in undergraduate education. *AAHE Bulletin, 39* (7), 3–7.

Chickering, A. W., & Reisser, L. (1993). *Education and identity* (2nd ed.). San Francisco, CA: Jossey-Bass.

Chopp, R. (2001, November 17). *Beyond the founding fratricidal conflict: Scholarship of religion and a renewed public academy.* Presidential address to the American Academy of Religion, Denver, CO.

Chopp, R., Frost, S., & Jean, P. (2001). What's old is new again: Alternative strategies for supporting faculty. *Change, 33,* 43–46.

Collie, S., & Chronister, J. (2001). In search of the next generation of faculty leaders. *AAC&U Peer Review, 3,* 22–23.

Corporate Impressions. (1998). New York, NY: Successories, Inc.

Covey Leadership Center. (2002). *4 roles of leadership.* Retrieved February 2002, from https://register.franklincovey.com/register/moreinfo_4roles.cgi?program_id=8andsource=WEB0121

Cowley, W. H. (1949). Some history and a venture in prophecy. In E. G. Williamson (Ed.), *Trends in student personnel work* (pp. 12–27). Minneapolis, MN: University of Minnesota Press.

Creamer, E., & Scott, D. (2000). Assessing individual advisor effectiveness. In V. Gordon & W. Habley (Eds.), *Academic advising: A comprehensive handbook* (pp. 339–348). San Francisco, CA: Jossey-Bass.

Crookston, B. B. (1972). A developmental view of academic advising as teaching. *Journal of College Student Personnel, 13,* 12–17.

Daller, M., Creamer, E., & Creamer, D. (1997). Advising styles observable in practice: Counselor, scheduler and teacher. *NACADA Journal, 17,* 31–38.

Deci, E. (1978). Applications of research on the effects of rewards. In M. Lepper & D. Greene (Eds.), *The hidden costs of reward: New perspectives on the psychology of human motivation* (pp. 193–204). Hillsdale, NJ: Lawrence Erlbaum.

Deci, E., & Porac, J. (1978). Cognitive evaluation theory and the study of human motivation. In M. Lepper & D. Greene (Eds.), *The hidden costs of reward: New perspectives on the psychology of human motivation* (pp. 149–176). Hillsdale, NJ: Lawrence Erlbaum.

Deming, W. E. (2000). *Out of the Crisis.* Cambridge, MA: MIT Press.

Diamond, R. (1993). Changing priorities and the faculty reward system. In R. Diamond & B. Adam (Eds.), *Recognizing faculty work: Reward systems for the year 2000* (pp. 5–12). New Directions for Higher Education, No. 81. San Francisco, CA: Jossey-Bass.

Diamond, R., & Adam, B. (1995). *The disciplines speak: Rewarding the scholarly, professional and creative work of faculty.* Washington, DC: American Association for Higher Education.

Diamond, R., & Adam, B. (2000). *The disciplines speak II: More statements on rewarding the scholarly, professional and creative work of faculty.* Washington, DC: American Association for Higher Education.

Dickeson, R. C. (1999). *Prioritizing academic programs and services: Reallocating resources to achieve strategic balance.* San Francisco, CA: Jossey-Bass.

Dillon, R., & Fisher, B. (2000). Faculty as part of the advising equation: An inquiry into faculty viewpoints on advising. *NACADA Journal, 20,* 16–23.

Dreisbach, C. (1990). *Retention and advising: Paternalism, agency, and contract.* Paper presented at the Noel-Levitz Conference on Student Retention, Washington, DC. (ERIC Document Reproduction Service No. ED 331 412)

El-Khawas, E. (1996). Student diversity on today's campuses. In S. R. Komives & D. B. Woodward, Jr. (Eds.), *Student services: A handbook for the profession* (pp. 64–80). San Francisco, CA: Jossey-Bass.

Emporia State University. (1993a). *Mission statement.* Internal communication.

Emporia State University. (1993b). *Strategic plan.* Internal communication.

The Family Educational Rights and Privacy Act (FERPA), 20 U.S.C. Section 1232g (1974).

Ferren, A., Kennan, W., & Lerch, S. (2001). Reconciling corporate and academic cultures. *AAC&U Peer Review, 3,* 9–11.

Fiedler, F. E. (1967). *A theory of leadership effectiveness.* New York, NY: McGraw-Hill.

Finkelstein, M., & Schuster, J. (2001). Assessing the silent revolution. *AAHE Bulletin, 54,* 3–7.

Fox Valley Technical College. (2001). *Academic/faculty advising guidelines.* Appleton, WI: Author.

Frost, S. H. (1990). A comparison of developmental advising at two small colleges. *NACADA Journal, 10* (2), 9–13.

Frost, S. H. (1991). *Academic advising for student success: A system of shared responsibility* (ASHE-ERIC Higher Education Report No. 3). Washington, DC: ERIC Clearinghouse on Higher Education, George Washington University.

Frost, S. H. (1993). Developmental advising: Practices and attitudes of faculty advisors. *NACADA Journal, 13* (2), 15–20.

Frost, S. H. (1994). Advising alliances: Sharing responsibility for student success. *NACADA Journal, 14* (2), 54–58.

Frost, S. H. (1995). Designing and implementing a faculty-based advising program. *NACADA Journal, 1,* 27–32.

Frost, S. H. (2000). Historical and philosophical foundations for academic advising. In V. Gordon & W. Habley (Eds.), *Academic advising: A comprehensive handbook.* San Francisco, CA: Jossey-Bass.

Gehring, D. D., & Letzring, T. D. (Eds.). *The College Student and the Courts* (quarterly newsletter published by College Administration Publications).

Glennen, R. E. (1975). Intrusive college counseling. *College Student Journal,* 9, 2–4.

Glennen, R. E., & Baxley, D. M. (1985). Reduction of attrition through intrusive advising. *NASPA Journal, 22,* 10–15.

Glennen, R. E., Farren, P. J., & Vowell, F. N. (1996). How advising and retention of students improve fiscal stability. *NACADA Journal, 16,* 38–41.

Glennen, R. E., & Vowell, F. N. (Eds.). (1995). *Academic advising as a comprehensive campus process.* Manhattan, KS: National Academic Advising Association.

Glotzbach, P. (2001). Conditions of collaboration: A dean's list of do's and don'ts. *Academe, 87.* Retrieved August 2002, from www.aaup.org/publications/Academe/01mj/mj01glot.htm

Gordon, V. N., Habley, W. R., & Associates. (2000). *Academic advising: A comprehensive handbook.* San Francisco, CA: Jossey-Bass.

Gray, W. H., III. (1997). *The case for all-black colleges.* The Washington Post Writers Group.

Greenwood, J. D. (1984). Academic advising and institutional goals: A president's perspective. In R. B. Winston, Jr., T. K. Miller, S. C. Ender, T. J. Grites, & Associates, *Developmental academic advising* (pp. 70–71). San Francisco, CA: Jossey-Bass.

Griffin, B. (2001). Instructor reputation and student ratings of instruction. *Contemporary Educational Psychology, 26,* 534–552.

Grites, T. (1985). *Advising satisfaction questionnaire.* Unpublished manuscript, Stockton State College, Pomona, NJ.

Gumport, P. (2001). Divided we govern. *AAC&U Peer Review, 3,* 14–17.

Habley, W. R. (1983). Organizational structures for academic advising: Models and implications. *Journal of College Student Personnel, 26* (6), 535–540.

Habley, W. R. (Ed.). (1988). *The status and future of academic advising.* Iowa City, IA: The American College Testing Program.

Habley, W. R. (1992). *Fulfilling the promise? Final report of the fourth national survey on academic advising.* Iowa City, IA: The American College Testing Program.

Habley, W. R. (1993). *Fulfilling the promise?* Iowa City, IA: The American College Testing Program.

Habley, W. R. (1994). FIRE! (Ready–Aim): Is criticism of faculty advising warranted? *NACADA Journal, 14* (2), 25–31.

Habley, W. R. (1995). Advisor training in the context of a teaching enhancement center. In R. E. Glennen & F. N. Vowell (Eds.), *Academic advising as a comprehensive campus process* (pp. 75–79) (Monograph Series No. 2). Manhattan, KS: National Academic Advising Association.

Habley, W. R. (2000). *Critical topics in assessing and rewarding faculty advisors.* National Academic Advising Association's Summer Institute on Academic Advising.

Habley, W. R., & McCauley, M. E. (1987). The relationship between institutional characteristics and the organization of advising services. *NACADA Journal, 7* (1), 27--39.

Habley, W. R., & Morales, R. H. (1998). *Current practices in academic advising: Final report on ACT's fifth national survey of academic advising* (Monograph Series No. 6). Manhattan, KS: National Academic Advising Association.

Hamilton College. (n.d.). *Hamilton College statement on advising.* Internal document.

Hamilton College. (2002). *Academic advising at Hamilton College.* Handout at the American Association for Higher Education Conference on Faculty Roles and Rewards, Phoenix, AZ.

Hardee, M. D. (1970). *Faculty advising in colleges and universities.* Washington, DC: American Personnel and Guidance Association.

Harris-Bowlsbey, J. A., Dikel, M. R., & Sampson, J. P. (1998). *The Internet: A tool for career planning.* Tulsa, OK: National Career Development Association.

Hartford, B., & Bardovi-Harlig, K. (1992). Closing the conversation: Evidence from the academic advising session. *Discourse Processes, 15,* 93–116.

Haskell, R. (1997a). Academic freedom, tenure and student evaluation of faculty: Galloping polls in the 21st century. *Education Policy Analysis Archives, 5.* Retrieved August 2002, from http://epaa.asu.edu/epaa/v5n6.html

Haskell, R. (1997b). Academic freedom, promotion, reappointment, tenure and the administrative use of student evaluations of faculty: Views from the court. *Education Policy Analysis Archives, 5.* Retrieved August 2002, from http://epaa.asu.edu/epaa/vol5.html

Isaacson, L. E., & Brown, D. (2000). *Career information, career counseling, and career development.* Needham Heights, MA: Allyn and Bacon.

James MacGregor Burns Academy of Leadership. (2002). *Mission statement.* Retrieved January 2002, from http://www.academy.umd.edu

Johnson, C., & Pinkney, J. (1980). Outreach: Counseling science impacts on faculty advising of students. *Journal of College Student Personnel, 21,* 80–84.

Johnson, C. S., & Cheatham, H. E. (Eds.). (1999). *Higher education trends for the next century: A research agenda for student success.* Washington, DC: American College Personnel Association.

Kanter, R. M. (2001). *Evolve!: Succeeding in the digital culture of tomorrow.* Watertown, MA: Harvard Business School Publishing.

Kapes, J. T., & Whitfield, E. A. (2001). *A counselor's guide to career assessment instruments* (4th ed.). Tulsa, OK: National Career Development Association.

Kaplan, W. A., & Lee, B. (1995). *The law of higher education* (3rd ed.). San Francisco, CA: Jossey-Bass.

Kaun, D. (1984). Faculty advancement in a non-traditional university environment. *Industrial and Labor Relations Review, 37,* 592–606.

Kelly, J. (1995). Faculty speak to advising. *New Directions for Teaching and Learning, 62,* 13–24.

Kerr, T. (2000). Recognition and reward for excellence in advising. In V. Gordon & W. Habley (Eds.), *Academic advising: A comprehensive handbook* (pp. 349–362). San Francisco, CA: Jossey-Bass.

King, M. C. (Ed.). (1993). Academic advising: Organizing and delivering services for student success. *New Directions for Community Colleges, No. 82.* San Francisco, CA: Jossey-Bass.

Kramer, G. L. (1995a). Redefining faculty roles for academic advising. In G. L. Kramer (Ed.), *Reaffirming the role of faculty in academic advising* (pp. 3–9) (Monograph Series No. 1). Manhattan, KS: National Academic Advising Association.

Kramer, G. L. (Ed.). (1995b). *Reaffirming the role of faculty in academic advising* (Monograph Series No. 1). Manhattan, KS: National Academic Advising Association.

Kramer, G. L. (2002). Online advising. *ECAR Research Bulletin, 15,* 2–10.

Kramer, G. L., & Childs, M. W. (Eds.). (1996). *Transforming academic advising through the use of technology*. Manhattan, KS: National Academic Advising Association.

Kramer, G. L., & Childs, M. W. (2000). *The "e" factor in delivering advising and student services.* Manhattan, KS: National Academic Advising Association.

Kramer, H. (1986). Faculty development: The advising coordinator's changing scene. *NACADA Journal, 6,* 31–42.

Kramer, H., & Gardner, R. (1983). *Advising by faculty.* Washington, DC: National Education Association. (ERIC Document Reproduction Service No. ED 235 742)

Kuh, G. D. (2000). *National survey of student engagement: Conceptual framework and overview of psychometric properties.* Bloomington, IN: Indiana University, Center for Postsecondary Research and Planning.

Larson, M., & Brown, B. (1983). Rewards for academic advising: An evaluation. *NACADA Journal, 3,* 55–60.

Leslie, P., Harvey, P., & Leslie, G. (1998). Chief academic officers' perceptions of the relationship between faculty research and undergraduate teaching. *Sociological Spectrum, 18,* 185–199.

Licata, C., & Morreale, J. (2001). Implementing post-tenure review. *AAHE Bulletin, 54,* 3–5.

Light, R. J. (2001a). *Making the most of college: Students speak their minds.* Cambridge, MA: Harvard University Press.

Light, R. J. (2001b, March 2). The power of good advice for students. *The Chronicle of Higher Education*, p. B11.

Lipschultz, W. P. (1999, January). What can and should we do with e-mail? An outline for a systematic approach. *The Mentor: An Academic Advising Journal, 1* (1). Retrieved February 15, 2002, from http://www.psu.edu/dus/mentor

Lunneborg, P., & Baker, E. (1986). Advising undergraduates in psychology: Exploring the neglected dimension. *Teaching of Psychology, 13,* 181–185.

Lynch, M. (2000). Assessing the effectiveness of the advising program. In V. Gordon & W. Habley (Eds.), *Academic advising: A comprehensive handbook* (pp. 324–338). San Francisco, CA: Jossey-Bass.

Magolda, M. B., & Terenzini, P. T. (1999). Learning and teaching in the 21st century: Trends and implications for practice. In C. S. Johnson & H. E. Cheatham (Eds.), *Higher education trends for the next century: A research agenda for student success.* Washington, DC: American College Personnel Association. Retrieved February 2002, from http://www.acpa.nche.edu/seniorscholars/trends/trends4.htm

Mahoney, J., Borgard, J., & Hornbuckle, P. (1978). The relationship of faculty experience and advising load to perceptions of academic advising. *Journal of College Student Personnel, 19,* 28–32.

Mahoney, M. (1991). *Human change process.* New York, NY: Basic Books.

Manning, M. M. (1999). *Liberal education for our life's work.* Keynote address at the National Conference of the Association for General and Liberal Studies, Richmond, VA.

McAnulty, B., O'Connor, C., & Sklare, L. (1987). Analysis of student and faculty opinion of academic advising service. *NACADA Journal, 7,* 49–61.

McCalla-Wriggins, B. (2000). Integrating academic advising and career life planning. In V. N. Gordon, W. R. Habley, & Associates (Eds.), *Academic advising: A comprehensive handbook* (pp. 162–176). San Francisco, CA: Jossey-Bass.

McGillin, V. (1996). A theory base for developmental advising. In J. Burton, B. Crow, W. Habley, V. McGillin, F. N. Vowell, & T. Kerr (Eds.), *NACADA faculty advising training facilitator's manual* (pp. 18–21). Manhattan, KS: National Association for Academic Advising.

McGillin, V., & Kornfeld, M. (1998). *Advisor recognition and reward.* Paper presented at the National Academic Advising Association national conference, San Diego, CA.

Mittler, M., & Bers, T. (1994). Qualitative assessment: An institutional reality check. *New Directions for Community Colleges, 22,* 61–67.

Moore, L. V., & Upcraft, M. L. (1990). Theory in student affairs: Evolving perspective. In L. V. Moore (Ed.), *Evolving theoretical perspectives on students* (pp. 3–23). New Directions for Student Services, No. 51. San Francisco, CA: Jossey-Bass.

National Academic Advising Association. (1994). *NACADA statement of core values of academic advising.* Retrieved 2002, from http://www.nacada.ksu.edu/Profres/corevalu.htm

National Academic Advising Association. (1995). *NACADA faculty advising training video* [Video]. Manhattan, KS: Author.

National Academic Advising Association. (1999). *Academic advising: Campus collaboratives to foster retention* [Video]. Manhattan, KS: Author.

National Academic Advising Association. (2000). *Mission statement and strategic plan 2000–2005.* Retrieved February 2001, from http://www.nacada.ksu.edu/Associnfo/stratpln.htm

National Academic Advising Association. (2001). *Academic advising: Discover the many voices* (National Conference Program). Manhattan, KS: Author.

National Academic Advising Association. (2002a). *Consultant's bureau.* Retrieved February 2002, from http://www.nacada.ksu.edu/Profres/consult.htm

National Academic Advising Association. (2002b). *NACADA statement of core values of academic advising.* Retrieved February 2002, from http://www.nacada.ksu.edu/Profres/corevalu.htm

National Academic Advising Association. (2002c). *National advising awards program.* Retrieved February 2002, from http://www.nacada.ksu.edu/Awards/advcall.html

National Academic Advising Association. (2002d). *Organizational structure.* Retrieved February 2002, from http://www.nacada.ksu.edu/Associnfo/structur.html#committeechairs

National Academic Advising Association. (2002e). *Outstanding advising program award.* Retrieved February 2002, from http://www.nacada.ksu.edu/Awards/procall.html

National Academic Advising Association & American College Testing. (2002). *Summer institute on academic advising.* Retrieved February 2002, from http://www.nacada.ksu.edu/Summer Inst/brochure02.htm

National Career Development Association. (2001). *NCDA mission statement.* Retrieved January 2002, from http://ncda.org/about/mission.html

Neal, J. (1995). Overview of policy and practice: Differences and similarities in developing higher education accountability. *New Directions for Higher Education, 91,* 5–10.

Nelsen, W. (1981). *Renewal of the teacher scholar: Faculty development in the liberal arts college.* Washington, DC: Association of American Colleges.

Newman, J. H. (1993). The idea of a university. In C. Eliot (Ed.), *Essays, English and American.* Danbury, CT: Grolier.

Noel-Levitz. (2002). *Academic advising for student success and retention.* Retrieved December 2001, from http://www.noellevitz.com/ret_advising.asp

O'Banion, T. (1972). An academic advising model. *Junior College Journal, 42* (6), 62–69.

Pardee, C. F. (2000). Organizational models for academic advising. In V. N. Gordon, W. R. Habley, & Associates (Eds.), *Academic advising: A comprehensive handbook* (pp. 192–209). San Francisco, CA: Jossey-Bass.

Pascarella, E. T., & Terenzini, P. T. (1991). *How college affects students: Findings and insights from twenty years of research.* San Francisco, CA: Jossey-Bass.

Pennsylvania State University. (2002a). *Guidelines for advising web sites.* Retrieved March 2002, from http://www.psu.edu/dus/uac/webmain.htm

Pennsylvania State University. (2002b.) *Role of the adviser.* Retrieved March 2002, from http://www.psu.edu/dus/cfe/myrole

Pennsylvania State University, University Advising Council. (2002). *UAC assessment guidelines.* Retrieved August 2002, from http://www.psu.edu/dus/uac/aseval.htm

Peterson, M., & Augustine, C. (2000). Organizational practices enhancing the influence of student assessment information in academic decisions. *Research in Higher Education, 41,* 21–52.

Polson, C. (1981). The impact of advising skills upon the effectiveness of the departmental academic advising center. *NACADA Journal, 1,* 47–55.

Prochaska, J., & DiClemente, C. (1983). Stages and processes of self-change of smoking: Toward an integrative model of change. *Journal of Consulting and Clinical Psychology, 51,* 390–395.

Prochaska, J., DiClemente, C., & Norcross, J. (1992). In search of how people change: Applications to addictive behavior. *American Psychologist, 47,* 1102–1114.

Prochaska, J., & Velicer, W. (1997). The transtheoretical model of health behavior change. *American Journal of Health Promotion, 12,* 38–48.

Prus, J., & Johnson, R. (1994). A critical review of student assessment options. *New Directions for Community Colleges, 22,* 69–83.

Ramos, M., & Vallandingham, D. (Eds.). (1997). *Advising students with disabilities.* Manhattan, KS: National Academic Advising Association.

Reece, S., Pearce, C., Melillo, K., & Beaudry, M. (2001). The faculty portfolio: Documenting the scholarship of teaching. *Journal of Professional Nursing, 17,* 180–186.

Regents of the University of Michigan v. Ewing, 474 U.S. 214 (1985).

Rendon, L. (1994). Validating culturally diverse students: Toward a new model of learning and student development. *Innovative Higher Education, 19,* (1) 33–50.

Rhoades, G. (1996). Reorganizing the faculty workforce for flexibility; Part-time professional labor. *Journal of Higher Education, 67,* 627–659.

Rossman, J. (1968). Released time for faculty advising: The impact on freshmen. *Personnel and Guidance Journal, 47,* 358–363.

Rudolph, F. (1962). *The American college and university: A history.* New York, NY: Knopf.

Rudolph, F. (1977). *Curriculum.* San Francisco, CA: Jossey-Bass.

Ruedrich, S. L., Cavey, C., Katz, K., & Grush, L. (1992). Recognition of teaching excellence through the use of teaching awards: A faculty perspective. *Academic Psychiatry, 16,* 10–13.

Ruedrich, S. L., Reid, W. H., & Chu, C. (1986). Rewarding teaching excellence with cash: A faculty response. *Psychiatric Annals, 16* (6), 370-–373.

Ryan, K. C. (1992). Advising as teaching. *NACADA Journal, 12* (1), 4–8.

Sassen, S. (1991). *The global city: New York, London, Tokyo*. Princeton, NJ: Princeton University Press.

Schroeder, C. S. (1999). Collaboration and partnership. In C. S. Johnson & H. E. Cheatham (Eds.), *Higher education trends for the next century: A research agenda for student success*. Washington, DC: American College Personnel Association. Retrieved January 2002, from http://www.acpa.nche.edu/seniorsscholars/trends/trends7.htm

Scriven, M. (1995). Student ratings offer useful input to teacher evaluations. *Practical Assessment, Research and Evaluation, 4*. Retrieved August 2002, from ericae.net/pare/getvn.asp?v=4&n=7

Seagren, A., Creswell, J., & Wheeler, D. (1993). *The department chair: New roles, responsibilities and challenges* (ASHE-ERIC Higher Education Report No. 1). Washington, DC: The George Washington University, School of Education and Human Development.

Seldin, P. (1997). *The teaching portfolio: A practical guide to improved performance and promotion/tenure decisions* (2nd ed.). Bolton, MA: Anker.

Snyder, T. D. (Ed.). (1993). *120 years of American education: A statistical portrait*. Washington, DC: United States Department of Education, Office of Educational Research and Improvement, Center for Educational Statistics.

Spence, J., & Helmreich, R. (1983). Achievement-related motives and behaviors. In J. Spence (Ed.), *Achievement and achievement Motives: Psychological and sociological approaches* (pp. 7–74). San Francisco, CA: W. H. Freeman and Associates.

Srebnik, D. (1988). Academic advising evaluation: A review of assessment instruments. *NACADA Journal, 8* (1), 52–62.

Stark, J. S. (1989). *Student goals for colleges and courses: A missing link in assessing and improving academic achievement* (ASHE-ERIC Report No. 6). Washington, DC: George Washington University.

Strada, M. (2001). Assessing the assessment decade. *Liberal Education, 87,* 42–49.

Sun, A., & Valega, M. (1997). *Assessing reliability of student ratings of advisors: A comparison of univariate and multivariate generalizability approaches.* Paper presented at the annual meeting of the American Educational Research Association, Chicago, IL. (ERIC Document Reproduction Service No. ED 411 262)

Syracuse University. (2002). *Syracuse University statement on academic advising.* Handout at the American Association for Higher Education Conference on Faculty Roles and Rewards, Phoenix, AZ.

Teague, G., & Grites, T. (1980). Faculty contracts and academic advising. *Journal of College Student Personnel, 41,* 40–44.

Tharp, T., Hensley, B., & Meadows, D. (1996). *Current trends in the evaluation of academic counselors.* Retrieved August 2002, from www.nade.net/documents/SCP96/SCP96.20.pdf

Tinto, V. S. (1987). *Leaving college: Rethinking the causes and cures of student attrition.* Chicago, IL: University of Chicago Press.

Tinto, V. S. (1990). Principles of effective retention. *Journal of the Freshman Experience, 2,* 35–48.

Tinto, V. S. (1993). *Leaving college: Rethinking the causes and cures of student attrition* (2nd ed.). Chicago, IL: University of Chicago Press.

Tinto, V. S. (1998). Colleges as communities: Taking research on student persistence seriously. *Review of Higher Education, 21* (2), 167–177.

Trower, C., Austin, A., & Sorcinelli, M. (2001). Paradise lost: How the academy converts enthusiastic recruits into early-career doubters. *AAHE Bulletin, 53,* 3–6.

Upcraft, M. L., & Kramer, G. L. (Eds.). (1995). *First-year academic advising: Patterns in the present, pathways to the future.* Columbia, SC: University of South Carolina, National Resource Center for the Freshman Year Experience and Students in Transition.

U.S. Department of Education, National Center for Educational Statistics. (1995). *Digest of educational statistics.* Retrieved August 2002, from www.nces.ed.gov

Velicer, W., Prochaska, J., Fava, J., Norman, G., & Redding, C. (1998). *Detailed overview of the transtheoretical model.* Retrieved August 2002, from www.uri.edu/research/cprc/TTM/detailedoverview.htm

Veysey, L. R. (1965). *The emergence of the American university.* Chicago, IL: University of Chicago Press.

Vincow, G. (1993, January). *Annual address to the faculty.* Unpublished speech, Syracuse University.

Voigt, L. (2002). *Using assessment to foster a campus learning cycle and institutional effectiveness.* Paper presented at the Assessing Quality in Higher Education Conference, University of Vienna.

Volkwein, J., King, M., & Terenzini, P. (1986). Student-faculty relationships and intellectual growth among transfer students. *Journal of Higher Education, 57,* 413–430.

Vowell, F. N., Wachtel, E., Grites, T. J., & Rozzelle, R. W. (Eds.). (1993). *Designing an effective advisor training program.* Manhattan, KS: National Academic Advising Association.

Wergin, J. (2001). Beyond carrots and sticks: What really motivates faculty. *Liberal education, 87,* 50–53.

Western New Mexico University. (2002c). *Western New Mexico University academic advising mission statement.* Handout at the American Association for Higher Education Conference on Faculty Roles and Rewards, Phoenix, AZ.

Western New Mexico University. (2002a). *Advisor training for orientation.* Internal document.

Western New Mexico University. (2002b). *Training session for faculty advising in orientation.* Internal document.

Western New Mexico University. (2002d). *Western New Mexico University expectations for promotion and tenure.* Handout at the American Association for Higher Education Conference on Faculty Roles and Rewards, Phoenix, AZ.

White, E. R. (2000). Developing mission, goals and objectives for the advising program. In V. N. Gordon, W. R. Habley, & Associates (Eds.), *Academic advising: A comprehensive handbook* (pp. 180–191). San Francisco, CA: Jossey-Bass.

Winston, R., & Sander, J. (1985). *Academic advising inventory and advising conference record.* Athens, GA: Student Development Associates.

Woolston, D., & Lipschultz, W. (1997). *E-mail advising: Art, science, or waste of time?* Concurrent paper session at the 21st National Conference on Academic Advising, Kansas City, MO. Available: www.personal.psu.edu/faculty/w/p/wpl100/EMAILSAM.HTM

Yerian, J. M. (1988). *Putting the standards to work.* College Park, MD: Council for the Advancement of Standards for Student Services/Development Programs.

INDEX

A

AAHE (American Association for Higher Education), 185
ACPA (American College Personnel Association), 186
ACT (American College Testing), 25, 49, 73, 125, 129, 130, 139
Fifth National Survey of Academic Advising, 26, 32, 57, 111, 114, 139
Adam, B., 101
Advising
- a shared responsibility, 140
- administration of, 51–54, 66, 92, 103, 126, 154–155, 159–160, 166, 219–222, 240–241
- an integral component, 1, 2, 6, 21
- and new student orientation, 210
- as teaching, 1, 6, 7, 20, 31, 46, 223
- assessment and evaluation, 12, 32, 35, 36, 39, 49, 97, 98, 101, 110, 138, 170
- checklist, 215
- collaboration, 1, 2, 14–15, 19, 21, 43, 45, 179, 187, 196, 233, 235–236
- defined and examined activity, 225
- defined, but unexamined activity, 225
- definition, 42, 102, 137, 202
- delivery, 1, 2, 15, 26, 27, 35, 125, 127, 131–141, 154–155
- developmental, 3–5, 233–235
- diversity, 2, 19, 23, 50, 62, 77, 126, 156
- effective, definition of, 102–103
- expectations, 24, 55–56, 58–64, 70–72
- new students, 48–49, 210–211
- online, 261–263, 268
- outcomes, 18, 103
- practices, 1, 3, 7, 12, 19, 23, 31, 45, 47, 49, 67–69, 75, 82, 84–85, 99, 103, 109, 111–117, 128–134, 136–137, 138, 139, 146–147, 153, 155–156, 160–164, 167–169, 184, 186, 195, 201–202, 204–207, 209–215, 220, 223–226, 231, 238, 242, 274, 277
- programs, 4, 38, 195
- resources, 1, 176, 177–183
- services, 45
- staff, 135–136, 141, 165
- student needs, 8, 18, 19, 33, 36, 38, 152
- technology (see technology), 265–267
- training, 14, 72, 78, 137, 208–209, 276–277

Advisors and advisee, rights and responsibilities, 64–65, 257–258
Aims Community College, 67, 79, 85
Alexitch, L., 110
American Historical Association, 101
American Psychological Association, Joint Policy Board for Mathematics, 101
Arizona State University, 113,117
Arnstein, D., 98
Assessment, 1, 10, 95, 138, 207, 214–215, 279
methods and models, 13, 106–109
Astin, A. W., 18, 49, 153, 157, 189, 194
Astin, H., 98, 194
Atkinson, R. H., 91, 98
Augustine, C., 96
Austin, A., 93–94, 99
Auw, A., 236
Azusa Pacific, online guide, 168

B

Baker, E., 114
Ball State University, 134, 213
Banta, T., 12
Bardovi-Harlig, K., 110
Barnhartt, W., 114, 116
Baxley, D. M., 48
Beattie, J., 97
Beaudry, M., 105
Beede, M., 130
Beloit College, 128
Bender, T., 224
Bennis, W. D., 145
Berberet, J., 94, 98
Berdahl, R., 117
Berquist, W., 98–99
Biggs, D., 114, 116
Blackboard, to synthesize advising, 168
Blix, A., 99
Blix, G., 99
Bolles, R., 191
Bond, L., 97
Borgard, J., 118
Bowen, H. R., 148
Boyer Commission, 228, 235, 239
Boyer, E., 92,101
Bradley University (NAW), 156
Bridgewater State College, 211
Brigham Young University, 45

Brodie, J., 114, 116
Brown, B., 100
Brown, D., 191
Brown, R., 15
Buckley Amendments, 255–256
Burgan, M., 93–94
Burnett, D., 130

C

Career decision-making, life planning, resources, 18, 173, 189–191, 222
Carnegie Commission, 40
CAS (Council for the Advancement of Standards in Higher Education), 174
Cavey, C., 115
Center for Creative Leadership, 193
Change, 89–92, 249–250
Changing demography, 148–150
Chickering, A. W., 5, 18–19, 25, 76
Childs, M. W., 178
Chopp, R., 9, 224
Chronister, J., 93, 98
Claremont Graduate School of Religion, 111
Clark College Business Division (NAW), 161
Clark University, 116
Cloud County Community College, 117
Collie, S., 93, 98
Concordia University, 109
Contract law, 247–248, 253
Covey Leadership Center, 193
Cowley, W. H., 23
Creamer, D., 109
Creamer, E., 95–96, 100, 105, 109–110
Creswell, J., 95–97
Crookston, B. B., xxiii, 1, 4–6, 8, 151
Cross, K. P., 77
Cruise, R., 99

D

Daller, M., 109
Datatel (software), 265
Deci, E., 95, 98–99
Degree audit program, 265
Deming, W. E., 157–158
Diamond, R., 98, 101
DiClemente, C., 89–90
Digest of Educational Statistics, 149
Dikel, M. R., 190
Dillon, R., 115
Discover (software), 192
Dreisbach, C., 110
Due process, student, 251

E

East Carolina State University, 111
eLion, Pennsylvania State University, 270
El-Khawas, E., 19
Emporia State University, 47
Evaluation
  formative, 95, 113
  smart, 1, 10, 18, 77, 96, 138, 175
  summative, 96, 113
Extracurricular activities, 237–238

F

Faculty advising
  a CAO/CEO perspective, 40–41, 51–54
  evolution of, 3, 23–24
  framework for, 6, 7
  Faculty advisors
  development of, 1, 19, 52
  evaluation of, assessment, 10, 29, 94–95
  recognition and reward for, 1, 10, 19, 29, 94–95, 99–101, 114–115, 139, 169, 205–206, 238–239
  role of, relationship with, 8, 10–11, 18–19, 42, 49, 88, 126
  technology nexus, 280–282
  training for, 27–29, 52, 72, 74, 75, 77, 82, 137, 153, 208, 276
Faculty, promotion, tenure, merit pay, reward, 10, 69, 99, 101, 117–118, 168–169, 238
Faculty-student interaction, 1, 18, 24–25
Farren, P. J., 46
Fava, J., 90
FERPA (Family Educational Rights to Privacy Act), 72, 255–257
Ferren, A., 95
Fiedler, F. E., 154
Finkelstein, M., 93
Fisher, B., 115
Fox Valley Technical College, 133, 207, 215

Frost, S. H., 98, 25, 140–141, 146, 151–153, 224–226, 233–235
FYE (National Resource Center for the First Year Experience and Students in Transition), 188

G

Gamson, Z. F., 19, 25
Gardner, R., 112
Glennen, R. E., 46, 48, 178
Glotzbach, P., 92
Gordon, V. N., 153, 179
Gray, W. H. III, 149
Greenwood, J. D., 48
Griffin, B., 98
Grites, T., 112, 117
Grush, L., 115
Gumport, P., 95

H

Habley, W. R., xxiii, 2, 19, 25–26, 36, 100, 105, 109, 114, 125, 127–128, 138–139, 153, 179
Hamilton College, 68, 202
Handheld computers, 274
Hardee, M., 3
Harris-Bowlsbey, J. A., 190
Hartford, B., 110
Hartford College for Women, 146
Harvard College, University, 3, 23
Harvey, P., 97
Haskell, R., 96–98
Hayes, R., 3
Heath, D., 77
Heath, R., 77
Helmreich, R., 98
Hensley, B., 105, 110
Higher Education Research Institute at UCLA, 49
Hope Scholarships, 149
Hornbuckle, P., 118

I

Indiana University–Purdue University Indianapolis, 206, 211
Institutional mission, 91, 126, 174
Iowa State University, 112,114
Isaacson, L. E., 191

J

James MacGregor Burns Academy of Leadership, 194
Jean, P., 98
Johns Hopkins University, 3, 23
Johnson, C., 117
Johnson County Community College, 130
Johnson, R., 97

K

Kansas State University, 113, 115
Kanter, R., 21
Katz, K., 115
Kaun, D., 92
Kelly, J., 114, 116
Kennan, W., 95
Kerr, T., 116, 117
King, M., 18
King, M. C., 135
Korn, W. S., 189
Kornfeld, M., 116
Kramer, G., xxiii, 14, 16, 18, 177–178
Kramer, H., 112, 118
Kuh, G., 11

L

Lansing Community College, 134
Larson, M., 100
Leadership, advising resources, 193–194
Leading and managing faculty advising, 144, 160, 163, 174, 204
Learning, 4, 146–147, 151, 164–165
Legal concepts, 25, 175, 245–246
Lerch, S., 95
Leslie, G., 97
Leslie, P., 97
Licata, C., 97, 98
Light, R., xxiii, 1, 5, 18, 20, 100, 140, 151, 153, 167, 169, 173, 196, 201, 228, 232, 235, 238
Linfield College, 131
Lipschultz, W., 263
Lowry, S., 93, 94
Loyola University, 12

Lunneborg, P., 114
Lynch, M., 105

M

Magolda, M. B., 186
Mahoney, J., 118
Mahoney, M., 89, 100
Manning, M., 196
McAnulty, B., 110
McCalla-Wriggins, B., 192
McCauley, M., 213
McCauley, M. E., 125, 127
McGillan, V., 76, 116
Meadows, B., 105, 110
Melillo, K., 105
The Mentor: An Academic Advising Journal, 277
Michigan State University, 111
Middle Tennessee State University, 109
Mitchell, B., 99
Monroe Community College (NAW), 114, 161
advising awards, 207, 212, 214
Moore, L. V., 19
Morales, R. H., 19, 100, 105, 109, 114, 127, 128, 139, 179
Morreale, J., 97, 98

N

NACADA/ACT Summer Institute on Academic Advising, 180
NACADA Journal, 139
NACADA (National Academic Advising Association), 148, 174, 177, 215–216, 229, 276
- core values, 44, 176
- faculty advising training facilitator's manual, 76
- NACADA Award Winners (NAW), 144
- Outstanding Advising Program Award, 184
- Outstanding Advisor Award, 140

NACE (National Association of Colleges and Employers), 190, 191
Nanus, B., 145
NASPA (National Association of Student Personnel Administration), 188
National Guidelines for Academic Advising, 173
National Resource Center for the First Year Experience and Students in Transition (FYE), 188
National standards for advising, 173
National Student Engagement Survey, 10
NCDA (National Career Development Association), 189
Neal, J., 96
Nelsen, W., 95–97
Newman, J. H., 226–227
Noel Levitz, 189
Student Survey, 73
Nontenured faculty and advising, 93
Norcross, J., 90
Norman, G., 90
Northwestern State University of Louisiana (NAW), 164
NSF (National Science Foundation), 228

O

OASIS–University of South Florida, 160
O'Bannion, T., 8, 76, 151, 153, 189
O'Connor, C., 110
Ohio University, 116
Oklahoma City Community College, 133
Online guide, Azusa Pacific, 168
Oral Roberts University (NAW), 162

P

Pardee, C. R., 128
Parrott, S. A., 189
Pascarella, E. T., xxiii, 18
Pearce, C., 105
Pennsylvania State University, 109, 129, 156, 169, 206, 213, 215, 270, 277
Pennsylvania State University–Altoona, 117
Pennsylvania State University, Eberly College of Science, 109
Peoplesoft (software), 265
Peterson, M., 96
Phillips, S., 98–99
Pinkney, J., 117
Polson, C., 112
Porac, J., 95
Powell, L. F., 246
Prochaska, J., 89–90
Prus, J., 97
Purdue University Calumet (PUC), 212

Q

Quality control, 158

R

Ramos, M., 178
Redding, C., 90
Reece, S., 105
Reisser, L., 18
Rendon, L., 77
Rhoades, G., 93
Richard Stockton College, 131
Richland Community College, 231
Rossman, J., 117
Rowan University, 186
Rudolph, F., 23, 25, 223–224
Ruedrich, S. L., 115
Rutgers University, 238

S

Sampson, J. P., 190
Sander, J., 111
Sassen, S., 224, 232
SAT, 49
Sax, L. J., 189
Schenectady County Community College, 132
Schroeder, C. S., 187
Schuster, J., 93
Scott, D., 95–96, 100, 105, 109–110
Scriven, M., 110
SCT Banner (software), 265
Seagren, A., 95–97
Seldin, P., 239
Sigi Plus (software), 192
Sklare, L., 110
Snyder, T. D., 148
Sorcinelli, M., 93–94, 99
Southwest Missouri State University, 116, 185
Spence, J., 98
Srebnik, D., 111
Stanford University, 115
Stark, J. S., 5
Strada, M., 96
Students
  diversity, 2, 19, 23, 62, 77
  records, management of, 255–257
Sun, A., 110
Survey of Advisor Traits and Advisor Effectiveness, 112
Syracuse University, 68, 75, 112, 117, 164, 184, 202, 210

T

Tarrant County College Southeast Campus, 130
Teague, G., 117
Technology (Internet) and advising, 14–16, 19, 152, 167, 192–193, 212–213, 230, 258–259, 260–261, 264, 268, 274–275
Temple University, 117
Terenzini, P. T., 18, 186
Tharp, T., 105, 110
Tinto, V., xxiii, 18
Tort liability of faculty advisor, 254
Towson State University, 109, 117
Trower, C., 93–94, 99
Tuzin, D., 91, 98

U

U.S. Department of Education, 149
University of Alabama at Birmingham, 211
University of Arizona, 205
University of Central Arkansas (NAW), 134, 155, 204, 209, 214–215
University of Connecticut, 114
University of Georgia, 116
University of Hartford, Hillyer College, 167
University of Idaho, 117
University of Illinois, 116
University of Nebraska–Lincoln (NAW), 163
University of Pittsburgh, School of Engineering (NAW), 162
University of South Carolina, 115
University of South Carolina–Union, 113
University of South Dakota, 274
University of South Florida, 160, 168
University of Texas at Arlington (NAW), 164
University of Virginia, 274
University of West Alabama, 109
University of Wisconsin–Eau Claire (NAW), 153
University of Wisconsin–Whitewater, 117, 134, 184, 206, 210

Upcraft, M. L., 19, 178

V

Valega, M., 110
Valencia Community College, 242
Vallandingham, D., 178
Velicer, W., 90
Veysey, L. R., 223–224
Video conferencing, 275
Virginia Tech, 115
Voigt, L., 12
Volkwein, J., 18
Vowell, F. N., 46, 178–179

W

Walla Walla College, 111
Wartburg College, 131
Weisbuch, R., 93–94
Wergin, J., 99
West Carolina State University, 109, 113
Western New Mexico University, 69, 82, 84
Wheaton College, 109, 147
Wheeler, D., 95–97
Wilbur, F., 10
Winston, R., 111
Woolston, D., 263

X,Y,Z

Yerian, J. M., 174